HELPING THE ADDICT YOU LOVE

THE NEW EFFECTIVE PROGRAM FOR GETTING THE ADDICT INTO TREATMENT

LAURENCE M. WESTREICH, M.D.

A Fireside Book
Published by Simon & Schuster
New York   London   Toronto   Sydney

AUTHOR'S NOTE: The names and identifying characteristics of all the addicts I refer to in this book have been changed.

FIRESIDE
Rockefeller Center
1230 Avenue of the Americas
New York, NY 10020

FIRESIDE and colophon are registered trademarks of Simon & Schuster, Inc.

For information regarding special discounts for bulk purchases, please contact Simon & Schuster Special Sales at 1-800-456-6798 or business@simonandschuster.com.

Designed by William Ruoto

Manufactured in the United States of America

10   9   8   7   6   5   4   3   2   1

Library of Congress Cataloging-in-Publication Data is available.

ISBN-13: 978-0-7432-9213-9
ISBN-10:   0-7432-9213-8

This book is dedicated to my parents, Gil and Natalie

Contents

Introduction

When I served as the director of Bellevue Hospital's detoxification ward, I often met patients whose lives had been destroyed by addiction. I particularly remember one young man who, in addition to his heavy use of alcohol, smoked more than $100 worth of crack cocaine every day and had been admitted to the hospital in a drunken stupor. Given the life-threatening nature of his addiction, and our experience with individuals with similar stories who had died, our treatment team gave him the "full-court press." In addition to medications, counseling, group therapy, and Alcoholics Anonymous meetings, several of us sat down with him and his family and tried to convince him of how much danger he was in, and how important it was for him to change his behavior. But despite our entreaties, he left after four days, telling us that he appreciated our concern and that he would try to cut down his alcohol use, but that he had no intention of stopping his crack cocaine use. In our staff meeting, we agreed that we'd failed to reach this young man, and prepared ourselves for his readmission or news of his death.

Much to our surprise, however, the next we heard of him was several months later when he showed up, with several others from a local AA group, to lead a meeting on our ward. He told us that after leaving our ward and using crack cocaine a few times, he'd decided to try a few of the relapse prevention techniques we'd taught him and got his best friend to go with him to an AA meeting. From that modest beginning came full-fledged sobriety and the subsequent positive changes in his life.

Ever since then, whenever I find an addict who seems similarly "hopeless," I think back on my own hopelessness in that situation and how misguided it was. It reminds me that no case is hopeless and that the techniques for getting an addict into treatment—both those professionals use and those families and friends can use—are more powerful than we sometimes realize and can have long-lasting effects.

I wrote this book because, as a psychiatrist who treats addiction, I've had many similarly difficult and sometimes painful experiences with the friends and families of addicted people. Very early on in my practice I realized that although I could give some solid advice to my patients (such as encouraging them to join a twelve-step program), I had no such recommendations for the often frustrated family and friends of those addicts who would not even consider any kind of treatment. But over the fifteen years that I've worked in this field, I've developed a method for guiding friends and family to help get their loved ones into treatment without getting hurt themselves. That method—which I call "Creative Engagement"—is based on what I've learned from my teachers, what I've read in the psychiatric literature, and what I've found works best with the hundreds of patients I've treated. And I've written this book so I can share it with you.

Creative Engagement means, first, being willing to use every available strategy, even those you may be uncomfortable with, to convince your loved one to go into treatment. And, second, continuing to engage with the addict—to hang in there—rather than leave the addict to his or her own devices. That can mean trying to push him or her toward a program, looking for ways to help the addict avoid the dangers of the substance use, or simply being there to help as he or she suffers with the addiction. Creative Engagement, then, is essentially about focusing on solving the immediate problem of getting help for your addicted loved one, doing whatever you can to resolve it, and continuing to work on it until you have.

But in order for you to understand why I feel that Creative Engagement is such an effective method, I need to tell you something about how I think of addiction, some of which, frankly, goes against the conventional wisdom. The first and perhaps most important thing for you to understand is that addicts, almost by definition, are "reluctant patients." That is, they're at best ambivalent about and, at worst, in complete denial concerning their addiction. Of course, reluctance is a common enough human feeling. We're all reluctant to do necessary but sometimes unpleasant tasks, like getting out of a cozy bed on a cold winter's morning, or going to the dentist to have a cavity filled. We *know* we have to face the cold floor or the dentist's drill, but we just don't want to do it, at least not yet. The same is true for addicts—the problem must be faced, but the addict is invested in putting that moment off for as long as possible.

One reason for this is that, unlike other diseases such as high blood pressure or diabetes, there are actually some "upsides" to remaining addicted. Although people who have become addicted to substances usually feel very little actual "high," some of them need the substance to work effectively, and some are literally unable to function without it. For instance, if an individual addicted to OxyContin was to stop using it, he might find himself experiencing muscle cramps, diarrhea, and insomnia. Faced with a situation like that, taking the drug may seem like a very good idea, and it would be entirely understandable for him to be reluctant to face the uncomfortable effects of withdrawal in order to get back to a sober life. This, though, is where the "creative" aspect of Creative Engagement comes into play. If, instead of disagreeing with the addict when he or she makes such an argument, you acknowledge whatever upside there may be to the substance use, even if it means having to bite your lip, you can keep the lines of communication open and continue working toward convincing him or her to enter treatment.

This is important because, reluctant though they may be, addicts are desperately in need of treatment, and just as desperately in need of someone to help them get that treatment. And this is one example of how Creative Engagement conflicts with the conventional wisdom. Much of what's been written on addiction argues that, as a friend or family member, it's best for you to divorce yourself from the problem of your addicted loved one and simply do what you can to protect yourself. Of course, it's true that those who care about addicts have to work to keep from being taken advantage of by them, both emotionally and financially. But it's equally true that friends or family who take an active role in trying to save an addict from the wreckage of his or her life can have an enormous influence. And that's what Creative Engagement is all about—being proactive and positive instead of reactive and negative. It's also exactly what this book will teach you to do.

Conventional wisdom also says that you can't get people to make even beneficial changes in their lives unless they want to. In terms of addiction, this would suggest that, regardless of how much of an effort you make to convince, cajole, or demand that the addict you love deal constructively with his or her addiction, unless they're ready, it won't happen. And there is some truth in that. In my opinion, though, while you can't physically or legally force an addict into a treatment program, as his or her friend or family member, you have the right to encourage the addict to enter treatment. And whether or not the addict in your life is completely ready to change, there are still effective and potentially lifesaving steps that you can take.

If, for example, your loved one is a cocaine addict, you can absolutely refuse to be around her when she's using or intoxicated, but welcome her when she's not. Similarly, you can spend as much time as possible helping her do positive things like looking for a job or an apartment, but refuse to help when she needs a ride to pick up drugs. In other words, you can encourage those aspects of her thinking that are positive and aimed toward getting into treatment, and discourage those that aren't.

A third bit of conventional wisdom is that addicts have to "hit bottom" before accepting treatment and sobriety. But "bottom" for many addicts is death. So if you wait for that to happen, it may be too late. What you can do instead is help them "raise the bottom" to a more acceptable level, such as embarrassment, job loss, or even ill health. There are a number of ways you can do that, and I discuss several of them in this book.

At the same time, it's important for you to understand that your power to prevent an addict's use of drugs or alcohol is limited. You also have to let go of any unrealistic guilt feelings you may have for having caused or encouraged the addictive behavior. *No one other than the addict him- or herself is responsible for the substance use, and no one other than the addict can stop it.* That's the bad news. The good news is that once you have a realistic understanding of the limits of your power, you can focus that power on the problem at hand and become really effective. I've seen families unite to convince an alcoholic parent—a woman who had been in denial for years—to address her alcoholism. I've seen groups of friends band together to help a member of the group stop dangerous cocaine or heroin use. Pulling together, family and friends can act as powerful change agents in an addict's life.

One of the ways you can do this is through what I call "Constructive Coercion." The term Constructive Coercion essentially covers a number of different strategies that you and other friends and family members can use that are more forceful than those used to just convince an addict to enter treatment. This may sound like the well-known technique called intervention, but it's actually very different. Intervention is, essentially, a group of the addict's friends and/or family members getting together to surprise the addict, confront him or her about the addiction, and threaten to cut him or her off unless he or she goes into a treatment program. What distinguishes intervention from other methods is that element of surprise. Someone who doesn't want to deal with his or her addiction can avoid going to a therapist's office or an AA meeting but has no way of avoiding a confrontation that he or she isn't even expecting.

While I recognize that there may be some benefits to surprising an addict in this way, I don't recommend using this technique for a number of reasons, not the least of which is that it often doesn't work. Even more important, though, to my way of thinking the whole idea of a "surprise attack" is misguided. I think it's better—from both the emotional and practical standpoints—to frame the interaction with the addict as an attempt to help rather than as an attack. Constructive Coercion accordingly focuses on the friends' and family's concern for the addict rather than on whatever threats they may make. And while it also makes use of ultimatums to coerce addicts into treatment, those ultimatums are presented by different people over a period of time, instead of all at once, and don't include threats to cut off the addict unless he or she enters a program.

How, then, do you get the addict in your life to agree to enter a treatment program? This book lays out a plan for you to follow. Of course, I can't promise that, even if you follow it exactly, you'll be able to control the addict's substance abuse or get him or her into a program. But I know from experience that the power of Creative Engagement and, if necessary, Constructive Coercion, can help the addict in your life. I've seen many examples of the strategies contained in these pages tilting the balance toward sobriety, and am confident that, regardless of what efforts you've already made, I'll be able to show you some that you've never even thought of. More important, if you follow the plan, you can be sure that you'll have done the best you (or anyone) could do to help the addict you love end his or her dependence on drugs or alcohol.

In order to help you achieve this goal, the book is divided into four sections. The first—*An Addiction Primer*—helps you figure out whether or not your loved one is an addict, answers basic questions about the nature of addiction, and shows you both how addicts avoid dealing with the problem and what you can do about it. The second part—*Strategies for Getting the Addict into Treatment*—provides detailed suggestions for how, using Creative Engagement, you can gather information about addiction and addiction treaters and use that information to convince your loved one to go into treatment. It also explains when and, if necessary, how to use both Constructive and Legal Coercion. The third part—*Treatment Options*—explains what treatment is and what types of treatment are available, what to look for in evaluating a treatment facility, why and when detoxification may be necessary, the uses of psychotherapy in rehabilitation, the benefits of organizations like Alcoholics Anonymous, and some of the popular but, in my opinion, misguided strategies that you should avoid. The last part—*When Addiction Is Just One of the Problems*—discusses how to handle situations that can present special difficulties, such as dealing with addicts who have also been diagnosed with mental disorders.

As you read through this book, and work toward helping your loved one achieve sobriety, there's one other thing I'd like you to keep in mind. There's a wide range of treatments available for addiction, and even if one method doesn't work, that doesn't mean another won't. Too often those trying to help addicts give up out of frustration before exploring all the possible avenues. Sometimes they give up because they don't know there are other possibilities. More often, though, it's because they're unfamiliar or uncomfortable with other methods and afraid to try them, or because they're afraid of getting their hopes up for yet another "failure."

But the "failure" of any one particular addiction treatment doesn't mean that you should give up hope. It can mean that the treatment was ill-advised, that the addict wasn't ready for the particular treatment, that no treatment would have been effective at that particular time, or all three. In fact, even if the addict opts out of any treatment, or if multiple treatments have been tried and failed to help, the only disaster in addiction treatment is to stop trying without reassessing the situation and trying another strategy. We human beings can't tell the future, so we have to maintain our self-confidence and persevere through our doubts. Nowhere does this idea apply more powerfully than in addiction, where the addict's life can become a misery of suffering and self-doubt. So, too, for the family and friends of the addict, who must face down the strength-stealing loss of morale common in such a drawn-out battle against a resourceful enemy.

As someone whose profession is helping addicts, I am buoyed in my work by my memories of addicts who have "turned the corner" to a new life free from the agony of their addiction. Although I once thought that some addiction problems should be considered "terminal," as you've seen, I've learned over time that some of these seemingly hopeless individuals can—and do—find their way to sobriety and a better life. Although these transformations are due to the addict's own courage and faith, they serve to remind me that I must never abandon hope myself.

All the ideas presented here are based on my work with the friends and families of addicted people, and represent the techniques I've found to be the most effective. My primary goal is to provide hope and encouragement to people like you who are engaged in a battle to help their loved ones stop dangerous use of drugs and alcohol—to offer you tools and information that will make your difficult job a little easier.

Laurence M. Westreich, M.D.
New York, N.Y.

Part I

AN ADDICTION PRIMER

Chapter One

DO YOU HAVE AN ADDICT IN YOUR LIFE?

George and Emily had just finished dinner and were relaxing over coffee and dessert one evening when the phone rang. The call was from their son Sam's college roommate, who was calling to tell them that Sam had been hospitalized for "alcohol poisoning." Rushing to the hospital, they found Sam heavily sedated, with bruises all over his body, and surrounded by some very worried-looking nurses and doctors. They were relieved to hear that Sam's physical injuries were not life-threatening but surprised to discover that he'd experienced a severe alcohol withdrawal reaction in the hospital, hallucinating and even having a seizure. They were even more surprised, though, when Sam's roommate told them that he'd passed out from drinking several times over the previous semester. He was also, they learned, regularly using painkillers in pill form and had stopped attending classes several weeks before. Not knowing what to do, Sam's roommate had simply tried to keep him safe but hadn't called his parents or the campus infirmary. This time, though, when Sam passed out and threw up in his sleep, his roommate got scared and called 911.

You may not have had to face a situation like this yet, but you may soon, and I understand how worried you are. You have a son, a daughter, a parent, a brother or sister, a spouse, a boyfriend or girlfriend, or a friend who you're concerned may be an addict, and you don't know what to do about it. Let me tell you, first of all, that I've seen lots of people in the same place you are now, and difficult as it may be to believe, you will get through this. Just the fact that you're reading this book means that you care enough about the person to go out of your way to help, and that alone may well make the difference between life and death for him or her.

I'm going to tell you more about exactly what addiction is a little later, but for now all you need to know is that someone is an addict when he or she has lost control over his or her use of a substance, despite the negative consequences of that use. I know that's a very broad definition, but I mean it to be. I want you to understand that the word "addiction" can apply not only to physically addicting drugs like heroin or cocaine but also to alcohol, steroids, medications prescribed by a doctor, and marijuana, as well as sex and even food.

But what exactly do I mean by "lost control"? And exactly what are "negative consequences"? For our immediate purposes, people can be said to have "lost control" when they're using more of a substance than they intended, or for longer than they intended, or more often than they intended. "Negative consequences" are the harmful effects that the use of a substance has on someone's physical health, relationships, or ability to function at work or at school. Based on this definition, you may already believe that your friend or loved one is addicted. And you may be right. But before you do anything else, it's important that you make sure, and that's what this chapter is about.

The Signs of Addiction

Determining whether or not your friend or loved one is an addict is essentially the first step in Creative Engagement. It's possible, of course, that like George and Emily you may have already been confronted with incontrovertible proof that he or she is addicted, even if not quite so dramatically. You may, for example, have discovered that your wife is using so much cocaine that her nose bleeds and she feels her heart pounding so hard she can't sleep, or that your son's hangovers from alcohol leave him so depressed that he's contemplated killing himself. Even in the absence of such obvious signs, though, there are a number of ways you can tell whether or not someone is addicted.

The simplest—if not necessarily the most accurate—way to tell is to simply observe the individual for signs of addiction. Most addictions cause visible, if sometimes subtle, mental, behavioral, and physical changes in the addict, and for his or her sake, as well as your own, it's important that you know what they are. The general appearance of an addict—especially compared to his or her usual appearance—can provide clues to a serious problem. Obvious signs like an unsteady gait, sudden weight loss, a decreased interest in personal hygiene, or soiled clothing can be indications of a problem. But by the time someone is exhibiting signs like these, he or she has already been deeply drawn into addiction. That's why you should be on the lookout for the less obvious signs that will enable you to recognize that there is a problem and to do something to help before the situation gets to that point.

Among the most common mental signs of addiction are persistent sadness or depression, mood instability, and the hallucinations and delusions that psychiatrists call "psychosis." This psychosis might manifest itself by the addict's seeing bugs that aren't really there, being paranoid about other people's intentions, or worrying for no reason that the police are watching him or her. These mental signs can, however, be very subtle and can be easily mistaken for indications of other kinds of problems. For example, your friend may be depressed because she's using alcohol, but it may also be because she hates her job and is having difficulty finding one she likes. Similarly, your husband or wife might be having trouble sleeping because he or she is using cocaine, but it also might be due to stress at work. In fact, all of these mental signs of addiction can have other causes, but you should suspect addiction unless it's been absolutely ruled out.

There are also numerous behavioral signs of addiction that you should watch for. These include decreased success at work or in school, ill-defined problems in a relationship, or unexplained—even if minor—health problems. But as with the mental signs, recognizing these signs can be quite difficult. I recently worked with a family in which the parents told me they felt terrible about not noticing their twenty-year-old daughter's heavy heroin use until she'd been doing it for almost eight months. They'd noticed that she seemed very tired much of the time, and often dozed off while watching television, riding in the family car, and, sometimes, even while eating dinner. But because they thought her "sleepiness" was due to her heavy load of schoolwork—she was a college sophomore—all they did was suggest she learn to manage her time better.

They'd also noticed, though, that sometimes, particularly on weekends, she would be irritable, unable to sleep, and complain of cramps in her legs. It was only after she took a near-fatal overdose that they realized these were all signs of heroin addiction—the sleepiness during the week being a result of her using the drug, and the irritability and sleeplessness on the weekends caused by her inability to get any of it. Having no personal experience with addiction, the young woman's parents didn't recognize the signs because they didn't know what to look for. As is often the case, too, the problem was compounded by the fact that their daughter was not only trying to hide the signs from them but was also quick to provide excuses or rationales for those signs they did notice. She knew how they were used to seeing her and was able to lie effectively to make sure they would continue seeing her in the same way.

Another frequently seen behavioral sign of addiction is more-than-normal use of emergency rooms or doctors' offices. Many types of addiction can cause multiple medical problems that require frequent contact with doctors. One of the most common of these, particularly among alcoholics, is frequent bruising or aches and pains that the individual can't account for. In fact, they're usually caused by the alcoholic's falling down while intoxicated, even though he or she doesn't remember it. But physical trauma from falls and the well-known liver problems associated with alcohol are not the only medical problems that can suggest an addiction problem. I can't tell you the number of cocaine-addicted patients who have gone to specialists—sometimes for many years—complaining about frequent sinus infections, nosebleeds, or painful nasal passages, all of which were actually caused by snorting cocaine. There are also some common medical problems, like high blood pressure or diabetes, that can be considerably worsened by addiction.

Although the doctors themselves should be aware that these ailments might be signs of addiction, and should ask questions about them, the truth is that they don't always do it. And that means you'll probably have to put the pieces together yourself. In addition, if your friend or loved one is an addict, he or she may well be reluctant to tell a doctor about the substance use. In that case it would be best for you to go to the doctor with him or her to make sure that the actual problem is being addressed. Of course, if addicts acted logically they would tell their doctors everything they're taking into their bodies. Instead, they often try to hide the likely cause of the medical problem at the same time that they're trying to find the cause by going to the doctor. I know it doesn't make sense. It's called addiction, and it never does.

Finally, and most obviously, there are the physical signs of addiction. Some of these can be observed just by looking into someone's face. If your friend or loved one, for example, has reddened eyes, he or she may be using marijuana. Dilated—that is, enlarged—pupils can be the result of using stimulants like cocaine, methamphetamine, or crack. Conversely, opioid sedatives like heroin, oxycodone, and hydrocodone can cause very small "pinpoint" pupils, as well as droopy eyelids. A persistently bleeding or irritated nose suggests cocaine use, and the smell of alcohol or marijuana on the breath indicates the obvious.

Marks on your friend's or loved one's skin may also be a sign of certain types of addiction. Needle marks on the arms, as well as in less obvious places like the tops of the feet and behind the knees, are only the most familiar skin problems caused by drug addiction. Multiple skin infections, or abscesses on the arms or in other locations, might mean that he or she is "skin-popping"—injecting drugs under the skin. If someone has goose bumps on his or her skin, a runny nose, and tearing eyes, he or she may be an opiate user in withdrawal. (These signs, incidentally, are where the phrase "cold turkey" comes from.) Crack cocaine users often have a burned ridge on the thumb of their dominant hand, which is caused by the repetitive use of a lighter and crack pipe. Other burns on the lips, hands, and chin also suggest the use of crack.

But whether you're looking for mental, behavioral, or physical signs of addiction, the important thing is that you be vigilant and trust your instincts. If something seems to be "not right" about a friend or loved one, ask yourself if it could possibly be explained by the use of drugs or alcohol. Then ask everyone who might be able to provide you with some understanding—others in the family, friends, doctors, and anyone else you can think of. Finally, don't be afraid to ask the person you're concerned with about it, even if you think it might be embarrassing. Real concern from someone like you, expressed in a loving manner, can help an addict start thinking seriously about his or her actions as well as about the need for treatment.

Expressing Your Concern in a Constructive Way

But what's the best way to express your concern? And how do you do it without alienating the individual you're trying to help?

To be perfectly honest, there's no "right" way. However, I've found that the people who are most successful at approaching friends or loved ones about addiction are those who simply describe their worries while, at the same time, expressing their positive feelings for the individual. If, for example, you're concerned that your son may be smoking marijuana, you might raise the issue by saying something like, "Bill, Mom and I have been really worried lately when you come in late and we smell what seems like pot on your breath. We're just concerned that, if it is, you might hurt yourself while driving, or that it might be affecting your ability to study." Similarly, if you're worried that your father may be an alcoholic, you might invite him out to lunch and, during the meal, say, "Thanks for coming out for lunch with me, Dad. I wanted to spend some time with you, but I also wanted to tell you how worried I am about your drinking. It looks to me like it's making you depressed. I mean, you don't even seem to like golf anymore, and that's not like you."

In my experience, when people suspect addiction-related troubles in a friend or loved one, they're almost always correct. Even so, it's best to express your concerns this way because, when you do, you can avoid the individual's feeling that you're trying to "label" him or her as an addict, which is something that, not surprisingly, makes most people defensive. Also, by not specifically accusing the individual of anything, you acknowledge that you might be wrong and that the behavior you see could be due to something else.

But timing is also important in approaching someone you're concerned may have an addiction problem. There's an old axiom in psychotherapy that says, "Strike while the iron is cold," and that's good advice to follow in situations like these. When the individual is intoxicated or in withdrawal, there's probably not much value in your pursuing the subject. He or she may not be able to process what you're saying, be in such discomfort that nothing will get through, or be unable to even remember the conversation later. But when he or she is feeling relatively well—and you're feeling somewhat less panicky about the problem—you can sit down and express your concerns in a low-key, nonthreatening way.

The chances are that, if you raise the issue this way, even if it turns out that there's some other explanation, the worst thing that can happen will be that your friend or loved one will think you're being overly concerned about his or her well-being. More likely, though, you'll have accurately picked up on a problem. And if that's the case, by confronting the addict with the concrete evidence you see before you—even if he or she denies it—you'll have started chipping away at the addict's efforts to cover it up. In the best-case scenario, your raising the issue might even provoke the addict to ask for or seek the help he or she needs. Here's an example of how such a conversation might go.

"I Don't Use Cocaine That Much Anymore"

Boyfriend: Marie, I'm really worried about the way you've been using cocaine at parties lately. You talk a mile a minute and you act like everything is hilarious, and it's really scary. *[Bill just offers an observation rather than accusing Marie of anything.]*

Addict: Oh, please, Bill! I just snort a few lines to get up for the party. I work really hard all week, and if I didn't do some coke when we go out I'd be asleep by ten o'clock. You know that. *[Marie minimizes her drug use.]*

Boyfriend: I do know that, but it was really embarrassing at Tina's last week when she asked you to leave. Especially since she's such a good friend of yours! She told me that you were coming on to all the guys there and she couldn't take it anymore. To tell you the truth, it looked to me like you were flirting with *everyone* in the room, male and female. *[Bill offers more simple observation.]*

Addict: I was just kidding! Have you lost your sense of humor? [She pauses for a moment.] Okay, sometimes I worry about the way I use it, too. But I really don't use it that much anymore—only on weekends, after work is done. It's nothing like when we were in college.

Boyfriend: I know you're using less than you did in college. But the way you're using now really does scare me, and I'm worried about you. You look like you're going crazy when you use, and you act crazy. You won't stop, or pay attention to me, and you pester anyone who's got it to give you more. *[Bill (still) correctly sticks to description, not diagnosis, when confronting her about the problem.]*

Addict: That's not fair! I've cut down on my cocaine use, and now you're attacking me!

Boyfriend: I'm not attacking you. I'm worried about you.

Addict: [She's silent for few moments.] Anyway, you use coke, too.

Boyfriend: It's true, and I guess I shouldn't. The thing is, I'm willing to stop if you are, because I think it's hurting you, and it could hurt me, too. We could go to get some help together.

Addict: Oh, great! I can just see us in some AA group. A

couple of losers who aren't even alcoholics. *[Marie tries to deflect Bill's suggestion. But drug-addicted people often attend AA, as well as other groups like Cocaine Anonymous or Narcotics Anonymous.]*

Boyfriend: Well, at least we wouldn't be spending all our extra cash on drugs.

Addict: All right. I'll go to AA, but only if you go with me. I think your problem is as bad as mine.

Boyfriend: Great, I'll find an AA meeting for us to go to this Saturday night before we go out. *[Bill avoids rising to the bait of discussing his own use of drugs. He's gotten Marie to agree to go to a meeting, a first step in getting her the help she needs. And the specific commitment—an AA meeting on Saturday night—is better than just asking her to agree to "go for help."]*

This conversation obviously worked out well. To be fair, though, there is a possibility that, when confronted like this, your friend or loved one may react in an angry or, in extreme cases, even violent way. Of course, an angry response would suggest that there's a genuine and serious problem with addiction. If you think that he or she may become violent, it would be best to avoid the confrontation yourself and, instead, arrange for a professional to discuss the issue with him or her. I'll tell you more about the types of addiction treaters that are available and how to get an addict to see one later on in the book. As a start, though, you can make arrangements to do this by looking in your local phone book for psychiatrists, psychologists, social workers, or counselors who treat addiction. In addition, your local hospital may have resources available from the psychiatry department. You could also use the resources suggested in Appendix A: Where to Find Help.

Getting Toward a Diagnosis

Based on the definition of addiction I've suggested, or on signs you've observed, you may now believe that your friend or loved one is an addict or at least has a problem with a particular substance. If so, before you do anything else, it's important that you make sure. At the same time, though, you should remember that, as I mentioned earlier, in terms of seeking help, the actual diagnosis is secondary. Damage—and potential damage—to the individual's physical and mental health, relationships, and employment are much more important than quibbling over the exact diagnosis. Even so, there are several reasons why establishing a diagnosis is important.

First, the process of establishing a diagnosis—whether you're using a very simple method or one of the well-defined and scientifically validated approaches—can sometimes convince the addict that he or she has a problem and help solidify your own determination to help the individual. Second, just asking the kind of questions that need to be asked may enable both you and the addicted person to recognize additional consequences of addiction that you hadn't even considered. Finally, a standard diagnosis may be required for admission into a treatment program and/or to get a health insurer to cover the cost of the program.

How, then, can you determine definitively if your friend or loved one is an addict or has a substance problem? There have been a number of methods developed to do that. Among the best-known and widely used of these are the "Substance Dependence" criteria included in the professional handbook called the *Diagnostic and Statistical Manual of Mental Disorders,* Fourth Edition–Text Revision

(American Psychiatric Association, 2000), referred to as DSM-IV-TR; "The Michigan Alcoholism Screening Test (MAST)" (M. L. Selzer, "The Michigan Alcoholism Screening Test—The Quest for a New Diagnostic Instrument," *American Journal of Psychiatry* 127(1971): 1653–1658.); the CRAFFT test for adolescents; and the Alcohol Use Disorders Identification Test (AUDIT).

These tests were all developed—and are used—by professionals. In fact, if you should need to get your friend or loved one into a program, a clinician will probably administer one of them to him or her. They're all designed to get at the core of the issue, that is, the behaviors that lead people to suspect there may be a problem. By essentially providing lists of behaviors that indicate the existence of such a problem, these methods enable practitioners to determine whether or not a problem actually exists. Some of them, however, are quite complex, and for your immediate purposes there's a much simpler test you can use to determine if the individual is an addict or has a substance problem. It's called the "Three C's of Addiction."

The Three C's of Addiction

The "Three C's of Addiction" are "Lack of Control over Use," "Compulsive Use," and "Continued Use Despite Knowledge of Adverse Consequences." "Lack of Control over Use" distinguishes between the individual who has two beers on a Friday night and the addict who *says* he's going to have two beers and winds up drinking ten times that many. "Compulsive Use" refers to the repetitive use of a substance to the exclusion of other major life activities, such as working or maintaining relationships with other people. That is, it defines an addict as someone whose use of a substance is so all-consuming that it's more important than anything else in his or her life. Finally, "Continued Use Despite Knowledge of Adverse Consequences" essentially means that anyone who continues using a substance that he or she knows to be harmful is in all likelihood an addict. In fact, this criterion could alone be considered the very definition of addiction.

This method is appropriate for use by anyone trying to determine if someone has an addiction problem, because the "Three C's" put into words some commonsense criteria you can use to convince yourself (and perhaps your loved one) that there is a problem. Of course, these criteria are very general, so they're not as meaningful as the more detailed methods used by professional addiction treaters. If, however, you're interested in getting a better understanding of how addiction affects people, and in more accurately determining whether or not your loved one has a problem, you can also ask yourself the questions listed below.

Additional Questions to Ask

There are essentially five areas in which an addict is likely to exhibit behaviors that may be caused by whatever substance he or she is using—physical problems, mental problems, relationship problems, work/school problems, and legal problems. Using the professional tests I mentioned earlier, I've put together a list of questions in these five areas. If you suspect your loved one is having a problem in one of these areas, you should run down the list and see if he or she is having any of the other problems mentioned. If, on the other hand, you suspect the individual has a problem but you don't know whether or not it's true, you can simply browse through all the questions. Doing so should help you recognize those behaviors that are related to substance abuse, and if it appears that your friend or loved one is using a substance, you can use that information to press him or her to get help.

QUESTIONS ABOUT PHYSICAL PROBLEMS

- Has the individual become so tolerant of the effects of the substance that he or she has to take more to achieve the same effect?

- Does the individual exhibit symptoms of withdrawal from the substance when he or she stops using it?
- Does the individual continue using the substance despite its having negative physical effects such as skin infections, weight loss, or others?
- Has the individual ever physically harmed him- or herself—or anyone else—as a result of the substance use?

QUESTIONS ABOUT MENTAL PROBLEMS

- Does the individual take more of the substance than he or she intends?
- Does the individual continue using the substance despite negative emotional effects such as depression or anxiety?
- Does the individual use the substance to feel better?
- Does the individual forget what happens when he or she uses the substance?

QUESTIONS ABOUT RELATIONSHIP PROBLEMS

- Has the individual's marriage or other relationship(s) been affected by the substance use?
- Does the individual's substance use worry friends or family?
- Does the individual get into verbal or physical fights while using the substance?
- Does the individual, when using substances, have sex with people he or she would otherwise not have sex with?

QUESTIONS ABOUT WORK/SCHOOL PROBLEMS

- Has the individual's work productivity or attendance suffered as a result of his or her substance use?
- Has the individual's school grades or attendance suffered as a result of his or her substance use?

- Does the individual use substances while on the job or at school?

QUESTIONS ABOUT LEGAL PROBLEMS
- Has the individual been arrested for anything related to drugs or alcohol?
- Has the individual been stopped by the police for any reason related to drugs or alcohol?
- Has the individual committed any illegal act as a result of his or her substance use?

If the answer to even one of these questions is "yes," you certainly have reason to be concerned and should look into it further by asking your friend or loved one about it. Although social use of substances can occasionally result in a positive response to one of these questions, it's more likely that you've either identified an early sign of more serious substance use or just recognized the most visible of several such signs. In any case, you're better off asking about the issue than remaining silent and perhaps allowing your loved one to progress to a more dangerous level of addiction.

Is He or She Just an Addict, or Is There Another Problem, Too?

Being an addict is certainly enough of a problem for anyone. But sometimes—in fact, much more frequently than most people realize—addicts also suffer from a variety of other mental illnesses. A common example of this is the alcoholic who also has clinical depression. This kind of "dual diagnosis" can confuse the addicts themselves, their friends and family, and those who treat them, because symptoms of addiction and mental illness can mimic each other. Sadness, lethargy, and impaired sleep, for example, are found in both alcoholics and people with depression. Interestingly, the American Psychiatric Association's official diagnostic guidelines put substance dependence in the same category (AXIS I) as other psychiatric illnesses such as depression and schizophrenia. What this means is that addiction should be considered a disease in the same way that schizophrenia is. That is, while the sufferer should not be held responsible for *having* the condition, he or she should be held responsible for *getting it treated*.

The term "dual diagnosis" includes a virtually endless variety of combinations, from the anxious individual who smokes marijuana to the schizophrenic who uses crack cocaine. And since mental illnesses and addictions often occur at the same time, and mimic each other's symptoms, if you suspect that, besides being addicted to a substance, your friend or loved one suffers from another mental illness, you should make sure to contact a psychiatrist who's been trained specifically in the field of dual diagnosis. Such an individual will be able to assess the nature and extent of the addict's substance problem as well as of his or her mental illness. He or she will also be able to design and coordinate the kind of more complex treatment plan that the addict will need in order to deal with both of his or her problems. (There's more information on these kinds of treatment plans in chapter 7, as well as a discussion of how to deal most effectively with dually diagnosed addicts in chapter 13.)

Do You Have an Addict in Your Life?

- Be on the lookout for the mental, behavioral, and physical signs of addiction.
- Always trust your instincts. If something doesn't seem right, ask about it.

- Make sure your friend or loved one actually has a substance problem before taking any action.
- Focus on the addict's behaviors rather than on the diagnosis.
- Concentrate on getting help for the addict, not on "catching" him or her.
- Strive to be gently insightful rather than dramatic.
- Always address the big problems first.
- If you think the addict may also have a mental illness, have a trained clinician assess him or her to determine if it's so and, if necessary, design a comprehensive treatment program.

You now know how to tell if someone is an addict and should have a good idea of whether or not your friend or loved one actually has a substance abuse problem. In the next chapter I'm going to tell you more about what addiction really is, how and why people become addicted, and the kinds of things they become addicted to.

Chapter Two

WHAT ADDICTION REALLY IS

Before you try to help an addict, it's important that you know and understand exactly what addiction is. That is, why and how people become addicts and the kind of substances to which they become addicted. This, too, is part of Creative Engagement. Having this kind of information will help you—and help you help the addict—by enabling you to understand and appreciate how powerful a pull addiction has on those who are under its influence. This will, in turn, enable you not only to be more compassionate but also to maintain, over the long term, the desire you feel right now to help the individual rid him- or herself of the addiction. And that's ultimately what this whole process is about.

Why and How People Become Addicted

Trying to understand why and how your friend or loved one became an addict is one of the most painful and difficult tasks you're likely to encounter. To complicate matters, reasonable people can and often do disagree on the causes and explanations of addiction. And for that reason, there are a number of different theories, or models, of it. However, because each of these models approaches it from a somewhat different perspective, each one, except the one called the "Moral Model," can help explain at least some part of addiction, as well as some part of why the addict you love behaves in such a self-destructive way. There's something else, too, that these models have in common. They all make it painfully clear that once someone becomes an addict, because of the nature of addiction itself, he or she no longer has the ability to make choices in the same way that you and I do. The addiction, in effect, damages the "choosing mechanism" in his or her brain. And that's something you always have to take into account when dealing with someone who has a substance abuse problem. In practical terms, this means that no matter how clearly and logically you explain to your friend or loved one why the addiction must stop, he or she simply won't understand and will continue using the substance.

The Models of Addiction

Of the several models, or explanations, of addiction, the most un-fortunate—and least useful—is the one referred to as the "Moral Model." This model argues that all addicts are either evil, weak-willed, or both, and was used for years to explain the apparently inexplicable behavior of addicts. Although it's been convincingly disproved by several of the other explanations discussed below, even now family members hurt by an addict's behavior, health-care workers frustrated in their attempts to help addicts, or politi-cians looking for an easy target sometimes turn to this "theory" of addiction.

The "Learning Theory Model" of addiction, which is based on neurochemistry and psychology, suggests that people become addicts because, having experienced a beneficial effect from using a substance, such as feeling "high," they will seek out the substance again. This is known as "positive reinforcement." Of course, it's perfectly normal for people to want more of something that feels good. But our brains aren't designed to cope with the kind of substances we can become addicted to, so even though that kind of response may be psychologically appropriate, it can also be terribly destructive. In addition, according to this theory, once addicted, the individual may continue using the substance to avoid the painful effects of withdrawal. A prime example of this is the alcohol-dependent person who has to have a drink early in the morning to avoid the "shakes," one of the symptoms of the addiction itself.

Another model, the "Self-Medication Hypothesis," suggests that people become addicts by starting to use a particular addictive substance in order to "treat" a specific kind of emotional disturbance. An angry person, for example, might choose a depressant drug like heroin to calm the fury he or she feels inside all the time. By contrast, a depressed, lethargic person might choose a substance like cocaine to provide him or her with a burst of energy, even if only a temporary one. According to this theory, which has been best described by Dr. Edward Khantzian at Harvard University, it's the need to control these emotional disturbances that encourages the initial use of the substance. This, in turn, not only leads to the user's becoming dependent on the substance but also contributes to his or her relapses. Advocates of this theory don't claim that these drugs actually help addicts deal with their emotional problems over the long term, only that the need to exercise some control over those problems is what begins the cycle of addiction.

The "Biopsychosocial Model," as its name suggests, argues that addiction—like other types of psychiatric illness—is caused by a combination of factors and, accordingly, requires a combination of interrelated methods to treat it. This theory is based, at least in part, on the widely held although not conclusively proven belief that, in addition to psychological and social components, there's a biological or genetic component to addiction. Research studies on twins and children of alcoholics—although not on those dependent on other substances—show a clear tendency toward addiction in blood relatives. This doesn't mean that alcoholism is something you can inherit from your parents, like blue eyes or red hair. It only means you can be born with a predisposition, or vulnerability, to it.

According to the "Biopsychosocial Model," it's this vulnerability, when combined with psychological and social components, that can lead to substance abuse problems. Unhappiness, stress, or psychiatric syndromes like depression or psychosis can make someone with this genetic predisposition turn to substances for relief of their symptoms. Similarly, social factors like poverty, homelessness, and a general lack of social support can contribute to the likelihood of someone's becoming an addict. However, while this model may ultimately prove to be a useful explanation of the causes of addiction, right now it's actually most valuable as a prescription for treatment. As I'll explain later on, any addict is most likely to abstain from substances of abuse if he or she receives comprehensive treatment that addresses psychological problems, biological changes, and the environmental or social cues that encourage relapse.

Finally, there is the "Disease Model" of addiction, which is the one I find most convincing. This model defines addiction as a chronic, relapsing medical condition much like high blood pressure or diabetes. This definition fits the picture of addiction in many ways: like a medical illness, addiction has both a genetic and an environmental component. The genetic component, as I mentioned earlier, is the possibility that people can actually inherit a vulnerability to addiction, at least to alcohol if not necessarily to other substances. And environment becomes a factor because, just as a person with hypertension can lower his or her blood pressure by losing weight and avoiding salt, an addict can ward off relapse by avoiding situations that he or she knows will trigger a relapse, such as spending time with other addicts or in the local bar.

Also like individuals with physical ailments, however, addicts must bear responsibility for treating their condition, or suffer the consequences of neglecting that treatment. In the same way, for example, that a diabetic must take insulin on a daily basis to stay healthy, a recovering addict must attend self-help groups, have relapse prevention counseling, and take his or her prescribed medications. To my mind, though, the greatest advantage of the "Disease Model" may be that it removes the moral stigma from addiction. It presents the addict, like anyone suffering from an illness, as an unfortunate victim rather than as a "bad person" who is somehow to blame for his or her sickness. Unlike the "Moral Model," which essentially blames the individual for being ill, this model takes a more positive approach by emphasizing the action needed to treat the addiction and make the sufferer well again.

The Biology of Addiction

The various theories of addiction help explain why people become addicts, but it's the biological effects of substances on the human body that explain how it happens. And unless you understand both, you won't be able to sympathize with the addict who's fighting forces that are drawing him or her to the substance of abuse. And sympathy is not only necessary, it's also appropriate. If your friend or loved one had asthma, for example, and was having difficulty breathing, you would certainly sympathize with him or her. Addiction isn't any different. Asthma is a disease of the body, and addiction largely one of the brain, but both create strong biological drives. In fact, the addict's need for his or her substance of choice is like a starving person's primal need for food. Drugs and alcohol literally "hijack" the brain, physically and emotionally driving the addict to find, use, and keep using whatever drug he or she has chosen.

In fact, addiction is such a powerful force that laboratory rats that are allowed to self-administer drugs like cocaine will do so to the point of starvation, exhaustion, or even death. Of course, people aren't lab animals, but our addictive behaviors often show the same lack of concern for our physical well-being. These behaviors, in simple terms, are the result of chemical changes that occur when an individual uses an addictive substance. What happens is these substances cause an upsurge of neurochemicals in a part of the brain called the *nucleus accumbens,* which is sometimes referred to as the "pleasure center." These neurochemicals in turn cause changes in the brain that make it much more difficult to stop using the substance. The brain, in effect, says, "Get more of that!" and "Do it again!" And the addict does what the brain tells him or her to do.

Over the past twenty-five years, this biological explanation of the basis of addiction has come to be so widely accepted that *not* believing it is like saying that the world is flat. It's important to remember, though, that biology only explains *how* someone becomes an addict, not *why*. Nor, unfortunately, can it provide a cure—we still have only primitive medications for treating the disease. Of course, that doesn't mean you have to accept your friend or loved one's addiction. What it does mean is that in order to help him or her you have to address the other aspects of addiction—the addict's social and emotional environment. I'll tell you more about how to do that later on, but for now you just need to understand that addressing these aspects means, in large part, relying on nonbiological tools like Alcoholics Anonymous (AA) and relapse-prevention psychotherapy, both of which have proven to be very effective against addiction. Most important, you have to remember that what your friend or loved one needs most of all is your understanding and support in his or her struggle toward sobriety.

What People Become Addicted To

Addicted people often have a "drug of choice" and, unfortunately, there are many drugs from which they can choose. Addicts also

sometimes move back and forth between several different substances, particularly when, for one reason or another, they're trying to get off one of them. For example, a man trying to stop
using cocaine (a stimulant) might be able to do so by, instead,
starting to drink alcohol (a depressant). Even though the effects
of these substances are different—in fact, opposite—using them
allows him to alter his consciousness, which may have been what
he was trying to do in the first place. Since, however, an individual
who's become addicted to one substance is much more vulnerable
to becoming addicted to another, it's likely that he would eventually progress to the point where his alcohol abuse was as bad as his
cocaine abuse had been.

Despite the wide variety of drugs available, though, there are
actually only four basic categories of addictive substances, each of
which in turn includes numerous drugs. (The following table lists
the names, availability, use, and primary effects of these drugs.) The
categories are central nervous system (CNS) depressants, central
nervous system stimulants, hallucinogens, and other substances.
Although the biological effects of these drugs vary widely, their
destructive patterns are quite similar, as is their treatment.

Substances and What They Do

Category	Substance	Availability	Method of Use	Primary Effects
Central Nervous System Depressants	Alcohol	Legal for adults	Oral	Sedation Disinhibition
	Barbiturates: Fiorinal Fioricet Seconal Phenobarbital	By prescription	Oral	Sedation Disinhibition Pain relief
	Benzodiazepines: Valium Halcion Xanax Ativan Restoril Serax Tranxene Dalmane	By prescription	Oral	Sedation Disinhibition Memory loss
	Opiates: Heroin Percodan Percocet Vicodin Methadone Morphine Dilaudid Demerol Fentanyl Tylenol II, III, IV	By prescription	Oral Smoked Injected (into veins or under skin) Snorted	Sedation Disinhibition Pain relief

Category	Substance	Availability	Method of Use	Primary Effects
Central Nervous System Stimulants	Amphetamine	By prescription	Oral Smoked	Mood elevation Increased energy Weight loss
	Caffeine	Legal for adults	Oral	Stimulation
	Cocaine: Powder cocaine Crack cocaine Freebase cocaine	Illegal	Snorted Injected Smoked	Stimulation Euphoria
	Methamphet-amine in pill form	By prescription	Oral	Stimulation Euphoria
	Methamphet-amine in smokable form "Ice" "Crank" "Speed" "Crystal"	Illegal	Smoked	Stimulation Euphoria
	Nicotine	Legal for adults	Smoked	Stimulation
Hallucinogens	LSD	Illegal	Oral	Hallucinations Delusions
	Marijuana	Illegal (except for medical marijuana)	Smoked	Sedation Hallucinations
	MDMA: "X" "XTC" "E" "Ecstasy"	Illegal	Oral	Euphoria

Category	Substance	Availability	Method of Use	Primary Effects
Hallucinogens (cont.)	Mescaline	Illegal	Oral	Hallucinations Delusions
	Mushrooms	Illegal	Oral	Hallucinations Delusions
Other Substances	Anabolic-androgenic steroids	By prescription	Oral Injected (into muscles)	Muscle and endurance building Heart and liver disease Disinhibition
	Inhalants: Nitrous oxide Amyl nitrate "Poppers" "Whippits" Glue Solvents Gasoline	Legal (if bought for legitimate reasons)	Snorted	Sedation Disinhibition
	PCP ("Angel Dust")	Illegal	Oral	Stimulation Pain relief
	Ketamine	By prescription	Oral Snorted	Anesthesia Hallucinations

Central Nervous System Depressants

The broad category of central nervous system (CNS) depressants includes alcohol, barbiturates, benzodiazepine drugs like Valium, and opioids such as heroin, Vicodin, and Darvon. Although the ultimate effect of these substances is sedation, the immediate result of using them can be a loss of inhibitions, as anyone who has seen a "rowdy drunk" can testify. The brain mechanisms that normally prevent us from acting in offensive or otherwise inappropriate ways are deactivated by the drug, and the user appears to be energized or intoxicated by the supposedly "sedating" substance.

Too much of a CNS depressant causes fatigue, unconsciousness, and ultimately paralysis of the brain center that regulates breathing, which results in death. At what point this paralysis occurs depends on how tolerant a user has become of the particular substance. When someone develops a "tolerance" of a substance it means that he or she needs more and more of it to achieve the same effect. That is, a casual drinker usually needs less alcohol to feel high than someone who's accustomed to drinking a great deal. For that reason, while a high alcohol level in the blood can have little effect on a longtime alcoholic, it can be lethal to a first-time drinker. This is, unfortunately, demonstrated every fall when college freshmen, trying alcohol in large amounts for the first time, sometimes drink so much that they die of the alcohol's effects.

On the other hand, those who have developed a tolerance of CNS depressants are also vulnerable to several potential dangers. For example, even the knowledgeable heroin addict may inadvertently use much stronger heroin than he or she is used to, resulting in overdose and, sometimes, death. Similarly, someone who has, separately, drunk alcohol and taken barbiturates, and had no problem with either, might make the mistake of underestimating the effects of combining the two, which sometimes prove lethal.

Finally, withdrawal—that is, the effects of abruptly stopping the use of a substance—from CNS depressants can also result in death. *Delirium tremens,* which is a syndrome of impaired consciousness, hallucinations, and fluctuating blood pressure and pulse caused by withdrawal from alcohol or other CNS depressants, has a very high mortality rate. In fact, the potential for death from this syndrome is so great that withdrawal from alcohol is one of the few addiction diagnoses for which most insurance companies will pay for immediate inpatient treatment.

Central Nervous System Stimulants

The category of central nervous system (CNS) stimulants includes amphetamine, methylphenidate, methamphetamine, cocaine, caffeine, and nicotine. These substances all stimulate the production of chemicals in the brain that cause excitement, which in turn results in euphoria, irritability, elevated blood pressure, and sometimes paranoia.

Amphetamine and methylphenidate are both legal stimulants that are sometimes prescribed for attention deficit hyperactivity disorder (ADHD), depression, or hypersomnia. Amphetamine can also be abused, though, and is sometimes used as a "stay-awake" pill for truck drivers, a stimulant for athletes, or a medication to help people lose weight. Both medications are also sometimes abused by people who crush the pills and snort them in order to get an immediate "high."

Methamphetamine, in its oral (pill) form, is also a prescription drug. Marketed as Desoxyn and others, it's used for weight reduction as well as a few other purposes. It's also available illegally, however, in a smokable form. Known as "ice," "speed," "crank," or "crystal," this form of the drug has become increasingly popular, particularly on the West Coast and in the Midwest, over the last several years. Its initial effects are increased energy and weight loss but, as I've mentioned, it eventually leads to irritability, paranoia, aggressiveness, and often death. Because it's relatively easy to make using instructions and materials available on the Internet, law enforcement agencies have found it particularly difficult to stem the drug's flow into new communities.

Cocaine, another common stimulant, is also available in several forms, including powder cocaine, which can be snorted or injected, and crack and freebase cocaine, which are smoked. In the late 1980s and early 1990s, cocaine became known as a party drug and its use spread throughout society. A very potent and addictive stimulant, cocaine was used both for getting high and for enhancing—if only briefly—the user's thinking ability, which was helpful at work or in school. But many of its users became addicted and suffered from nasal problems from snorting it, heart attacks and strokes from its cardiovascular effects, and the same kind of social losses that every addiction brings with it. Although cocaine is no longer considered a hot new drug, there's still plenty of it around, and people are still becoming addicted to it.

And of course, there are caffeine and nicotine, both of which are, of course, legal and can be ingested, respectively, through coffee, tea, and soft drinks, and tobacco. Even though these stimulants are readily available, they can nevertheless cause problems on their own. For example, many people who stop using alcohol or illicit drugs increase their use of caffeine or nicotine. And as anyone who's had too much coffee knows, heavy caffeine use can cause heart palpitations, anxiety, insomnia, and withdrawal headaches. And nicotine, in the form of tobacco, kills more Americans every year—about 400,000—than alcohol, cocaine, and heroin put together.

When someone has too much of a CNS stimulant, the result is an extreme version of whatever effect he or she was trying to achieve in the first place. For example, the exuberance and heightened awareness that people feel when they've just used cocaine can quickly turn into irritability, self-absorption, and sometimes the break with reality called psychosis. In addition, the increased heart rate and blood pressure it produces can be not only dangerous but fatal. Conversely, withdrawing from CNS stimulants can make the user feel the exact opposite of what he or she felt while using the drug. And the "crash" that people go through after using cocaine can lead to suicidal feelings, physical lethargy, and hopelessness about the future. The cocaine user may feel high for a short period of time, but he or she pays for it by subsequently experiencing an emotional low that can last for days. As anyone who's tried to stop smoking knows, withdrawing from nicotine, although not dangerous, produces a craving for nicotine, agitation, and insomnia, which is why so many people go back to smoking. And, finally, the physically benign effects of caffeine withdrawal—headaches, lethargy, and a dulled mood—are what keep Starbucks in business.

Hallucinogens

The third category of addictive substances is hallucinogens, which include marijuana; lysergic acid diethylamide (LSD); and methylenedioxymethamphetamine (MDMA), which is known by a variety of names, including "X," "XTC," "E," and "Ecstasy," among others. Although these substances are generally considered to be harmless by many young people, they all change the user's consciousness in ways that are unpredictable, and can cause delusions, hallucinations, and paranoia. They can also cause profound lethargy and a lack of motivation that can lead to failure at work, in relationships, and in school. In fact, hallucinogens can destroy a person's life just as quickly as cocaine.

Marijuana is unique among these substances in that it's not only seen as relatively harmless but is also widely available. (In a survey conducted in 2005, 44.8 percent of twelfth graders said they had tried marijuana or hashish.) And it is true that many people show no apparent ill effects from occasional use of the drug. However, marijuana smokers can—and sometimes do—develop the same addictive behaviors associated with the "harder drugs." Also, although many people have doubts about the argument that marijuana leads to harder drugs, the fact is that it can. Because marijuana works as both a hallucinogen and a sedative, smoking even a small amount of it can impair a user's judgment just enough so that, given an opportunity, he or she might be willing to try one of the more dangerous substances. Unfortunately, if you're a parent, the prevalence of marijuana use among teenagers may make it difficult for you to convince your children to stay away from it. But since even apparently innocent experimentation with marijuana can cause unanticipated legal, social, and health consequences, it's best for you to be strict about the use of *all* drugs, including marijuana. It may not prevent your child from using it, but it can reduce the frequency of its use and increase the age at which it's first used, both of which are positive goals in themselves.

LSD, which was developed in a laboratory in the 1940s, can cause hallucinations that can persist for months and, sometimes, even years. In addition to these hallucinations, the "acid trip" it causes can include both delusions and a profound sense of self-reflection. Although the drug has been extensively studied for a variety of possible military and medical uses, it's been used consistently only for recreational purposes. It first became popular in the late 1960s, and then again as a "club drug" in the late 1990s. LSD users most often come to the attention of clinicians when they have a bad trip, which produces profound anxiety, bizarre perceptions, and the feeling that they're "going crazy."

MDMA is often used by young people at parties and dance "raves" to promote a sense of well-being and a connection with those around them. Those who use it say it provides a sense of warmth and open-mindedness toward others without the stirring of sexual desires. Since, though, MDMA acts as a stimulant, it can also cause rapid heart rate, increases in blood pressure, and dehydration. Although the drug is not fatal itself, deaths related to it have been reported in situations where there was no water available to users who were dancing vigorously in a hot room, became seriously dehydrated, and subsequently suffered kidney failure. MDMA has also been shown to cause memory problems in heavy users.

Other Substances

The fourth and final group of addictive substances includes anabolic androgenic steroids (AAS); inhalants like nitrous oxide, amyl nitrate, and solvents; phenyl cyclohexyl piperidine (PCP), which is also known as "Angel Dust"; and Ketamine.

Anabolic androgenic steroids are chemicals that are converted in the body to testosterone, the naturally occurring chemical that creates "masculine" traits in men. Developed during World War II, and first used by athletes in 1954, they can cause muscle growth, increased strength, and aggressive behavior. They're taken today, by both athletes and bodybuilders, in several forms, including pills, injections, and skin creams. Despite the fact that their use has been outlawed by the International Olympic Committee as well as virtually every professional sports league (including Major League Baseball, the National Football League, the National Basketball Association, and others), they're still being used illicitly by professional as well as high school and college athletes. Unfortunately, because they do what they promise to do, that is, make muscles grow larger and improve their users' abilities, the athletes' friends, family members, and coaches often turn a blind eye to their sudden spurt of muscle growth.

The fact is, however, that these substances are extremely dangerous, particularly to young people. They can, for example, cause early closing of the growth plates, which means that users may be shorter when they reach maturity than they would have otherwise been. The fact that many elite weight lifters are wide but short is probably no coincidence. Also, since the amount of testosterone in a user's body is considerably greater than normal, the body converts the extra testosterone to the female hormone estrogen, which causes men's breasts to grow. Female AAS users, conversely, suffer from the side effects of too much testosterone, including increased facial hair, deepening of the voice, and enlargement of the clitoris. Both men and women suffer side effects that include muscle and tendon tears, heart and liver problems, and serious depression when they withdraw from the drugs.

Inhalants are substances whose vapors can be snorted or taken in through the mouth, and include gasoline, kerosene, antifreeze, lighter fuel, and even general anesthetic agents like nitrous oxide (N_2O or "whippits"). They're legal as well as safe when used as intended but are nevertheless very dangerous when abused. For example, nitrous oxide, which is normally used by dentists, causes intoxication when overused by recreational users. More important, overdoses or long-term use of N_2O can bring about memory loss, hallucinations, and such severe nerve degeneration that it can cause paralysis. The most commonly used inhalants are paint thinners, gasoline, and glue. Their users are usually young, unable to obtain other substances of abuse, and blithely unaware of their potential dangers. People use inhalants because they cause a certain wooziness, even though side effects range from nausea to nosebleeds to a chronic cough. Over the long term, though, many of the inhalants can cause suppression of the bone marrow, kidney and liver failure, and neurological problems like paralysis.

Phenyl cyclohexyl piperidine, better known as PCP or "Angel Dust," was originally developed as a surgical anesthetic for use with humans. It was quickly abandoned, though, because its use tended to cause confusion, agitation, and hallucinations. PCP abusers use it as a powder or in flakes, often sprinkling it on marijuana cigarettes to heat it up, and inhale it as vapors, along with the marijuana smoke, to get its full effect more quickly. Because it acts as both a hallucinogen and a stimulant, the drug causes disorientation, visual hallucinations, and sometimes violent behavior. And, since these symptoms can continue for up to five or six hours after a single use, people intoxicated with it sometimes find themselves admitted to psychiatric hospitals on the assumption that they are mentally ill.

Finally, Ketamine, like PCP, was originally developed as an anesthetic, although for use with animals rather than with people. Known on the club scene as "K" or "Special K," it's usually smoked on marijuana or tobacco and produces hallucinations, confusion, and high blood pressure in its users. Also like PCP, an overdose can cause violent behavior, and heavy users sometimes experience long-term memory loss.

~~~~~~~~

What Addiction Really Is

- Addiction is not a choice.
- Addicts react to substances differently than other people do.
- Genetics and biology make addicts more vulnerable to addiction than other people.
- Addicts often deal with their emotional state by using substances.
- Addiction is a disease.
- Addicts change their "drug of choice."
- Depressants include alcohol and heroin.
- Stimulants include cocaine, Ritalin, and caffeine.
- Hallucinogens include marijuana, LSD, Ecstasy, and mescaline.
- Other addictive substances include steroids, inhalants, and PCP.

Now you know something about how and why your friend or loved one became an addict, as well as something about the kinds of substances to which he or she may be addicted. In the next chapter I'm going to tell you about the kinds of defense mechanisms addicts use to protect their addiction, as well as provide you with some guidelines on how you can manage those defense mechanisms for the addict's benefit as well as your own.

Chapter Three

HOW ADDICTS AVOID DEALING WITH THE PROBLEM AND WHAT YOU CAN DO ABOUT IT

As you learned in the last chapter, in order to help your friend or loved one rid him- or herself of an addiction, it's essential that you understand what addiction is and the kinds of substances to which people become addicted. There is, though, another aspect of addiction that it's very important for you to understand. And that's the fact that all addicts know, even if unconsciously, that their use of substances is detrimental to them and those around them. In order to protect themselves from that knowledge, though, and to avoid dealing with the problem, they use a variety of psychological defense mechanisms.

Defense mechanisms enable people to deal with unpleasant if not painful realities without being overwhelmed by them, and we all use them from time to time. In fact, sometimes using one of these mechanisms is a healthy response to a difficult situation. Humor, for example, can be a defense mechanism. Used to defuse a confrontation, it could enable someone to avoid violence (although it also prevents any resolution of the underlying disagreement). Similarly, when a loved one dies, using denial as a defense mechanism sometimes helps his or her survivors function more effectively in the days immediately following their loss.

However, when people use defense mechanisms to the extent that they're no longer dealing effectively with a problem (or problems), those mechanisms start to have negative rather than positive effects. And, unfortunately, that's particularly true when it comes to addicts. To make things even more difficult, instead of using one defense mechanism at a time, addicts often mix them together in a way that's both confusing and frustrating for their loved ones. There is, though, some good news. While you can't entirely stop your friend or loved one from using these mechanisms, you can use Creative Engagement to manage them, and later on in the chapter I'll show you how.

There are actually many types of psychological defense mechanisms, but there are a few that addicts tend to use more frequently than others. These include denial, rationalization, externalization, all-or-nothing thinking, acting out, passivity, conflict avoidance, flight into health, comparison, and—my personal favorite—the Popeye Defense. I've provided some information about each of these below. You should bear in mind, though, that these descriptions represent my take on how these mechanisms are used by most addicts and that not every doctor defines them in exactly the same way.

Denial

Denial is the most commonly seen defense mechanism in addicts and the one that most often infuriates friends and family. It occurs, essentially, when an individual unconsciously puts up a mental barrier to protect him or herself from an unpleasant truth. In the addict's case, this means refusing to recognize or admit that he or she is an addict, or that the addiction is negatively affecting his or her health, job, or relationships. It's important to understand, however, that even though it may seem like it, denial is not the same thing as lying. Lying is a conscious misrepresentation of the truth, and the addict who denies his or her addiction isn't doing so consciously. (Although, of course, addicts may also lie to protect themselves in other ways.) In fact, if an addict in denial was given a lie detector test and, under questioning, denied that his substance abuse had an adverse effect on his life, the machine would probably register his response as a truthful one. That's because the addict in denial actually *believes* what he or she is saying, and *must* believe it in order to keep functioning. Here's an example of an addict using denial as a defense mechanism.

"I'm Doing Fine"

Mother: Alex, Dad and I have been worried about how much marijuana you've been smoking.

Addict: What? I hardly smoke anymore!

Father: Alex, we can smell it on you when you come home from school. And you act like you're high.

Addict: That's only because the guys in my car pool smoke it in the car. And I'm not high. I'm just a little tired at the end of the day. That's nothing new.

Mother: You can't be serious! You're not tired, you're stoned! Your eyes are all red, you say silly things, and you can barely make it to your room. And that's not even our biggest concern. What really worries us is that you failed three classes last semester.

Addict: That wasn't because of pot! Those classes were upper-level classes, and they were really hard. A lot of other people failed them, too.

> **Father:** But Alex, you've always done well in math before. And the few times you didn't, you always made a point of getting help. This time you didn't even seem to realize that you were failing.
>
> **Addict:** Oh, please. I'm doing fine. I may just not be cut out to be a math major.

Rationalization

Although rationalization is sometimes considered to be a form of denial, it's also a defense mechanism on its own. Someone is rationalizing when he or she provides reasons or excuses for some (usually questionable) action or behavior that seem to be plausible but are actually inaccurate or illogical. Your alcoholic husband might, for example, claim—and actually believe—that going out drinking with colleagues is necessary for him to achieve success at work. By making this argument, he's able to convince himself, and sometimes others, that the addictive behavior is genuinely beneficial. Like most rationalizations, this one has some validity, but it falls apart when examined more closely. Fewer and fewer work environments even implicitly support alcohol use anymore, and alcohol-free socializing has become the norm rather than the exception. In fact, in today's business environment, being alcohol-dependent is more likely to limit than to enhance someone's likelihood of success. Unfortunately, unlike denial, rationalization isn't always so easy to detect. Sometimes you may not recognize it until an experienced addiction treater points it out to you. Here's another example of an addict using rationalization.

"It's Part of the Business"

Addict: So, Tommy, are we going out tomorrow night?

Friend: I don't think I can go out with you tomorrow. I'm getting worried about all those pills you're taking.

Addict: What? Why?

Friend: Because I see you getting all bleary-eyed after a few hours. It looks to me like those uppers are making you confused.

Addict: Are you kidding me? I just take them to stay awake when I hang out with you guys.

Friend: I thought you said you take them for work.

Addict: I do. Sometimes I'm driving for twenty-four hours straight, and there's no way I could stay up that long without them. But everybody does it. It's part of the business.

Friend: You take them so you can drive all day and night?

Addict: Yeah.

Friend: But you said you're half-asleep when you drive. And then you can't get to sleep when you get to the truck stop.

Addict: Well, yeah, but just think how tired I'd be if I didn't take the pills!

Externalization

Externalization occurs when people claim that others are responsible for their behavior, thereby theoretically absolving themselves of any blame for it. Like rationalization, externalization can enable addicts to avoid taking responsibility for dealing with their problem as well as prevent them from even recognizing that they have a problem. A common example of using this type of defense mechanism is the addict who blames his or her spouse for the addiction: "My husband is so difficult that I have to keep using cocaine just to deal with him." Under the right circumstances, this kind of argument can actually sound quite convincing. If, for example, your friend were to tell you something like this, you might get so caught up in sympathizing with her that you wouldn't even realize she was refusing to take responsibility for her own destructive behavior.

Similarly, using a difficult academic environment as an excuse for abusing a substance can sound reasonable if you don't think about it too much. You might, for example, hear a young woman say, "These exams I've got to take are so hard, if I don't snort Ritalin [a stimulant] for a day or two before I take them, it'll be a lot tougher for me to get good grades. It's no big deal. And it's worth it because it'll help me get into a good law school." Sounds logical, doesn't it? Unfortunately, though, if she gets into the habit of snorting Ritalin to get ready for these tests, and gets into law school, she'll have to use more and more of the drug to prepare for the even more difficult law school exams. And that can lead to a full-blown addiction. An addict using this defense mechanism might sound something like this.

"He's Just Driving Me Nuts!"

Addict: Oh, man, do I need a beer! Let's go out tonight.

Wife: Hold on, there. I thought you said we were going to stay home tonight and watch a movie.

Addict: Forget that! Jerry's making me crazy at work, and I need to go out and unwind some.

Wife: But you said he was acting like that because you missed work on Monday and Tuesday.

Addict: No, that's not it. He's just driving me nuts with all his demands, like always. I'd like to belt him one.

Wife: So you're going to take a few belts instead?

Addict: Very funny. But I'm telling you, if you worked for that maniac you'd drink, too.

Wife: So it's his fault you drink?

Addict: Well, if it wasn't for him, I sure wouldn't need to!

All-or-Nothing Thinking

Someone who uses all-or-nothing thinking as a defense mechanism basically paints everything in the world as either black or white, and then rejects one or the other because he or she is unable to see any shades of gray. Let's say, for example, that your brother is a heroin user who's been told that in order to rid himself of his addiction he has to get immediate inpatient treatment, make a lifelong commitment to Narcotics Anonymous, and maintain a permanently sober lifestyle. Faced with such an apparently exhausting and all-consuming commitment to sobriety, if he's seeing everything in black and white, he's very likely to consider his present lifestyle to be preferable. That's because he can't see that, even though a commitment to sobriety is necessary for successful treatment, life after heroin doesn't have to be boring and flavorless. It's true that some recovering addicts remain sober by a single-minded pursuit of their goal, but others find sobriety in a more balanced way. The addict who uses all-or-nothing thinking, though, is unable to see that middle ground. Here's another example of how this works.

"X Is the Only Thing That Makes Me Happy"

Addict: So, are we going dancing tonight?

Friend: I want to, but I really don't want to get high tonight. I have to work tomorrow.

Addict: Okay, we won't smoke. But we can use a little X. It'll be great.

Friend: That's what I mean. I don't want to smoke or get high at all.

Addict: Why not?

Friend: Because when you do, you get all blank on me, and then we don't hang out for the rest of the night, and I don't like it. It seems to me that doing X is the only way you can have fun now.

Addict: X is the only thing that makes me happy. Everything's so boring without it!

Friend: So, what? You can't enjoy anything without using it?

Addict: I guess I can't . . . but there's plenty of X in the world, right?

Acting Out

People most often use the term "acting out" to describe a child's bad behavior. What "acting out" really is, though, is releasing negative emotions through action rather than through thought. The child who's upset about having to go to bed early, but can't deal with it in a rational way, may respond by taking some action, like throwing a tantrum. The addict "acts out" in the same way. That is, when faced with uncomfortable emotional situations, such as arguments with loved ones, setbacks at work or school, or health problems, he or she responds with action, in this case using his or her substance of choice. For the addict, behaving this way actually serves two purposes. It not only enables him or her to avoid dealing with the immediate problem, it also makes it possible to maintain the addiction by at least temporarily eliminating the possibility of examining his or her self-destructive behavior and figuring out how to stop it. Here's an example of an addict who's acting out.

"I Just Had to Get Drunk"

Father: Sammy, I know that you came home drunk last night. What's going on?

Addict: Well, Sarah and I finally broke up—for good this time—and I was really bummed out.

Father: I can understand that, but why get drunk?

Addict: Are you kidding? What was I supposed to do? I just had to get drunk.

Father: But it seems like you're getting drunk all the time now.

Addict: This kind of stuff keeps happening to me.

Father: I understand some bad things have happened lately, but isn't there any other way you can deal with your feelings besides getting drunk?

Addict: Like what?

Passivity

Like people suffering from depression, those who use passivity as a defense mechanism do so because they feel so hopeless that they can't see any point in even trying to alleviate a difficult situation. For that reason, if you were to suggest a course of action to someone who's feeling that way, his or her response would probably be something along the lines of, "What's the use?" Addicts who use this defense mechanism basically take the position that their addiction is inevitable and that there's accordingly no sense in fighting it. They will not, however, admit as much. When confronted about his or her addiction, a "passive" addict is likely to say something like, "We'll just have to see what happens." In practical terms, of course, what that really means is that he or she will continue using the addictive substance. So despite what it's called, this "passive" response is actually an active plan to continue the addictive behavior. An addict using passivity as a defense mechanism might sound like this.

"Let's Just See What Happens"

Addict: I need to go out and get some air.

Friend: Don't B.S. me, Sean. I know you're going to get some more heroin.

Addict: Well, yeah. So what?

Friend: I know you're addicted. But I also know where you can get some help.

Addict: Don't bother.

Friend: I am bothering. I care about you and I don't want to see you OD again. And I know there's a detox place downtown where they'll take you on the spot.

Addict: Really, I haven't been using as much lately.

Friend: I guess not. But your use always ramps up.

Addict: Let's just see what happens. Maybe I'll just grow out of it.

Friend: I don't think you ought to wait around for that, my friend. It's going to get bad again.

Addict: You're just being pessimistic. I think it'll all work out on its own. . . .

Conflict Avoidance

Slightly more subtle than passivity, and therefore harder to recognize, is the defense mechanism called conflict avoidance. People who use this mechanism are able to avoid inner conflicts, as well as conflicts with others, by basically refusing to admit to themselves exactly how real a problem actually is. Addicts use it, of course, to avoid dealing with their own conflicted feelings about their addiction. If, for example, your sister is a cocaine addict, she might try to smooth over her inner conflicts about using drugs by making a bargain with herself that, since cocaine is admittedly harmful, she'll limit its use to Saturday nights.

But addicts also use this mechanism to avoid conflict with others by trying to limit the harmful effects of their addiction to certain areas of their lives. Physicians who are addicts, for example—and there are, regrettably, a good number of them—are sometimes able to "keep it together" at work even while their home lives, relationships, and even physical well-being deteriorate. By avoiding the appearance of any problems in their professional lives, though, they can avoid conflict with their colleagues, medical boards, and patients. In addition, using this defense mechanism enables them to convince themselves that, "If it doesn't affect my work, it can't be that bad." Here's another example of an addict using this defense mechanism.

"I Only Drink at Home"

Husband: Jenny, I'm really worried about your drinking. I know you've been having some more trouble with it.

Addict: Trouble? What trouble?

Husband: Well, for one thing, you've been going to bed soused. At least I think you have, but I can't really tell if you're just sleepy or you're bombed.

Addict: Hey! That's not fair! You said you were worried about me driving home from work drunk, so I stopped drinking anywhere out of the house. I only drink at home now. That's what you wanted, isn't it?

Husband: Well, yeah. At the time . . .

Addict: So don't bug me about it. I didn't think it was such a big deal in the first place, but you seemed so worried about it that I figured I'd be a good wife and do what you asked.

Husband: I guess what I'm really worried about is you, not just your drunk driving.

Flight into Health

Addicts who use this defense mechanism decrease or even stop their use of substances for the purpose of "proving" to themselves and others that they have no problem and therefore don't have to deal with it by going into treatment. At first glance, this may sound like a good thing. After all, wouldn't you be happy if your friend or loved one cut down on or stopped using an addictive substance? Unfortunately, though, when an addict takes this "flight into health," it can present problems of its own. Let's say, for example, that your son has a serious drinking problem but has cut down to the point where he's only drinking on weekends. While this is obviously a move in the right direction, there's still a problem because, without a structured support system to help him fight the addiction, he's very likely to start drinking heavily again at some point in the future. In fact, even if he were to stop drinking altogether, unless he got into a program, he'd still be susceptible to falling off the wagon. Of course, relapse is always a possibility, even with help, but without it the risk is greater. An addict using flight into health as a defense mechanism might sound something like this.

"I Just Stopped!"

Friend: So, Allan, how's it going with those AA meetings?

Addict: I don't know. I haven't gone to any this month.

Friend: I thought you said you were going to go every day?

Addict: Yeah, but I decided I didn't need it. I'm not an addict, really.

Friend: Is that what the therapist said?

Addict: Actually, I'm not seeing her anymore either.

Friend: So what are you doing to avoid using anymore?

Addict: I just stopped! Isn't that what you wanted?

Friend: Yes, but don't you need some help to stay stopped?

Addict: No, I don't. And stop looking at me that way. You told me you wanted me to stop, and I did. So what are you bothering me about?

Friend: I'm worried you'll start using again. I mean, you always have in the past.

Addict: Are you betting against me now?

Friend: Of course not. I just want you to have the best odds for staying sober.

Addict: Stop bugging me! I did what you wanted, now back off!

Comparison

This defense mechanism is a way for addicts to convince others, and perhaps themselves, that they're all right because others use more of their particular substance, use it earlier in the day, or have worse problems because of it than they do. And, in fact, in a lot of cases their arguments may be entirely true. The problem is that no matter how true they may be, they're irrelevant. There's no such thing as a "safe" level of substance abuse, and no matter how much of a substance someone else may use, anyone who abuses it is in danger.

In fact, it all depends on the individual. The person who has three cocktails before dinner every evening but has no problems with his or her health, relationships, or work life because of it, doesn't have an addiction problem. On the other hand, the person who drinks three cocktails once a month and gets into a car accident every time he or she does it, does have a problem. The total volume of alcohol consumed makes no difference—it's the effect that matters. The simplest way for you to respond when your friend or loved one makes this kind of argument, then, is to say, "I don't care if someone you know drinks more. I care about you!" Here's an example of someone doing just that.

"What's the Big Deal?"

Wife: Honey, I'm getting so worried about your drinking—you came in late again last night.

Addict: Oh, it's no big deal. Half the guys drink more than me. In fact, I'm the lightweight of the bunch.

Wife: Well, I don't doubt it, but that's not the point. Have any of them had any problems because of drinking?

Addict: Not that I know of. Besides, like I said, some of them drink much more than me.

Wife: I know, but maybe you're just more susceptible to alcohol.

> Addict: No way. Have you seen how much they drink?
>
> Wife: I don't know about them. I only know that you've been arrested twice for drunk driving, and I'm not sure I can take this anymore.
>
> Addict: What? That's ridiculous. Look, I never drink before six o'clock, I don't drink as much as the other guys, and I never drink alone. What's the big deal?

The Popeye Defense

If you remember the cartoon character Popeye, you'll probably remember his claim that "I yam what I yam." In saying that, what Popeye was actually doing was exhibiting his individuality as well as his pride in his rather offbeat sensibilities. Addicts who use this defense claim to have the same sort of free-spirited joy in being an outsider, even though—as with all addicts—they actually know that their substance use isn't a good thing. What this defense does, then, is enable the addict to put the best possible face on a terrible situation and, at the same time, ask his or her friends and family to go along with the delusion.

This defense is actually a combination of several defenses. Like addicts who use the externalization defense, one young heroin addict I worked with insisted that his use of heroin was an inevitable result of his difficult family situation, genetic makeup, and addictive personality. But when his parents pointed out his inability to stay in school, to pay for his own apartment, or to avoid being arrested, he replied, like an addict using the passivity defense, that since he actually had no choice in the matter, there was no point in trying to do anything about it. Like Popeye, though, he also argued that he didn't agree with their value system and that they should respect him for who he was. In fact, of course, despite his claims, he wasn't choosing a lifestyle, he was trapped in one, and no matter how hard he tried, he couldn't hide it.

These, then, are the psychological defense mechanisms that addicts use most frequently in their efforts to avoid dealing with their addiction. As you can see, some of them are relatively easy to recognize and counter while some are considerably more formidable. They can all, however, be managed, at least to some extent, and in the next section I'm going to show you exactly how you can do that.

How to Manage the Addict's Defense Mechanisms

Dealing effectively with someone who's using defense mechanisms is always a difficult task, but it's especially hard when the individual is an addict. That's because addicts who use these defenses become particularly rigid, separated from reality, and likely to engage in dangerous behavior. Of course, faced with someone who's acting illogically or irrationally, your first inclination would probably be to confront him or her about it. And that's a perfectly natural reaction. Unfortunately, directly confronting addicts like that almost never works. Because they're not even consciously aware that they're using these mechanisms to avoid dealing with the problem, addicts are unlikely to believe anything you tell them. This, though, is a good opportunity for you to use Creative Engagement.

One way to do that is by finding out how the addict understands his or her own situation, that is, by trying to understand how he or she thinks about the problem. And you can do it by asking him or her as many questions as possible, like the questions in the dialogues throughout this book. It's very important, though, that you avoid expressing any value judgments. I'm not suggesting, of course, that you have to agree with the addict's way of thinking, only that you shouldn't make a point of disagreeing with it. If you engage your friend or loved one in this kind of conversation, he or she is likely to see your effort to understand as being respectful, and it will put the two of you on the same page rather than at odds with each other.

This is actually what therapists do when faced with a delusional patient. Just telling the individual that there's no giant pink rabbit in the room doesn't do any good. But asking him or her about it enables the therapist and patient to open a dialogue to explore how the patient came to that conclusion. In the same way, asking an addict, for example, about the effect that cocaine has on him or her can open up a discussion. If you ask about what he or she considers to be the benefits of using the drug, the addict will probably tell you that, at least at first, it feels good, makes it easier to talk to people, and heightens sexual pleasure. Having asked about the upside, though, you then have the right—in the addict's mind—to ask about the downside, too. And it's when the addict starts to talk about that downside that he or she has started on the road toward sobriety.

Bear in mind that your goal is not to overwhelm the addict's defenses by force (that is, unless he or she is in such immediate danger that you have to call 911). Your goal is to undermine those defenses while, at the same time, avoiding getting caught up in extraneous issues. That means, for example, that if your cousin is in denial about his addiction to methamphetamine but has also irritated the family for years because he's refused to look for work, you have to concentrate on the addiction and let the other issue go for now. The other important thing for you to remember while making this effort is that it's a process. That is, there isn't going to be any "Aha!" moment at which your friend or loved one nods, smiles broadly, and thanks you for clearing up his or her misunderstanding. It's only through slow, steady, and loving pressure that you'll be able to help the addict recognize that the perceptions he or she is using the defense mechanism to support are, in fact, misperceptions. Below are some of the techniques you can use to do that.

Use Benign Stupidity

One way of getting a dialogue started is by using a technique called "benign stupidity." This technique was developed by therapists as a means of treating schizophrenics with delusions and can be useful in dealing with addicts, too. It has the advantages of being honest and respectful of your friend's or loved one's perceptions as well as being likely to help you better understand how he or she is thinking. If, for example, your daughter were to tell you that her cocaine use actually helps her in her schoolwork, your first thought would probably be to say something like, "Are you nuts? You slept through most of your classes last week! And it could kill you!" Obviously, though, that wouldn't be very helpful in opening a dialogue. Instead, you might try something like, "Really! I didn't know cocaine could do that. How does it work?" In all likelihood, she would reply with her own version of how cocaine helps her, and you'd get a much clearer idea of her perspective.

I've often seen addicts start to respond to questions like this and then stop halfway through when they realize how crazy they sound. That's because even though an argument for the continued use of a substance may make sense inside the addict's head, once it hits the open air it's a lot harder to support. And when the addict realizes that, he or she is much more likely to be able to see exactly how skewed his or her take on reality is. So if your friend or loved one responds this way, you'll have gotten off to an extremely good start. But even if he or she doesn't, you'll have started a conversation rather than simply having engaged in a shouting match, and that's exactly what you want to do.

Point Out Alternatives

Arguing with addicts about their perceptions is useless, but one effective way of dealing with them is to point out alternatives. Let's say, for example, that your brother is an OxyContin addict who's stuck in a passive state and believes he can't change anything. In a situation like this, the first thing you have to do is acknowledge his perception by saying something like, "I can see how you might feel that way." Again, it's very important to avoid appearing disrespectful toward your friend's or loved one's beliefs, even if you totally disagree with them, because if you do, he or she will simply ignore everything you have to say.

Next, though, you should point out alternatives, such as, "Maybe if you had some help you could change" or "Maybe the drugs are making you feel that way." While every situation is different, at least to some extent, when you make suggestions like these the addict is likely to at least consider the possibility that you may be right. Even if you suggest to your brother that his Oxy-Contin use is what's making him feel so lethargic, and he totally rejects the idea, you'll still have tried to connect with that part of him that is still logical. And, more important, you'll have planted a seed, or seeds, for him to think about later.

Set a "Trip Wire"

As I mentioned before, defense mechanisms are all essentially means of enabling addicts to deny their addiction. So a good way to manage those mechanisms is to help the addict set a "trip wire" for acknowledging that he or she actually has a problem. If, for example, your son is addicted to methamphetamine, you might approach him by saying, "I understand that you don't think you have a serious problem with meth, but I'm wondering what you would consider to be a serious problem. I mean, what would a serious problem look like?" He might respond by providing you with some examples, such as missing work for two days in a row, spending the rent money on meth, or losing his girlfriend because of it. You can then make use of this information by writing it down so that when one of these things does in fact occur—and chances are they will—you can use his own definition of a problem to convince him that there is one and that he needs to get into treatment.

Hide the Hurt While Helping the Addict

Effectively managing these defense mechanisms is hard work, and the best way to do it is as gently and gradually as possible. At the same time, I understand that you're probably feeling a lot of pain and anger about your friend's or loved one's addiction and that it's difficult for you to hide that. It's also, though, very important that you do, because if you vent your anger and frustration on the addict, you and your feelings will become the center of attention rather than his or hers. This doesn't mean, of course, that you can't vent these feelings at all. But when you do, it's best to do it either with a sympathetic friend, at a meeting with other friends and families of addicts, or in a therapist's office.

Don't Support the Blame-Laying

Although no one can really "make" someone else use drugs or alcohol, as you've seen, addicts sometimes use the defense mechanism of externalization to blame others for their addictions. One of the primary purposes of your talking to your friend or loved one, then, is to get the addict to acknowledge his or her own personal responsibility and to stop blaming incompetent parents, cruel bosses, or distant spouses for the addictive behavior. But how do you do that? When your friend or loved one tries to lay the blame for his or her addiction on someone else, the most appropriate—and effective—way for you to respond is to acknowledge that other people can sometimes be incompetent, cruel, or distant, but to make it clear at the same time that they can't be held responsible for the addict's problem.

Gentle disagreement, quiet listening, and forceful confrontation—all of which are aspects of Creative Engagement—can be used in this situation, and it's up to you to determine which is most appropriate. If, for example, your teenage son tells you that, despite your disapproval, his use of steroids is necessary for his success in football, you can gently disagree by suggesting that his goal might suffer if he's tested and found to be using them. This will make it possible for you to get into a discussion of why he's really using the steroids. If he then says that he's willing to take the chance of getting caught in order to play at the college or professional level, you might quietly listen to what he has to say and then ask, in a respectful way, about his perceptions of the risks of using the drugs. This will both provide you with a better understanding of his thinking and arm you for a confrontation if it should become necessary.

If and when your son subsequently tells you that the risks from steroids are overblown, or that it's worth taking the chance if it can lead to a career in professional sports, that would be an appropriate time to confront him. Before you do, though, you should gather the evidence of how dangerous steroid use is for young people—and there's plenty of it—as well as about the likelihood that he won't get to be a professional athlete even if he does use steroids. You might start your confrontation by saying something like, "I think I understand where you're coming from about using steroids, but I have to tell you that where your health is concerned, I can't hold back my worries. You could really hurt yourself with steroids, and I'm really worried about it!" By presenting your thoughts this way, even though you're being confrontational, you're not shutting off communications, which is essential when you're trying to get through to an addict.

Finally, it's very important to remember that, while you're trying to help an addict avoid blaming others for his or her addiction, you have to avoid blaming the addict him- or herself. There's a big difference between responsibility and blame. Asking someone to take responsibility is essentially doing something positive, but blaming someone is suggesting that they did something shameful, and doing that in a situation like this is neither helpful nor constructive. One good way to avoid blame-laying is to say something like, "I don't care whose fault it is, I just want to see you get better!" or "Let's put aside whose fault this is and just focus on what we all can do now so you get better." Think of the situation as if it were a house on fire. You wouldn't obsess about what caused the fire. You'd rescue the people and put the fire out, and only then think about how it got started.

As I mentioned earlier, although some addicts tend to use only one or another of these defense mechanisms, most make use of several. Here's a conversation between an addict and his wife that shows not only the various kinds of mechanisms that addicts use but also how they can be managed for the addict's benefit.

"But Everybody in the Office Drinks!"

Wife: Eric, you're starting to scare me. I know you're trying to make partner at your firm, but I just don't see how you're going to do it if you keep drinking like this.

Addict: C'mon, Ellen, I don't drink any more than anyone else. And less than some! *[Eric uses the comparison defense.]*

Wife: The other associates drink as much as you do? *[Ellen tries to open up the conversation.]*

Addict: More! And anyway, you know the kind of crazy hours we keep. Anyone would drink in that environment.

It's just a way for us to blow off steam. *[Eric uses the externalization defense—it's the tough work environment that's to blame.]*

Wife: I don't know, Eric . . .

Addict: Look, Ellen, you're making way too much of this. I really don't have a problem with drinking. *[Eric uses the denial defense.]*

Wife: Really? Last week Bill told me that he was getting worried about you drinking all the time. *[Ellen tries gentle confrontation.]*

Addict: Bill? That lush? He's right in there drinking with me! We all do it, so we can hack those god-awful late-night and Saturday meetings.

Wife: But I know you miss a lot of those Saturday meetings. I can't believe that drinking helps you in your work. *[Ellen tries more gentle confrontation.]*

Addict: Are you kidding? It helps a lot! They see I'm a regular guy, that I can drink along with the best of them and still be a world-class lawyer. *[Eric uses the conflict avoidance defense.]*

Wife: Oh, come on! You didn't make partner last year, and I can't believe that your missing meetings didn't have something to do with that. *[Now Ellen tries more forceful confrontation.]*

Addict: That's your reality. You can think what you want,

but I know it's not a problem. If it's such a big deal to everyone, I'll just stop. I don't need a lot of psychobabble. *[Eric continues to deny he has a problem.]*

Wife: That sounds like a great idea! You could probably use some help with stopping. How about if I get a schedule for AA meetings? *[Ellen focuses on the positive (Eric said he would stop) rather than the negative (he still doesn't agree he has a problem).]*

Addict: No! I told you I don't need any help! It's not a problem for me to stop.

Wife: Well, okay. But what if your plan of going it alone doesn't work?

Addict: It'll work.

Wife: I hope so. And I certainly wouldn't bet against you. But how will we know if it's not working? I mean, what would have to happen for you to feel that there was a problem? *[Realizing that she cannot "outlogic" Eric's denial, Ellen attempts to set a trip wire to identify problems in the future.]*

Addict: I don't know. Maybe if I'm so hungover I can't make it to one of the Saturday meetings at work, or even if I get drunk at all. But it's not going to happen. I can stop without anyone's help.

Wife: I hope so, sweetie. Let's see what happens. . . .

~~~~~~

How Addicts Avoid Dealing with the Problem and What You Can Do About It

- Listen more than you talk.
- Focus on the addictive behaviors you can see.
- Avoid lengthy off-the-topic discussions.
- Monitor your own frustration level and stop if you start to feel too frustrated.
- Don't try to do it alone.
- Talk to others who care about the addict. You may learn something useful.
- Be persistent.
- Respect the addict's defenses. He or she has taken a long time to build them up, and it's going to take a long time to bring them down.

Now you've learned something about the kind of defense mechanisms your friend or loved one is likely to use to avoid dealing with his or her addiction, as well as something about what you can do to manage those defense mechanisms. In the next chapter I'm going to tell you how to develop a plan of action that will enable you to help the addict in your life get the kind of help he or she needs to overcome addiction.

Part II

STRATEGIES FOR GETTING THE ADDICT INTO TREATMENT

Chapter Four

WHAT FRIENDS AND FAMILY CAN DO:

Gathering and Evaluating Information About Addiction Treaters

Now that you've determined that your friend or loved one is an addict, and learned something about the nature of addiction and the kinds of defense mechanisms addicts use to protect themselves and their addictions, the time has come for you to do something about it. And that "something" is to convince the addict in your life to enter treatment. It's no exaggeration to say that your doing so could save his or her life. Continuing down the path he or she is on is likely to result in, at best, the loss of a job, a significant other, or a treasured relationship and, at worst, a fatal overdose. And you can help prevent these losses by using Creative Engagement.

But there are also other important reasons to help your friend or loved one decide to go into treatment. One of these is knowing that you've done your best for someone you care about. Another is showing those around you that addiction doesn't have to end in disaster. Since addiction runs in families, it's particularly important for the addict's immediate family to see that help is available, effective, and socially acceptable. It helps keep hope alive!

The simple fact that you're reading this book is proof that you care about the addict in your life and that you're willing—even eager—to do what you can to help. And that fact alone means that he or she has a better chance of recovering from addiction. In fact, the role that you and other friends and family can play in recovery can't be overestimated. And the most important way you can help is to develop a plan of action to determine the most appropriate type of treatment program and to convince the addict to enter it. In this chapter and the next I'll show you exactly how to do that.

Developing a Plan

Why is it so important for you to develop a plan? There are several reasons, the most significant of which is that it enables you to establish a clear set of priorities. This is essential because, if your friend's or loved one's addiction is life-threatening, you have to address that issue first, and as aggressively as possible. Another reason is that having a clear and agreed-upon plan makes it possible for all those who care about the addict to focus their attention on the most likely path to success and to pull in the same direction. This is important because if even one friend or family member suggests that the plan is too involved, intense, or time-consuming, the addict might latch on to that individual as the one who knows best. Finally, when you have a formal plan, all those who are trying to help will know sooner rather than later if the plan is failing or getting offtrack and will be able to do whatever needs to be done to set things right again.

This kind of plan consists of three steps. The first is gathering information about the different kinds of professionals in your area who work with addicts, including psychiatrists and other physicians, psychologists, social workers, addiction counselors, and others. The second step is evaluating that information so you can determine which type of professional, and which specific individual, would be most appropriate for the addict—that is, who would be most likely to help your friend or loved one rid him- or herself of the addiction. The purpose of these steps is to make it possible for you to recommend someone who can help the addict as soon as he or she agrees to start treatment. As you'll see, convincing an addict to get help can be very difficult, and once you have, it's important that you take advantage of the opportunity immediately. The third step, of course, is actually convincing the addict to start that treatment. It would be ideal if he or she could do all this him- or herself, but most addicts will do no such thing. Just admitting they have a problem and need help may be all they can handle for the moment. And what that means is that if anyone is going to take these steps, it will have to be you.

Now, I understand that you may not be comfortable with the idea of bringing a "stranger" into what up to this point has been primarily a family affair. And it's true that some drug and alcohol problems can be dealt with without any professional help at all. There's no need to bring in a professional when, for example, a husband who's gotten drunk and acted silly at a few barbecues stops drinking as soon as he's warned by his wife. Or when a teenager experiments with marijuana once or twice and then stops because it makes him "feel funny." In situations like these, even though the substance use is potentially dangerous, if it can be reined in so easily, it never rises to the level of an addiction. This isn't to say, of course, that it's a good idea to get drunk or smoke marijuana, only that the behaviors themselves don't necessarily require professional involvement.

Unfortunately, though, even when the situation is more serious, the shame and stigma attached to addiction can sometimes prevent families from seeking professional help. In fact, if you think of addiction as a sign of bad character, poor parenting, or moral weakness, it wouldn't be at all surprising for you to be reluctant about bringing your friend or loved one to a professional. The truth is, though, that addiction has little to do with how good or bad a family is. Addiction occurs in loving, attentive, and caring families, as well as in families that exhibit none of these traits. Ultimately what addiction is about is the addict's need for a particular substance, and that's all you really have to concern yourself with.

When, then, should you call in a professional? Whenever you'd call in a professional about any kind of health issue. If your child was to fall and scrape her knee, you wouldn't rush her to the emergency room. But if she was hit by a car it would never occur to you to try to keep the injury a "family matter." In the case of addiction, my opinion—admittedly biased because I'm an addiction professional—is that you should bring in a professional as soon as the idea occurs to you. Because a true addiction problem can worsen rapidly, it's important to get professional help at the earliest possible moment. I've found that, more often than not, by the time a friend or family member calls me about his or her addicted loved one, there's usually much more going on than meets the eye. That is, not only is there almost certainly a problem, the problem is almost invariably larger than the friend or family member suspects, and it's important that it be addressed as soon as possible. But what exactly can a therapist do for your friend or loved one?

Professionals Who Work with Addicts

As I mentioned, there are several different kinds of professionals who work with addicts, including psychiatrists and other physicians, psychologists, social workers, addiction counselors, and others. Although they can all be very helpful in enabling addicts to escape their addiction, they all have different training, abilities, and styles of working with patients. Because it's likely that one type will be more effective than the others in helping your friend or loved one, it would be in your—and the addict's—best interests to determine which type that is. We'll start with the professionals who hold medical degrees—psychiatrists and other physicians.

A psychiatrist is an individual who holds a degree from a four-year medical school and has completed a three-year residency in general psychiatry, and is therefore trained in diagnosing and treating mental illnesses like depression, bipolar disorder, and addiction. (Yes, again, addiction is considered a mental illness.) Since psychiatrists have medical licenses, they're able to prescribe medications. Some, like me, have taken additional training in addiction and hold certificates of Added Qualifications in Addiction Psychiatry from the American Board of Psychiatry and Neurology (ABPN). Psychiatrists can help addicts in a variety of ways, including making diagnoses, coordinating an addict's medical and psychiatric care, prescribing medications, and conducting psychotherapy. Other physicians, such as internists and anesthesiologists, sometimes also study addiction and can become certified as specialists by the American Society of Addiction Medicine (ASAM). Physicians like these are usually highly competent in treating addiction.

A psychologist is someone who attended undergraduate and graduate school for between four and seven years, where he or she earned a doctorate (a Ph.D.) in psychology. A psychologist's course of study usually focuses on the emotional processes that affect behavior, and most psychologists either conduct psychotherapy or do research once they've completed their schooling. All modern psychology training, however, also includes substantial education on the biological processes that underlie human behavior, and many psychologists are very knowledgeable about the functioning of the brain. Unlike psychiatrists, psychologists do not hold medical licenses and therefore, except in very rare circumstances, may not prescribe medications. Like psychiatrists, however, they may take advanced training in treating addiction and can get the kind of supervised work experience that's so important in learning how to treat addicts. Psychologists who work with addicts are particularly adept at helping patients with the emotional and social problems associated with addiction, and may work with a psychiatrist who will prescribe any needed medications.

A third group of addiction treaters consists of individuals who hold undergraduate degrees and attended graduate school for two years in order to become licensed social workers. Many social workers take advanced training in psychotherapy, and some specialize in addiction. They can accordingly help addicts in a variety of ways, including, like psychiatrists and psychologists, serving as individual and group therapists.

Addiction counselors, like all the clinicians discussed above, are state-licensed, but requirements for licensing in this field vary widely from state to state. Some states are relatively lax, while others have very rigorous requirements for education and on-the-job and ethics training. In New York, for example, an addiction counselor must work in a licensed facility for three years under the direction of a licensed professional before he or she is able to practice. Addiction counselors are like other addiction treaters in that they can provide both individual and group therapy for addicts. They are, however, different in that they don't necessarily have the same training in other psychiatric conditions that other types of clinicians do. As long as there are no other psychiatric issues, however, addiction counselors can provide excellent care for addicts.

Finally, because in many states no particular training is required for an individual to call him or herself a "therapist" or "counselor," there are some addiction treaters who have no professional certification of any kind. In fact, I know of some individuals who have developed large "therapy" practices despite their lack of education in the field. Although these individuals can certainly help some of the addicts who come to them, they can't even begin to address the needs of others and will frequently not even realize when they're in over their heads. Although even a thorough education and a professional degree do not guarantee competence, any therapist who doesn't have them is unlikely to be able to help your friend or loved one, and for that reason I recommend that you avoid such individuals.

What Professional Therapists Bring to the Table

But what exactly can a therapist do for your friend or loved one? There are essentially three things that a therapist can offer an addict—knowledge, skills, and an appropriate attitude. The best addiction therapists—whether they're psychiatrists, psychologists, social workers, or counselors—have a broad understanding of addiction and the available treatments for it. Although their knowledge may have started with their own experience with addiction—a fairly large percentage of addiction therapists are former addicts themselves—that knowledge must be augmented by both formal education and supervised work experience, both of which are necessary to help the therapist understand different substances, personality styles, and treatment possibilities.

In fact, any therapist who knows only one method of treatment will not be suitable for you or the addict you love. This includes the counselor who only recommends AA, the psychiatrist who says that medications will take care of the problem, the psychologist who claims that his intensive psychotherapy always does the trick, or the therapist employed by a facility who only recommends that facility. A knowledgeable therapist will of course recommend a particular course of treatment for a specific addict, but the therapist should be able to clearly articulate why he or she chose that type of treatment rather than others and be ready and able to modify it if necessary.

In order to be effective, an addiction therapist must also have certain skills, both those that are required of all therapists as well as some specialized ones. Every therapist should be empathic and understanding, but an addiction therapist must also be willing and able to handle potentially dangerous situations that the general therapist is unlikely to encounter. An addiction therapist may, for example, have to deal with an addict who is indulging in the extremely self-destructive habit of smoking methamphetamine (Ice). In such a situation, the therapist must be able to confront the patient while, at the same time, maintaining a caring attitude so as not to alienate him or her. Such therapists also sometimes have to take other actions that are rarely required of general therapists, such as breaking a patient's confidentiality by calling a member of the addict's family or contacting the police.

In addition to having these kinds of "emergency" skills, the addiction therapist must also be able to deal with the addict's inevitable lying, cheating, and manipulating. Addicts often lie about their use of substances, evade drug-screening tests by using agents that clean the substance out of their systems, and manipulate those around them by minimizing, disguising, or explaining away their use of the substance. In fact, this type of behavior is often aimed directly at the therapist, because, since he or she is trying to rid the patient of the addiction, the therapist is threatening the addiction itself. So the therapist must have the ability to recognize when the addict is being manipulative in order to "stay with" the addict who's trying to destroy, deflect, or ignore the therapist's attempt to help.

I think it's also important that the therapist has the right attitude, that is, one of compassion toward the addict, and without any cynicism or anger. There are, unfortunately, some therapists who come into the addiction field with very cynical attitudes, and some who come with ingrained anger toward addicts. There are also others who develop these feelings over the years. The best therapists, though, are those who can maintain a compassionate attitude toward their patients, even—and often especially—in the face of the deceptive and manipulative behavior that many addicts exhibit. These therapists understand addiction and recognize that this kind of behavior is part of the addiction itself, not an indication of animosity toward any particular individual.

Choosing the Right Kind of Therapist

Now that you understand the basic types of therapists who work with addicts, and what they can do, you have to choose which you think will be most likely to help your loved one. It may be, of course, that there's only one clinician near you, in which case you won't have a choice. If you do, though, there are three things you should take into consideration.

First, in addition to being an addict, does your friend or loved one have a mental illness? If he or she has not been formally diagnosed, it's unlikely that you'll be able to do the diagnosis yourself. If, however, you know that the addict suffers from bipolar disorder, depression, or some other mental illness, it would be best for you to choose a psychiatrist to work with him or her. Individuals with such diagnoses are likely to need medication of some sort—which, of course, requires a doctor to prescribe—and nonphysicians may be unable to recognize or treat the mental problem appropriately.

Second, is the addict in physical withdrawal? If so, before you do anything else, he or she must be assessed by a physician, whether that person is a psychiatrist, a family practitioner, or an internist. In fact, even if you were to take an addict in withdrawal to some other type of addiction treater, that therapist would in all likelihood send him or her to a physician. Once that issue has been resolved, you can then choose an appropriate addiction treater.

Third, does your friend or loved one *want* psychotherapy? If he or she has benefited from it in the past, and/or has a good feeling about it, then a psychologist, social worker, or other trained addiction therapist might well be the best choice. On the other hand, if the addict is uncomfortable with the idea of psychotherapy, it would make more sense for you to find a clinician from one of the other disciplines who will serve less as a therapist and more as a coordinator for the other forms of treatment. I've often served as such a coordinator myself. Typically—although not always—the addict eventually becomes sufficiently comfortable with me not only to allow me to coordinate his or her anti-addiction activities but also to discuss the various difficulties in his or her life. This is really no different from therapy, but it's called something else, at least at the beginning, in order to avoid spooking the addict.

Finding the Right Individual

Once you've determined which type of professional would be most appropriate for your friend or loved one, the next step is to find the individual who will best be able to help him or her. There are several tried-and-true methods for finding such a professional.

The best way to find a good addiction treater, as with any health professional, is through a personal referral. Your own physician may know of a specialist in addiction psychiatry or addiction medicine, or may be able to refer you to a colleague who does. You may also have friends or neighbors who can suggest someone you might contact. If, however, you have no local contacts, a good way of getting referrals is by attending an open AA meeting (AA does not require those attending open meetings to have an addiction problem themselves, and local meetings can be found on the Internet at www.alcoholics-anonymous.org). At the meeting, or in the social hour afterward, you can ask if anyone can recommend competent therapists or facilities in the area. It's true that some AA members believe the organization itself should take care of all problems associated with addiction. However, there are others who have benefited considerably from working with professional therapists and would in all likelihood be happy to provide referrals. In fact, recommendations from such people are particularly valuable, as they are very actively engaged in their own recovery.

If, though, you're unable to get any referrals through these means, there are several other websites you can consult. The American Academy of Addiction Psychiatry (www.aaap.org/home .htm) and the American Society of Addiction Medicine (www .asam.org) can both refer you to addiction-knowledgeable physicians in your area. The Association for Addiction Professionals (http://naadac.org) has a website that will direct you to local chapters which, in turn, can refer you to local counselors. The National Clearinghouse for Alcohol and Drug Information (http://ncadi.samhsa.gov) can provide referrals to treatment facilities all around the country and also has a lot of free materials on addiction. Finally, the membership list of the National Association of Addiction Treatment Providers (www.naatp.org) also includes information about treatment facilities around the country. (These and other possible sources of referrals are also listed in Appendix A: Where to Find Help.)

It's best, of course, to get as many referrals as possible, so that you'll have more choice when it comes to actually selecting an individual to work with your friend or loved one. You should, in any case, try to get the names of at least three possibilities. Once you've developed a list of possibilities, the next step is to contact each of the people on the list to arrange for an exploratory meeting. All you have to do is call each of their offices, explain the situation, and ask for an appointment to meet with the therapist. Addiction professionals know that not every therapist is right for every patient and have no problem with going through these kinds of "interviews." You are, after all, considering entrusting them with your loved one's well-being, and therapists understand that. Before you actually meet with anyone, though, I'd suggest that you think about the kind of questions you're going to ask. As I mentioned earlier, the three things a therapist can offer an addict are knowledge, skills, and an appropriate attitude. These interviews are your opportunity to determine to what extent the therapists you meet can provide your loved one with what he or she needs.

The first area to ask about, then, is the therapist's knowledge. Depending on what kind of therapist you've chosen, you should ask what university he or she attended, what degrees he or she holds, and whether or not the therapist has received any additional certification in addiction treatment. You'll also want to find out as much as you can about the therapist's experience. How long has he or she been in practice? Where has the therapist worked in the past? Exactly how successful has he or she been in helping addicts rid themselves of their addiction? You should also ask if the clinician is familiar with a wide range of treatment methods. Just as no one therapist is ideal for every addict, no one method is always the best. The clinician should accordingly have experience with several methods and be willing and able to use whichever one fits the situation, or—if not—at least be able to refer the addict to someone who can.

As you would expect, it's easier to find out about a potential therapist's knowledge than about his or her skills and attitudes. But you can actually learn a good deal about these as well, providing you ask the right questions. One area you can ask about is your friend's or loved one's specific problem. Having described the problem, you might, for example, ask the therapist how he or she would treat the addict. If the therapist responds by providing examples of other similar addicts he or she has worked with, you'll know that particular therapist will probably be able to handle the situation. If, on the other hand, he or she has little experience with individuals addicted to the same substance as your loved one, it would probably be best to consider working with someone else. Similarly, if your friend or loved one has been diagnosed with a mental illness in addition to the addiction problem, it would be a good idea to ask the therapist about his or her experience working with the dually diagnosed. You might discover, for example, that a psychologist you're talking to has no experience in that area, while a social worker you're considering was employed for many years on an inpatient psychiatric unit and, accordingly, developed the skills required to work effectively with dually diagnosed patients.

Another way to learn more about the therapist's skills and attitude is to ask about his or her understanding of what addiction is and how it's taken hold of your loved one. Although this is, admittedly, a very broad question, the clinician's response may help you decide whether he or she would be appropriate for your loved one. If, for example, a therapist is very biologically oriented and focuses on the changes that addiction causes in the brain, he or she might be an excellent choice if your loved one is particularly concerned about how he or she deals with those changes. On the other hand, if your loved one is using a substance to "medicate" his or her anxiety, a therapist who emphasizes the inability addicts often have to deal with anxiety might be a good match.

There are also two particularly good ways of learning about the therapist's attitudes. The first is to ask how he or she sees you and others being involved in the treatment. Since you're reading this book, you'll probably want to be as involved as possible, so you should be looking for a therapist who emphasizes outside involvement rather than one who focuses on the one-to-one relationship between the therapist and the patient. The second good way is to ask the therapist how he or she normally responds when a patient slips, relapses, or even goes on a binge. Although therapists are likely to differ somewhat in their responses, what you're looking for is someone who appreciates that missteps are a part of recovering from addiction, and that recovery is rarely achieved on the first attempt.

One additional question I'd advise you to ask the clinicians you interview is whether or not they are themselves recovering addicts, as it may provide you with some insight into their style in working with their patients. There are advantages and disadvantages to working with a therapist who is him- or herself recovering from addiction. One of the greatest advantages is that he or she will in all likelihood be able to relate to the addict on a more personal level. Such an individual may also be more sympathetic to other addicts and may have developed a more extensive network of facilities, AA groups, and other clinicians to whom he or she can refer patients. On the other hand, the fact that a clinician is in recovery does not guarantee better treatment. For example, a clinician whose life was saved by a particular treatment method but who is ignorant of other methods will not be of much use to an addict who needs something different. Clinicians who are in recovery are also vulnerable to relapse, regardless of how long they've been sober.

Of course, even clinicians who have never experienced addiction themselves, but are open-minded and have taken the opportunity to learn from those who have, can certainly provide good treatment. Although I generally avoid talking much about my personal life to patients, this is one area in which I recognize that both they and their families have a genuine need to know something about me. When asked about myself, I tell addicts and their loved ones that although I do not have personal experience of addiction, I've learned from many addicts over the years about the power, destructiveness, and involuntariness of addiction. If, nevertheless, the person I'm talking to prefers to see a clinician who is in recovery, I help him or her find one who is well trained and has experience with a variety of treatment methods.

There is one other issue that may come up about the kind of therapist you choose. Sometimes an addict will say that he or she would feel more comfortable working with either a man or a woman. Although I know from experience that competence is neither a peculiarly male or female trait, whenever I come across an addict who feels this way I simply help him or her find the kind of therapist he or she is looking for. Although I'm usually curious about why the addict should feel this way, I recognize that the most important thing to do at that point is simply to get the addict to a good therapist so his or her life-threatening problem can be dealt with. Determining at some point why he or she feels more comfortable with a therapist of one gender than the other would be a good idea, but it can wait until the more immediate problem has been resolved. Bear in mind, though, that on occasion an addict will use the "need" to find a therapist of a specific gender, race, or even appearance as a way to deflect those who wish to help. In situations like these I usually give the addict two or three choices, regardless of whether or not they have the "qualifications" the addict is asking for, and insist that he or she pick one.

It's important to understand that all the suggestions I've made regarding selecting an appropriate therapist are based on the assumption that you are dealing with a somewhat rational addict, that you will be able to convince him or her to follow your suggestions, and that you will be able to get him or her to work with the therapist you think is most appropriate. It's entirely possible, however, that that won't be the case, and you may find yourself in a situation in which, for one reason or another, you have to jump at whatever opportunity presents itself. You may, for example, have difficulty scheduling an appointment with your first choice, in which case you might have to see whoever else is available. You may also find yourself in a situation in which the addict gives you only a small window of opportunity. An addict who, for example, has been embarrassed at work one day and is willing to see a clinician that afternoon may no longer be willing to by the next morning. In this kind of situation you're better off taking the addict to see whoever is available rather than waiting, possibly until he or she is no longer willing to seek help.

Similarly, as I've already mentioned, your friend or loved one may fixate on a particular type of individual—or even a particular individual—as the only one he or she will work with. In all of these situations, though, you have to remember that your main goal is to get the addict into treatment however you can and not let anything distract you from attaining that goal. This is another aspect of Creative Engagement. Think of the addict in this situation as a man drowning in the ocean who's thrown a life preserver. You don't ask what color the life preserver is, you just grab it and hang on for dear life!

Finally, as you gather and evaluate this information, you should, if possible, enlist the cooperation of the addict or at least make sure that he or she knows you're doing it. This sort of "transparent" process can help give the addict reason to trust you, as well as show him or her that you're concerned enough to be looking for ways to help. Realistically, though, because addicts are almost always reluctant patients, it's unlikely that your friend or loved one will want to help in gathering information, or even agree on the need to do so. In that case, you should go ahead and gather the information on your own and, once you've evaluated it, use it to try to convince the addict that he or she needs help.

Beyond Friends and Family: Gathering and Evaluating Information

*   Develop a plan that all those who care about the addict can follow.

- Don't hesitate to get professional help for the addict.
- Determine which kind of therapist is most appropriate for your situation.
- Avoid untrained and unlicensed therapists.
- Develop a list of two or three possible therapists.
- Interview each of the therapists about their training, skills, and attitude.
- Look for therapists who are familiar with many different treatments.
- Go with the first good therapist you find.

Finding and deciding on the best therapist for your friend or loved one can, frankly, be a lot of work. But it is absolutely essential if you want to help the addict rid him- or herself of the addiction. Again, though, these are only the first two steps in the process. The third step is trying to convince the addict that he or she needs help, and that's the subject of the next chapter.

Chapter Five

WHAT FRIENDS AND FAMILY CAN DO:

Convincing the Addict to Enter Treatment

Once you've done your research into the addiction treaters available in your area, and selected an appropriate therapist to help your friend or loved one, the next step in the process is for you to do what you can to convince the addict in your life to take advantage of that help. I won't pretend to you that this step is an easy one. If it were easy, you would have already done it. It is, though, an essential one and could very well mean the difference between life and death for your loved one. This is a step in which Creative Engagement is particularly important.

But how do you convince an addict to go into treatment? There are several ways to do it, and in this chapter I'm going to tell you exactly what they are and how you can use them. First, though, there's something very important that you have to understand about addiction: addiction is not logical. That is, addicts don't sit down and make well-thought-out, rational decisions to continue their dangerous addictive behaviors. If they could do that, they wouldn't be addicts. So trying to reason with an addict in order to convince him or her to stop using is very unlikely to yield positive results. More often than not, what does lead addicts to stop is the realization of what may happen to them if they don't—things like losing a job, running into problems with relationships, having financial difficulties, or experiencing physical deterioration. And you can help the addict in your life come to that realization by providing him or her with a realistic assessment of those possibilities. Among the methods I suggest you use to do that are using addiction emergencies to promote treatment, motivational interviewing, logical consequences, removing temptation, and harm reduction.

Utilizing Emergencies to Promote Treatment

Addicts face several potentially life-threatening complications from their behavior. Ironically, though, when handled correctly, situations like these can actually help start addicts on the road to recovery. Not only can they help convince friends and family who witness them that it's time to act, they can also help addicts themselves realize the consequences of their addiction. I've seen cases in which an unpleasant emergency room experience has helped an addict declare a "bottom"—to say, "This is it. I'm going to get help for my problem"—rather than continue the behavior until he or she has lost a job or a spouse. And you can be instrumental in this change process. By handling these "emergencies" thoughtfully, you can help motivate the addict to seek treatment, which will in turn make similar emergencies less likely to occur in the future. Although the most obvious kinds of emergencies are suicidal behavior and accidental overdose, there are several others that are much more common. Among these are the potentially dangerous behavior caused by the intoxication itself, the physical dangers of withdrawing from alcohol, and the dangerous situations addicts must often face in order to get their drug of choice.

Common Possibilities for Drug-Related Harm

Whenever someone is intoxicated with an addictive substance, there's a danger that his or her impaired judgment will result in some sort of injury. An individual who causes an accident while under the influence of alcohol or drugs, or one who participates in unsafe sex while intoxicated are good examples. There are, though, other, less obvious dangers. One, for example, is the powerful central nervous system (CNS) depression caused by alcohol in an individual who doesn't have a tolerance for it, which can stop his or her breathing. Another is the possibility of an intoxicated individual choking to death on his or her own vomit. A third is the increased likelihood of a heart attack or stroke in someone who's using cocaine, which can be brought on by spasms of the heart's blood vessels, a serious heart rhythm abnormality, or the sudden, massive increase in blood pressure that cocaine causes.

When faced with emergencies (or potential emergencies) like these, in addition to the treatment that's needed immediately to preserve the addict's life and well-being, it's essential that the underlying addictive disorder be treated as well. Unfortunately, in such cases the intoxicated person usually can't understand the need for treatment, and attempts to convince him or her are usually a waste of time. Nevertheless, if you find yourself in such a situation, you should take the opportunity to insist as strongly as possible that the addict receive treatment for the addiction.

One way to do that is to enlist the help of emergency department personnel. These individuals have access to treatment programs, both inpatient and outpatient, and you should ask them to refer your friend or loved one to a program, tell him or her that they're doing so, and insist that he or she go to the treatment. Even in an intoxicated or semi-intoxicated state, most people will recognize when all those around them are arguing for a certain course of action, in this case getting treatment, and are more likely to follow it. This is using peer pressure for a good purpose!

Emergency department personnel also have the ability to hold a patient, even against his or her will, if there's an immediate danger to his or her well-being. Although laws vary from state to state, an emergency department physician (or any physician in a hospital) can hold a patient until any such danger has passed, or until a hearing can take place before a judge. For that reason, holding an intoxicated patient is usually acceptable, especially if family members can't assure the physician that they'll be able to get him or her home safely. Holding an addict who's in need of treatment but no longer intoxicated is much more complicated and requires a judge's order. In many cases, though, it can be done, and you should speak with the hospital's lawyer if you think this might be a good idea.

Of course, even if your friend or loved one doesn't end up in the emergency room, he or she may still be making poor life choices because of the addiction. If that's the case, you're faced with a more subtle but no less important task. If, for example, you know that your brother is putting himself in danger by having multiple sex partners and/or unsafe sex, you should try to point out to him the connection between the drug use and the dangerous choices. Again, calmly but persistently expressing how you feel about the problem will be more effective with most addicts than a major emotional confrontation. Also, as I mentioned before, it's important in such situations that you not allow any side issues to distract you from the life-threatening issue at hand. That is, you have to remember that you're not addressing your brother's sexual orientation, or which neighborhood he chooses to live in, or how he spends his salary. You have to focus on your concern about drugs leading to unsafe sex, which can, in turn, lead to death.

Suicidal Behaviors

Suicidal intentions or behaviors present the most immediately life-threatening emergency for the addict. This is one case where calling 911 may save a life, and if faced with such a situation you shouldn't hesitate to make that call, even if it provokes the addict's anger at having his or her suicidal or physically aggressive behavior stopped by the police or an ambulance crew. Although the urge to commit suicide may be due to psychiatric and/or addictive disorders, whatever the underlying reason, addiction to any substance substantially increases the risk for suicide. One study found that alcohol dependence made a person thirty-two times more likely to commit suicide than the average individual. And, often enough, suicidal addicts have the method for ending their lives—whether intentionally or not—literally in their hands at the exact moment they feel the most suicidal.

Of course, if someone was to tell you that he or she intends to commit suicide, you'd have to take immediate action to keep him or her from doing so. But you also have to be constantly on the lookout for less obvious clues of suicidal behavior, such as saying goodbye to friends, giving away valued possessions, or talking about the afterlife. In fact, any mention or hint that the addict makes regarding suicide can mean he or she has become severely disturbed. In situations like this, a complete psychiatric evaluation is called for, including a mental status examination and an effort to determine if the patient actually has the means of committing suicide. Although not even the best clinician can consistently predict another person's behavior, a careful examination will often not only reveal how serious the suicide threat is but also enable those who care about the addict to provide appropriate support. In extreme situations, such support may even mean involuntary hospitalization, and it's important to remember that suicidal behaviors or intentions are one of the few available legal rationales for involuntarily hospitalizing an addict.

Longer-term suicidal behavior, in which the addict doesn't appear to be in any immediate danger, is rarely as obvious and is accordingly much more difficult for friends and family to detect. Examples of this type of behavior include chronic use of cocaine, which can lead to sudden death, or use of alcohol in situations in which the addict should not be impaired at all, such as when he

or she is behind the wheel of a car. Moreover, even if such behavior is recognized, unless there's an immediate threat, the police
can't intervene. But that doesn't mean there's nothing you can do.
When you become aware of any kind of suicidal tendencies, you
can point them out to your friend or loved one as both cause for
concern and evidence that he or she needs help, and present him
or her with a reasonable plan for getting into treatment. This is an
especially valuable use of Creative Engagement.

Accidental Overdose

Although perhaps not consciously suicidal, accidental overdoses can—and sometimes do—kill. But even if an addict is lucky
enough to survive an overdose, it's a true psychiatric emergency
and doesn't bode well for his or her future. If your friend or loved
one has overdosed, whether accidentally or not, he or she is very
near bottom and is seriously in need of treatment. In such a situation you should certainly use the overdose itself as an argument for
him or her to enter a program. If, however, he or she is resistant,
it may be necessary to use coercion. I'll tell you more about involuntary treatment options in the next chapter. For the moment,
though, it's important for you to bear in mind that exercising one
of these options will be easier if you can provide a judge with
evidence that your friend or loved one has taken an overdose. For
that reason, it's essential that you remember the circumstances of
the overdose, gather medical records, and be prepared to assist the
hospital and, eventually, legal authorities who have the ability to
mandate treatment.

Motivational Interviewing

When an addict apparently doesn't want to stop using drugs or
alcohol, it may seem like no one can change his or her mind.

But even though no one can force someone else to give up these substances, a thoughtful campaign of persuasion can confront the addict's denial and help his or her life-affirming behaviors win out over the destructive ones. One of the techniques I recommend using to do that is motivational interviewing.

This is a method of working with addicts that enables the interviewer to learn more about the extent of the addiction while, at the same time, encouraging the addict to change his or her behavior. Despite its name, this method is really more of a series of conversations than interviews, although the conversations are conducted by the "interviewer" using certain strategies. William R. Miller and Stephen Rollnick, who developed the method, recommend five such strategies: (1) ask open-ended questions; (2) listen reflectively; (3) affirm your understanding; (4) summarize; and (5) elicit self-motivating statements.

Ask Open-Ended Questions

The first strategy is based on the idea that if you ask your friend or loved one questions about the addiction, rather than bombarding him or her with your concerns and doubts, you're much more likely to get a positive response. No one likes having to defend him- or herself, and if you put an addict into a situation in which he or she has to do so, all you're going to get is more resistance. In addition, if you ask open-ended questions, rather than "yes" or "no" ones, it encourages the addict to express his or her own thoughts and worries about the drug or alcohol use. And it's important that the addict expresses these thoughts and worries, because they can become the motivating force for getting him or her into treatment. What motivates us to change differs from person to person, and your friend or loved one may be motivated to start treatment for reasons that are unfathomable, or at least unknown, to you.

I learned this from a young woman I worked with very

early in my career. Although she was clearly addicted to alcohol, she apparently wasn't worried about either the impending loss of her executive position or of her fiancé, who had brought her into my office. She acknowledged that she might be "a little bit" in denial, but didn't seem at all concerned about the fact that her liver wasn't functioning normally. After several sessions it became clear to me that she was coming to my office mostly just to humor those who were worried about her and had no intention of stopping the drinking that was causing her so much emotional and physical damage. During one session, though, she made an offhand remark about not being able to fit into a dress she'd bought several weeks earlier. Much to my surprise, when I observed that the amount of alcohol she was drinking was probably causing her weight gain and bloating, she was horrified! We discussed it for about thirty minutes, and by the time we were through she'd decided to enter an inpatient program. Although she eventually identified other problems associated with her drinking, the turning point was clearly the thought of unacceptable weight gain. I learned then to always start with the addict's concerns rather than my own.

Of course, unless you know what's important to the addict, you can't make any use of it. For that reason, the best kind of questions to ask are open-ended ones like, "Well, never mind what your wife thinks, does your drinking bug you?" or "Has your cocaine use caused you any physical problems?" or "I understand that you don't see any problem with using cocaine now, but what would you consider to be a problem?" It's also, however, very important that you listen respectfully, because doing so when the addict is talking about the "upside" of his use of the substance entitles you to also ask about the "downside." Here's an example of what this conversation might sound like.

~~~~~~~~~~~~~~~~~~~~~~~~~~~

"What's the Deal with the Cocaine?"

Friend: So, Fran, what's the deal with the cocaine you were using last night? *[The friend doesn't ask, "Why were you using all that cocaine last night?" a much more threatening and provocative question.]*

Addict: Why? Do you think it was too much?

Friend: I was just wondering about it.

Addict: Yeah, I've been wondering if it's too much. Sometimes I feel like the things I do when I'm on coke are a little wacky. But it hasn't been a problem until the last few months. It's not like it's that expensive or anything, and my work has been fine.

Friend: Oh? *[The friend doesn't pounce on the addict's denial.]*

Addict: But you're the third friend who's brought it up to me this week. Seems like a pattern.

Friend: I guess so.

Addict: And what good is all the money and promotions if I'm wacked-out all the time?

Friend: Yeah, I know what you're talking about. . . .

Listen Reflectively

The most effective way to respond initially to an addict's statements is by reflecting back what he or she says about the drug use. For example, if your friend is a pill addict who says it's embarrassing to go to a doctor's office to get prescriptions, you might agree that the process of getting the drugs is a real hassle. If your son is taking steroids and tells you that he feels a little "jumpy" and "emotional" during his steroid use cycles, you might respond with, "That sounds really unpleasant." And if your niece is an alcoholic who says, "I know that alcohol makes me jittery in the mornings," you could answer with, "Wow! I can't imagine how bad it must feel to wake up in the morning feeling like that."

Responding this way is important for three reasons. First, by reflecting back what the addict says, you enable him or her to hear the same thoughts expressed in someone else's voice, which can solidify the meaning of the statement. Second, hearing such things out loud is more likely to result in behavior change. We're all locked up inside our heads so much of the time that actually hearing something spoken out loud can be a refreshing—and sometimes startling—experience. And third, reflective listening reassures the addict that his or her concerns are being taken seriously, without negative judgments. (Note that reflecting back the addict's points doesn't mean that you necessarily agree with them, only that you've heard them.) Such a conversation might sound something like this:

"It's a Good Year, Huh?"

Addict: Man, I'm doing great on the football team this year.

Friend: It's a good year, huh? *[The friend simply reflects the addict's thoughts.]*

Addict: Yeah, the coach says if I can keep my weight up and keep up a C average I'll be able to start for sure next year.

Friend: Sounds good, Phil. *[The friend offers another reflection.]*

Addict: I guess the 'roids are helping me. . . . I hate the shots, though.

Friend: They hurt?

Addict: Naw, I just get so down in the dumps after a few days. . . . I have to start taking them again so I don't beat the crap out of Jane.

Friend: You beat the crap out of her? *[The friend doesn't jump on the problem of the addict getting angry at his girlfriend but simply reflects back the obvious dilemma.]*

Addict: Nah, I don't, but I feel like it. She says that she'll break up with me if I yell at her again.

Friend: Sounds like a problem—I know how much you care about Jane.

Affirm Your Understanding

Another effective strategy is more actively expressing your understanding of what the addict says and clarifying anything that's unclear. For example, if your brother says to you, "I know Mom and Dad are concerned about me using Ecstasy," you might respond with, "So, if I understand you right, the harm you see in

using it is that it worries our folks." Word choice is very important here. It's essential that you avoid using words or phrases that
seem to make judgments, because they could undermine your
efforts to help the addict open up and change. If, for example,
you were to say, "So, the *only* harm you can see in using Ecstasy is
that it worries our folks?" your brother could easily see the word
"only" as a judgment of his behavior. It's also important that you
keep a calm tone in your voice. Remember that the goal here
is to affirm that you understand what the addict is saying about
his addiction, not convince him of the error of his ways. It's only
getting the addict's own ideas about the addiction on the table
that will enable you to do something about it. This part of such a
conversation might sound like this:

"That *Would* Be Painful!"

Sister: You looked a little down this morning when you got up, Eva.

Addict: You're not kidding! And then I had to face work for eight hours with a raging hangover. My supervisor kept saying that I looked tired, but I could tell she knew it was a hangover. It's a bummer, because I really need that job.

Sister: Do you think she might fire you? *[The sister raises an obvious question.]*

Addict: Nah . . . Well, maybe.

Sister: That would really suck. *[The sister makes an obvious observation.]*

Addict: I don't know what I'd do—maybe go back to live with Mom and Dad . . .

Sister: So I guess the worst thing about you drinking too much is that you'll end up with Mom and Dad again.

Addict: Now that *would* be painful!

Sister: Horrible! [They both laugh.]

Summarize

After asking questions, listening reflectively, and affirming your understanding, the next step is to summarize what you've heard the addict say during your conversations. This means offering a full—but brief—overview of the addict's situation as he or she sees it. Once again, you have to avoid injecting your own biases into the conversation. For instance, you might say, "From what you've said, I understand that your smoking crack has an upside and a downside for you. It makes you feel great, but then you crash afterward, which doesn't feel so terrific. Also, you and your girlfriend get along when you're using it, and you feel it makes your sex life better. But you're also starting to worry about the physical effect it's having on you, and that you could be fired from your job if your boss finds out you're using it. So—and again, correct me if I'm wrong—you're starting to think that it would be a good idea for you to stop using crack, and that's why we're talking." Notice that this phrasing simply restates what the addict has said and then connects the dots to a desire for treatment. Here's how a similar conversation—this one about excessive alcohol use—might go.

"Sounds Like You Know You Should Stop Drinking"

Sister: I really felt bad for you Sunday morning. It can't be fun having a headache like that.

Addict: Yeah, I kept telling myself I will *never ever* drink that much again!

Sister: Sounds like a plan. *[The sister is being nonconfrontational.]*

Addict: I guess I'm just getting too old for this. But I don't know what I'd do if I didn't go out drinking with my friends most nights.

Sister: Would you feel left out?

Addict: Maybe a little. But it seems like we don't go out together that much these days anyway. Some of my friends actually say they want to study at night. It's weird.

Sister: They study on weekend nights too?

Addict: I think so. Or maybe they just want to be conscious on Sunday morning so they can study. [She laughs.]

Sister: Do you study on weekends?

Addict: I have to now, because the classes are harder. But I can't seem to avoid drinking after classes. And it's a lot easier to study without a hangover!

Sister: So what I'm getting is that you'd be joining the crowd if you stopped drinking and saved yourself for studying. *[The sister merely rephrases what the addict has said.]*

Addict: Yeah.

Sister: But it's been hard to stop?

Addict: Yeah, I guess . . .

Sister: Wow! Sounds like you know you should stop drinking or cut down but you can't actually do it. You sound worried. . . . *[The sister summarizes the most important points—the addict knows it's a problem but can't stop on her own. Most important, because she hasn't attacked the addict with, "Aha! You're an alcoholic!" and, instead, waited for her to say it on her own terms, the lines of communication remain open.]*

Addict: I guess I am.

Elicit Self-Motivating Statements

This last type of conversation involves your asking leading questions to get the addict to make motivating statements on his or her own. If, for example, your son's grades had improved when he stopped using alcohol and marijuana for a short period of time, you might ask, "What happened with your schoolwork last year when you stayed sober over the fall term?" And he'd be likely to reply with something like, "Well, I could just concentrate better, and I didn't have to sleep off hangovers on Sunday morning, so I could study."

In this exchange, by incorporating some details into the

question, you would have gotten him to expand on the simple fact that his schoolwork improved. The details, particularly in this case, are very relevant because they provide hard evidence that staying away from drinking and drugs is directly connected to doing better in school. What's even more important, though, is that having the *addict* say it, rather than you, helps the idea sink in further, so he's more likely to retain it. One other thing you should take into consideration here is that patience is the key. In a half-hour discussion, the addict may make only three or four self-motivating statements. As the "interviewer," it's your responsibility to mentally note down these statements so you can bring them up later. This sort of conversation might sound like this.

"Well, That's Something, Anyway"

Mother: Good to see you. It must be nice to be done with your exams. *[The mother makes a simple observation to her son.]*

Addict: It sure is. Now I can relax and do nothing for the whole vacation!

Mother: What were the tests like?

Addict: Hard! I don't think I was ready for that calculus final. It really threw me for a loop, but I know I passed the class.

Mother: Calculus is a killer. *[The mother agrees.]*

Addict: Right. And the teaching assistant was only available from eight to ten in the morning.

Mother: Could you make it there that early?

Addict: I wasn't happy about getting up that early. It's not fair. But at least this semester I wasn't zoned out in the morning from partying all night.

Mother: I suppose that helped you face calculus at that hour. *[The mother gently suggests that there's some connection between his not partying and his ability to concentrate the next day.]*

Addict: I guess it did. I could concentrate on calculus and not get a headache or have that fuzzy feeling in my head. *[The addict says it himself.]*

Mother: Well, that's something, anyway. *[The mother gently reinforces the addict's assessment without overstating the case and potentially provoking him.]*

Addict: I suppose so.

Here the addict has acknowledged that he has a problem. He may have defined the problem as having a fuzzy head or difficulty studying rather than as alcoholism, but the issue is now on the table. This is where you can start making suggestions about him getting help. It's important, though, that you present these suggestions as something that will enable him to resolve the problem as *he* sees it. You could accordingly say something like, "Well, getting rid of that fuzzy head and being able to study sounds like a great goal, and it seems to be the alcohol that's keeping you from doing it. I've heard that a lot of people have gotten help with that kind of thing by going to a counselor or to Alcoholics Anonymous. I could even help you get hooked up with something like that. . . ."

Imposing Logical Consequences

In his book *Choices and Consequences,* addiction counselor Dick Schaefer defines "natural consequences" as those that happen to the addict of his or her own accord, without intervention from friends or family. These include hangovers from alcohol, arrests for driving under the influence (DUI), or financial loss as a result of drug use. Logical consequences, by contrast, are those that are arranged or imposed by the addict's friends or loved ones in an effort to maintain the addict's safety, encourage him or her to change, and promote treatment. These might include things like restricting use of the family car if a home urine toxicology test is positive or refused, denial of an agreed-upon allowance if the addict uses alcohol, or refusing to go with the addict to a party where drugs will be used.

As you can see from these examples, it's essential that any consequences you impose on the addict be reasonable, directly tied to the dangerous substance use, set up in advance, and easily enforceable. This is extremely important because if they're not, then the consequences will seem—and will be—just punishment and won't be helpful in any way. In fact, setting up consequences like these isn't only better for the addict, it's also better for his or her family or friends. If you and other friends and family feel that the consequences are too severe, you'll probably feel uncomfortable about using them, in which case no one will benefit.

Such consequences work because they set up the dynamics that make people change their behavior. For example, once you get a parking ticket for letting the time run out on a meter, you're not likely to let it happen again. Of course, forgetting to put another quarter into a meter isn't the same thing as being an addict. Addiction is a very powerful thing and usually only partly under the addict's control. But it's that part—the controllable part—that logical consequences can help with. And you can set up those logical consequences to help the addict control what he can control!

One family I worked with decided that if their twenty-six-year-old alcoholic son drank at night they wouldn't allow him to use his car. Since he lived at home, they could usually tell when he'd been drinking so they would be able to enforce it. The son was aware of the dangers of drunk driving, so he agreed that the plan made sense and said he would give up his keys if he drank. Two weeks later, when he came home from work with alcohol on his breath, his younger sister asked for his keys. There was a shouting match, during which he called her a "controlling bitch," but he gave her the keys.

The next morning over breakfast he told the family that he might be better off living on his own. His mother said that they would miss him and worry about his well-being but couldn't stop him from leaving. Weeks passed, and the son said little to his parents about the restriction they'd placed on him or about his threat to leave the house. But he didn't drink, either, and eventually he came to accept his parents' policy about drinking, because he acknowledged the logical nature of the consequences and appreciated his parents' concern for his well-being.

Removing Temptation

Our society promotes addiction in a variety of ways. We're bombarded every day with advertisements for alcohol and cigarettes that suggest that our using these substances will make us youthful, sexy, and sophisticated. Even popular magazines and newspapers help promote addiction. For example, one recent issue of a mainstream women's magazine contained several articles that touched on the subject, including "Drugs at the Office," "9 Ways Boozing It Up Makes You Beautiful," and "Caviar, Avocados and Speed." In addition, many of us use substances that, while we may not be addicted to them, can be abused and lead to addiction. Needless to say, if an addict is trying to free him- or herself from drugs or alcohol, all of this only serves to make it that much more difficult.

How do you protect your friend or loved one from all this temptation? Unfortunately, the ubiquitous nature of alcohol and cigarette advertising makes it virtually impossible to remove it from most people's daily environment. All you can do in the face of lies and false promises from the media is counter them with the truth of the addict's experience—physical damage, impaired relationships, and lost opportunities. However, you *can* do something about removing the "people, places, and things" in the addict's surroundings that Alcoholics Anonymous rightly identifies as cues for relapse.

There are a number of ways to do this, and the more you do it, the better off your friend or loved one will be. For example, even though you or others around the addict may not be addicts yourselves, if you continue to use addictive substances in the addict's presence it's only going to make it harder for him or her to stop using them. Imagine your alcoholic wife, who is trying to stop drinking, kissing you and smelling alcohol on your breath! How easy is it going to be for her to stop? This is assuming, of course, that you and others around the addict *can* stop using such substances. If you can't, it might be a good idea to take a good hard look at your own use!

If those around the addict can't refrain from using these substances, changing friends may be the only option available. Doing so may be quite difficult for the addict, especially if all his or her friends are similarly addicted, but that may be the price of sobriety. Alcoholics Anonymous and other peer-led support groups can be very useful in helping addicts who are dropping abused substances form new friendships with people who have productive and gratifying lives. You can foster this by not only encouraging your friend or loved one to attend an open AA meeting, but by going along with him or her to show your support.

Changing the "places" that promote drug use can be as easy as avoiding bars or as difficult as moving out of a neighborhood you've lived in your whole life. As a rule, addicts should avoid going to restaurants, bars, and even friends' homes where they've used substances in the past. The lure of addiction is so strong that the addict can experience cravings just by walking into an old haunt. For the same reason, AA advises addicts to avoid the "things" associated with their addiction. For some types of addiction, these things are obvious, such as crack pipes or heroin needles. For others, however, it may not be that simple. I had one patient who felt a nearly irresistible craving for crack cocaine every time he saw aluminum foil, because his drugs had always come wrapped in it. Since aluminum foil is all over the place and can't be avoided, we worked out a plan for him to put into effect whenever he saw it. He was to let himself experience whatever he felt, but call his sponsor and Narcotics Anonymous (NA) friends until he reached someone who could talk him down. By anticipating the inevitable, and preparing himself for it, when faced with the craving he was able to keep from being overwhelmed. An additional benefit of this strategy was that, because his sponsor and NA friends became aware of how he reacted to aluminum foil, they were able to talk about it with him and help him learn to control his behavior.

Harm Reduction

Harm reduction means different things to different people. It is, however, usually defined as putting more emphasis on reducing whatever damage may be caused by an activity than on reducing the activity itself. One common example of harm reduction is a program that provides condoms to teenagers. Although hardly anyone thinks thirteen-year-olds should be having sexual relations, making condoms available to them is an acknowledgment that many of them do, and that they need to protect themselves from HIV and pregnancy.

In terms of addiction, harm reduction means, first, trying to reduce the harm to the addict and, second, finding ways to minimize the amount of the drug used and the length of time it's used. Although the concept of harm reduction has actually been a component of most addiction treatment programs for many years, there is some disagreement about it among those who administer these programs. Some believe it should be used only as an interim measure until abstinence is within reach. Others, at the opposite end of the spectrum, teach addicts how to use drugs as safely as possible, sometimes to the point of providing clean needles and showing them how to inject themselves sterilely. But even those clinicians who insist on abstinence as the primary goal acknowledge that at the beginning of treatment, slips, relapses, and binges are quite common and should be prepared for. And harm reduction can be very helpful in such instances.

Friends and family should, out of necessity and common sense, practice the harm reduction philosophy. (Most people do but don't call it by that fancy name!) Bear in mind, though, that the less lethal the drug use, the easier it is to practice the philosophy. When an addiction worsens to the point of clearly destructive behavior, many people find it difficult to "stand idly by" while their friend or loved one suffers. Harm reduction, however, is not standing idly by, nor is it acquiescing to the addict's view of the inevitability of the substance abuse. It's actually an acknowledgment of the addict's essential autonomy. And barring a rationale for calling the police to rescue an addict from a life-threatening situation, it represents the most effective way for you to place yourself in a position to help when and if the addict is ready to accept that help. In other words, it's another good way to use Creative Engagement.

There are a number of ways that you can implement this philosophy with your friend or loved one. If, for example, the addict injects him- or herself with drugs, you might get him or her to enroll in a syringe exchange program (SEP). These programs, which are state-sanctioned and publicly financed in many states, acknowledge the high rate of HIV associated with sharing needles and work with injecting drug users on a wide range of problems. For the addict reluctant to accept treatment, an SEP can provide a welcoming, nonjudgmental environment—probably the *only* environment he or she will even consider voluntarily entering at this point.

In addition to clean needles, SEPs offer a wide range of services, including medical care, drug treatment, housing, child care, family services, employment information, education, legal help, and counseling. They also require neither identification nor insurance from their clients and are willing to meet them "where they're at" emotionally. This sort of service might make people who hold more traditional views uncomfortable, but SEPs have been proven to have a high rate of success for engaging and persuading the reluctant patient. You can find out if such a program is available in your state by contacting your state's public health department or a big city public hospital.

Another way you can help your friend or loved one is to get him or her to reduce the frequency of using a substance, or to switch from a more- to a less-dangerous one. Since it's relatively rare for addicts to stop their substance abuse "cold turkey," for most there is a middle phase in which they're moving toward abstinence but not yet there. So even if the individual refuses to commit to abstinence, but is willing to cut down on his or her use of the substance, that's clearly a good thing. Many—probably most—of those who eventually achieve abstinence start out with the idea of cutting down. Even AA says that the commitment to sobriety should be made "one day at a time," and sometimes one hour, or one minute, at a time. It's likely, of course, that you will continue to hope for abstinence and encourage your friend or loved one to achieve it. But in the meantime, supporting harm reduction methods like these can only help.

As you can see, there are several ways in which you can help encourage the addict in your life to enter a treatment program. Depending on the situation and the individuals involved, of course, some work better than others, but at various times I have seen all of these methods used successfully. I must also admit, though, that sometimes, no matter what you do, an addict will put up an emotional "brick wall" against any and all suggestions, confrontations, or pleas you may make. What can you do in the face of this sort of overwhelming resistance? You can do the same thing that I and other experienced addiction treaters do—rather than ramming directly into the brick wall, you look for a way around it, or a way to encourage the wall to crumble. In other words, as one of the ancient rules of medicine suggests, "If what you're doing isn't working, try something else." For example, if you've been yelling at your daughter that the cocaine she's using is bad for her, stop yelling and try another tactic. Enlist the help of some of her friends, withdraw financial support, or set limits on visits home. Try motivational interviewing, logical consequences, or removing temptation. The point is that you shouldn't give up. Her life may depend on it.

What Friends and Family Can Do: Convincing the Addict to Enter Treatment

- If there's a crisis, use it to promote treatment.
- If necessary, don't be afraid to call 911.
- Try to learn the addict's reasons for using the substance by using motivational interviewing.
- Set up consequences that are logical and enforceable.
- Remove as many temptations as possible.
- Do whatever you can to help reduce the harm the drugs or alcohol are causing.
- If whatever you're doing doesn't work, try something else.

Unfortunately, sometimes even the best efforts of family and friends aren't enough to convince an addict to go into treatment. But even if you've exhausted all the means I've discussed and still haven't convinced your addicted loved one to seek help, there are still other—more extreme—steps that you can take, and that's the subject of the next chapter.

Chapter Six

WHEN NOTHING ELSE WORKS:

Using Constructive and Legal Coercion

What do you do if you've found several possible addiction treaters to help your friend or loved one and tried a variety of ways to convince him or her to go into treatment, but still haven't gotten the addict to agree? The one thing you don't do is give up. Although it may seem like you've exhausted all the possibilities, there are still other ways to get your loved one the help he or she needs. The first, and easiest, is to seek the advice of one or more of the professionals you've already contacted in regard to treatment for the addict. The second, and more extreme, is to use one of the methods available to coerce the addict into treatment. In this chapter I'll tell you about both of them.

Seeking the Advice of Professionals

If you find yourself in a situation in which it's necessary for you to seek the advice of professionals to convince an addict to go into treatment, the most important thing to remember is that you shouldn't blame yourself for not having been able to do it on your own. Just as it's not your fault that the individual is an addict, it's not your fault that you haven't gotten him or her to seek help. In fact, there's a good reason why, more often than not, friends and family can't help their loved ones attain sobriety single-handedly: they're too close to the addict. I know, for example, that if one of my own children were to start behaving in a self-destructive way, I'd be very concerned and eager to help. I would also, however, be terribly frightened, angry with him or her for putting the rest of the family into a difficult situation, and worried that I hadn't done my job as a parent. And even though that fear, anger, and self-reflection might be justified, those feelings would certainly get in the way of my solving the problem. So even with my professional expertise in dealing with self-destructive behavior, it would be very difficult—if not impossible—for me to effectively help my child.

Of course, having already interviewed a number of professional addiction treaters in your area, you should have at least two or three you can call on for help. When you call, you should explain the situation to the professional and ask if you can come in to speak with him or her. In my own practice I've found that face-to-face meetings are usually more productive than phone conversations because they help me understand the situation better and make it easier for the friend or family member to get a better sense of me, my recommendations, and how urgent I think the situation is. The professional will charge you for his or her time, but a meeting like this is likely to be a lot more helpful than a hurried phone call.

During the meeting you should go over the facts of the situation and tell the professional about whatever methods you've already tried to get the addict into treatment. Of course, not having the addict in the room will put the therapist at a disadvantage, as he or she will have to try to assess the problem through your eyes. But the professional will still be able to help you in several ways. He or she can assess how serious the situation is, suggest other methods of convincing or coercing the addict to go into treatment, and give you the names of inpatient treatment facilities and mental health lawyers who can help you. The important thing here is that, by taking this step, you're using Creative Engagement, refusing to give up, and moving a step closer to getting your friend or loved one the help he or she needs.

Using Coercion to Get an Addict into Treatment

If an addiction professional isn't able to help you convince the addict to start treatment, there's still one other method you can use to accomplish your goal. It's not the best way, and I recommend it only as a last resort, but it does work and, if necessary, I would advise you to use it. This method is generally referred to, for lack of a better term, as coercion.

According to the dictionary, the word "coerce" means "to force to act or think in a given manner by pressure, threats, or intimidation." I'm sure that, like most people, you probably don't like the idea of trying to force anyone to do something he or she doesn't want to do. The truth is, though, that once you've exhausted the other possibilities, if you want to help that friend or loved one, you really have no alternative. And, in fact, most addiction treatment is coerced in one way or another. The spontaneous revelation that leads to abstinence, though well publicized by Bill W., the founder of Alcoholics Anonymous, doesn't happen very often, and most addicts need at least a little "push" from somebody or something in order to be sufficiently motivated to change.

This may sound to you like the technique called "tough love" that's sometimes used to get addicts to go into treatment, and it's true that there are some similarities. There are, however, also some extremely important differences. Tough love generally refers to someone showing love for another individual by clearly expressing his or her expectations and setting boundaries regarding the other person's behavior. The idea behind it is that sometimes the only way to get someone to behave appropriately is to "get tough" with him or her. But there are considerable differences in what people mean when they talk about tough love, and while some expressions of it are perfectly reasonable and can be helpful in bringing about the desired effect, there are others that, in my opinion, are not only counterproductive but can make the situation even worse.

It's these variations in the way tough love is applied that make it problematic. At its gentlest it can just mean setting a "tough" set of boundaries for what one considers acceptable behavior. Applying it to your addicted friend or loved one, then, might mean telling the addict that unless he or she comes home sober you won't speak to him or her. Or that unless the addict stops using marijuana he or she won't be allowed to go on a family vacation. And, in fact, setting boundaries like these is always important, because without them there's little impetus for the addict to stop his or her addictive behavior.

There are advocates of this technique, however, who argue that even stronger measures are both appropriate and advisable. Some, for example, suggest that all emotional support for the addict should be cut off until he or she stops using. And there are others who advocate even more extreme measures, such as simply abandoning an addict to his or her fate, sometimes with no reasonable expectation of receiving help of any kind, much less treatment. This kind of tough love may sound reasonable to some, but in practice it can be very destructive, particularly when the addict is in physical withdrawal or exhibiting signs of mental illness, such as experiencing hallucinations or contemplating suicide. Unfortunately, even though friends or loved ones of addicts who use these measures are often simply following well-intentioned advice, it can sometimes lead to disaster.

For example, in George McGovern's book, *Terry: My Daughter's Life-and-Death Struggle with Alcoholism*, the former senator wrote in regard to his and his wife's following a recommendation to use tough love: "I regret more than I can describe the decision Eleanor and I made under professional counsel to distance ourselves from Terry in what proved to be the last six months of her life. No matter how good the intentions or great the wisdom of the counselor, this was not the right course. . . . If I could recapture Terry's life, I would never again distance myself from her no matter how many times I had tried and failed to help her. Better to keep trying and failing than to back away and not know what is going on. If she had died despite my best efforts and my close involvement with her life up to the end, at least she would have died with my arms around her, and she would have heard me say one more time: 'I love you, Terry.'"

Of course, as I mentioned, tough love doesn't have to be so extreme, nor, fortunately, does it have to end the way it did for the McGoverns. Even so, I've seen so many instances in which using tough love had negative effects that I usually counsel against it. Although families who use it certainly intend to emphasize the "love" aspect of the approach, what the addict hears more often than not is the "tough" part, so the whole message doesn't get through. And while the idea of getting tough might be appropriate under certain conditions, it's not the emphasis that's likely to be most helpful for the addict. The emphasis should, I think, be on actual treatment, such as therapy, medications if necessary, and the assistance of peer-led groups like AA.

Coercion is, in fact, similar to the milder versions of tough love, but it's preferable exactly because it does emphasize these things. Perhaps a better way of looking at it is to see it, as suggested by addiction psychiatrist Sheila Blume, as various "levels of voluntariness." While coercion implies force, levels of voluntariness can just refer to a choice that's made from among many alternatives. And this isn't just a euphemism. There actually are several levels of coercion, and not everything people do to coerce their friends or loved ones into treatment is harsh. In fact, several of the methods I've already suggested could easily fall under the definition of coercion, including a wife's refusal to go to a party with her husband if he's going to use cocaine, or a parent's refusal to let a child use the car if he smokes marijuana. Of course, these methods are at the low end of a spectrum that extends from mild pressure applied by friends and family, to more forceful pressure from family members or employers, to court-mandated treatment with jail time if the addict leaves the program.

So when are these more forceful means of coercion appropriate? The answer, unfortunately, is far from simple and has to be answered on a case-by-case basis. In general, though, these means of coercion should be used only when all other remedies have been exhausted, and when the potential benefits outweigh the risks. And make no mistake about it, using coercion does have risks. It can make the addict angry at those who are doing it, harden his or her resistance to getting help for the addiction, and lead to the addict's refusal to have any further contact with those who are coercing him or her, which of course eliminates the possibility of any future help. On the other hand, there are real benefits to using these methods, including protecting the addict from the harm an addictive substance can cause, preventing the loss of a job or a significant other, and, of course, the possibility of establishing long-term abstinence. Although the eventual outcome always depends on the individual involved, generally speaking it's fair to say that the results of coercion are better than the alternative. However, deciding what kinds of coercive methods to use is ultimately a judgment call and one that you may have to make.

Although there are a variety of ways in which addicts can be coerced into entering treatment, they all fall into just two general areas—those that you and other friends or family members can exercise, which I call Constructive Coercion, and those that can only be exercised by the courts, which I call Legal Coercion.

Constructive Coercion

As I've mentioned, the chances are that you've already used some
coercive methods in your efforts to get the addict in your life to
enter a treatment program. Most of these required you to use as
little coercion as possible, which is advantageous because, as you
would expect, the more voluntary the alternative, the less of a problem the addict is likely to have with it. There are actually several
benefits to a friend, family member, or employer using this kind of
Constructive Coercion. One is that, when you use these methods,
all the decisions you make about treatment are designed specifically
for the individual addict and are more likely to be appropriate for
him or her. Another is that you make those decisions entirely for
therapeutic rather than legal or political reasons. And a third is that,
because the addict is involved in developing the plan, he or she per-
ceives his or her participation as being more voluntary than not. If,
however, the methods you've tried so far haven't worked, there are
several other—more coercive—steps you can take.

Constructive Coercion by a Spouse or Significant Other

If you're married, or living with someone, and want to coerce your partner to go into treatment, one thing you can do is
to arrange for unpleasant consequences unless he or she agrees to
do so. The most extreme consequence would probably be your
leaving him or her, but there are any number of less extreme
consequences that you can threaten. You could, for example, refuse to go anywhere with the addict if he or she is using, not let
the addict drive if your children are in the car when he or she is
intoxicated, or threaten to tell the addict's friends, other family
members, or employer about his or her use. If you choose to try
any of these methods, however, there are three things you should
keep in mind. First, you should never make any threats that you're
not willing and able to follow through on. Making empty threats

doesn't do anyone any good. Second, you should think very carefully and as unemotionally as possible before issuing any such ultimatums. And third, you should present these ultimatums to the addict as rationally and lovingly as possible.

Of course, the addict in your life isn't likely to respond very enthusiastically to threats like these, and he or she may well get angry. Sometimes, though, you have no other choice. Think about it this way: if the only alternative to making such threats is to passively watch the addict kill him- or herself, you're certainly better off trying whatever may have a chance of succeeding. Remember, too, that even if the addict reacts negatively to the consequence, you will have at least put your concerns on the table and given him or her a specific, concrete way to move forward. Here's an example of how a husband might use Constructive Coercion to get his pregnant alcoholic wife to seek help.

~~~~~~~~~~~~~~~~

"You Went Behind My Back?"

Husband: You know, I'm worried about your drinking, Carrie. That's the third beer you've had tonight, and drinking's supposed to be bad for the baby. *[Bob starts off well by concentrating on a specific, concrete danger.]*

Addict: Right! [She laughs.] You're one to talk, you big boozer. Relax, have a beer. *[Carrie uses humor in an effort to distract Bob from talking about her drinking.]*

Husband: No, really! I'm worried that the baby could be deformed or something. I saw it on the news. *[Bob doesn't let Carrie's attempt at humor deflect him.]*

Addict: Listen, Dan Rather, you've been watching a little

too much of the old boob tube. I could get hit by a car just crossing the street, too, you know.

Husband: Yeah, that's true, but getting hit by a car probably wouldn't be your fault. Sometimes drivers just lose control. But you're doing the drinking, and I think we'd both feel terrible if something happened to you or the baby because of it.

Addict: Oh, right, Mr. Holier-than-thou, as if you don't drink plenty. Don't you dare judge me! [Her voice begins to rise.] Don't blame me in advance for our baby being sick. This is your baby, too. *[Carrie switches to anger in her attempt to fend off Bob's continuing confrontation about her drinking.]*

Husband: I'm not trying to judge you or blame you. I'm just worried about our family. *[Bob stays relentlessly on message.]*

Addict: Worry about yourself, then!

Husband: I *am* worried about myself. You know, your drinking affects me, too, and I'd certainly be affected if there was anything wrong with the baby. That's why I looked into the county's Addiction Intervention Program. I think they could help. *[Bob uses the effects of drinking on his own life to explain why he's taken the extraordinary step of finding treatment for his wife without her permission.]*

Addict: What? You went behind my back? [Now she's shouting.]

Husband: Yes, I did. I thought it was the only way to

get some help—for you, me, and the baby. I made an appointment for tomorrow with the program's admissions counselor. *[Bob has taken some concrete action.]*

Addict: Good for you. You can go alone. There's no way I'm going down there!

Husband: The admissions counselor said I should go by myself if you wouldn't come. I told her what's going on, and she said that if you didn't want to get involved in this they might consider asking for a court order to evaluate the situation here when the baby is born.

Addict: What? You called child welfare on me?

Husband: No, I didn't. But I'm scared enough about this that I'm glad the counselor suggested it.

Addict: I can't believe you! You're a total asshole. You don't care about me at all! [Carrie is both screaming and crying now.]

Husband: I didn't know what else to do, Carrie. I'm really worried about the baby, and about you and me. And you wouldn't listen to just me.

Addict: So this is what you do? Call child welfare? I think you just don't want me to have this baby, and you don't want to be a family. I don't have a problem with drinking. It's you who drives me to all of this. I don't care. I don't care anymore. *[Bob remains silent but stays with Carrie, as the counselor had instructed him to do.]*

Constructive Coercion by Friends and Other Family Members

Friends and family members can, of course, make some of the same kinds of threats that spouses and significant others can in order to get an addict to go into treatment. If you're in this situation, though, you probably won't have the same kind of leverage with the addict that those who are closer to him or her do. On the other hand, if you are a friend or family member, simply because you're not as close to the addict, you may have some advantages that others don't. It may, for example, be easier for you to offer and follow through on an ultimatum with the addict because you don't have to interact with him or her on practical, day-to-day issues like child care. It's also possible for you to join together with other friends and family members in an effort to get the addict to seek help.

If you choose to do this, the first step is to contact people who you think would be interested in helping the addict. This group could include the addict's spouse, family members, friends, coworkers, or even employers, but not more than five people all together. When you first get in touch with them, you should say something like, "I'm calling about Sarah Allgood because I'm very worried about her. You've probably noticed that she's been drinking a lot lately, and I'd like to find some way of convincing her to get some help for it. I thought maybe if you and I and some of her other friends and family could get together, we might be able to get her to go into some kind of treatment program." The chances are that, if you've gauged the individual correctly, he or she will be more than happy to join you in your efforts.

When you've gotten everyone together, you should talk, first, about the addict's problems as you see them, second, about what you consider to be the most immediate priorities, and finally, about how you think the group can work together to convince the addict to go into treatment. You should also solicit and listen to what the others have to say, as they may see things some-what differently than you do, so that everyone's perspective can be taken into account when you make plans.

Such plans might call for each member of the group to talk with the addict about his or her particular concerns, separately, over the next several days, to express his or her belief that the addict should go into treatment, and to threaten the addict with unpleasant consequences if he or she doesn't comply. The adult daughter of an alcoholic might, for example, tell her father that she's worried about him being tipsy around his grandchildren and say that she won't allow him to visit with them when he's intoxicated. A coworker might tell the addict that his behavior at work is worrying others and say that she won't work with him if he comes to the office under the influence of alcohol. Whatever consequences are threatened should, of course, relate directly to the individual's concerns and be designed to minimize damage from the addiction, to both the addict and to those around him. The idea behind all this is that the cumulative effort of the addict's friends and family will help coerce him or her to go into treatment.

Although this may sound a lot like the technique called Formal Intervention, in fact it's very different. Formal Intervention was first developed by Vernon Johnson in the mid-1960s and since then has become so widely accepted that it's the first thing most people think of when they're interested in getting an addict into treatment. The technique is, essentially, a group of the addict's friends and/or family, usually with the help of a professional, getting together to surprise the addict, confront him or her about the addiction, and try to convince him or her to enter a treatment program. Its purpose, in Johnson's words, is to present "reality to a person out of touch with it in a receivable way."

During the actual intervention, the leader—usually a professional—explains to the addict why the group has gotten together, and then each of the participants talks about the damage the addict has done to him- or herself as well as to the others because of the addiction. In order to make their point more effectively, participants don't just say, "I hate your cocaine use," but, rather, something more specific, like, "Your using cocaine at the party last week made you act silly, and you embarrassed yourself and me." Because something coming from a group of people is more convincing than something coming from one individual, statements like these can serve to break down the addict's denial. Once all the participants have had their say, they lay out a very specific plan for getting help. Most interventions are designed to end with the addict going to a previously designated treatment center, where a bed is waiting for him or her. The leader will often accompany the addict to the treatment facility, even if that means an extra airline ticket.

Formal Intervention was neither the first nor the only method of group confrontation developed for use with addicts. Others include Alcoholics Anonymous, various types of group therapies, and Network Therapy, all of which are discussed later on in the book. It is, though, similar to all of these in that it presents the addict with the focused, hard-to-ignore concerns of the people who are most interested in him or her. What distinguishes Formal Intervention from the other methods, and provides what its proponents consider to be its greatest advantage, is the element of surprise. The addict who is reluctant to address his or her addiction can avoid an AA meeting or a therapist's office but can't avoid a confrontation that he or she doesn't even know is coming. In addition, unlike the other forms of group confrontation, Formal Intervention concludes with a clear ultimatum, usually that the addict will enter inpatient treatment or lose the support of those around him or her.

While I recognize that there may be some benefits to giving an addict an ultimatum, I don't recommend using this technique. One reason is that it often doesn't work, and once you've tried it, there's nothing else you can do. Some addicts confronted in this way just walk out, and many of those who stay simply agree to do whatever is asked of them and then forget about it as soon as the confrontation is over. Even worse, sometimes addicts break off contact with all those who participated in the intervention, which of course makes it even less likely that they'll receive any help. There have even been instances in which already unstable individuals have attempted suicide as a result of being confronted in such a dramatic way.

Even more important, to my way of thinking, the whole idea of a "surprise attack" is misguided. It's essentially based on the assumption that the addict is so deeply in denial that the only way to get him or her out of it is to use what amounts to a kind of shock treatment. It's entirely possible, though—even likely—that that's not the case. It's true, of course, that some addicts are very deeply in denial, but most of those who confront addicts in this way haven't even asked them about their addictive behavior, so they have no way of knowing what the addict is thinking. And, in fact, there's a big difference between someone who's reluctant to address his or her addiction and someone who will go into treatment only if he or she is ambushed by friends and family. My experience suggests that most fall into that middle ground, which is why I think it's better—from both the emotional and practical standpoints—to approach the addict expressing a desire to help rather than to attack him or her.

The method I've suggested of getting a group of friends and family together to coordinate the effort to convince an addict to go into treatment doesn't include any kind of "surprise attack," nor does anyone threaten to cut off all contact with the addict unless he or she enters a treatment program. As a result, the focus remains on concern for the addict rather than on threats made by members of the group. Also unlike intervention, in this method whatever ultimatums are offered are presented to the addict not by a group but by several different people individually, and over a period of time. This makes it possible for the addict to think about the various recommendations he or she receives, so the addict has plenty of time to consider them. Although this sort of coercion from friends and family doesn't usually have an immediate effect, over time the efforts of all those who care about the addict usually convince him or her to enter a treatment program. Here are some examples of how the friends and family of one addict might exercise this kind of coercion.

"I Can't Hang Out with You Anymore"

Friend: So, Rob, I want to talk to you about something.

Addict: Are you going to break up with me?

Friend: Ha-ha. No, I'm serious here, I'm really worried about you.

Addict: Not this again, Sam.

Friend: I don't want to bug you about this, but we're all really worried about you. Mary even called me again yesterday and said that you might be heading for an overdose. *[Sam is up-front about the discussions regarding his friend.]*

Addict: Oh, great. My wife is calling my best friend to rat on me.

Friend: No one's ratting on you. But a lot of people are worried about your heroin use, me included.

Addict: I appreciate your concern, but I've got it under control. I used less today than I used yesterday, anyway.

Friend: You've said that to me a lot lately, and it doesn't look to me like you can cut down, much less stop. I think you need to go to a detox, and so do Mary and all your other friends.

Addict: What, are all you guys talking about me?

Friend: Yep. People are scared out of their minds about you. In fact, I just can't hang out with you when you're high, I'm so worried that you'll OD.

Addict: You *are* breaking up with me.

Friend: Ha-ha. No, I'm not, smartass. But when you're using I can't be around you—it looks to me like you're going to die. I'll gladly help you get to detox, though. *[Sam clearly states the consequence: he will not spend time with Rob if he's high.]*

Addict: Well, I'm not high now.

Friend: I know. So just tell me when you want to go to detox, and I'm there for you, bro.

Addict: But you really won't hang with me when I'm high?

Friend: Right. Neither will anyone else.

Addict: You're tough.

Friend: Just trying to do the right thing for my friend. . . .

"I Can't Let You Be Around the Kids"

Wife: Rob, I need to talk to you about the kids.

Addict: Are they all right?

Wife: Yes, they are. But I'm worried about you being around them when you're using.

Addict: Worried about what, Mary?

Wife: I'm worried that your judgment is off. Or if you drive them that you might be high and get into an accident. *[Mary is very specific.]*

Addict: That's not fair. I never drive them when I'm high.

Wife: I know you don't want to put them in danger. But when you're using or high, you just don't know what you're doing.

Addict: I said I've never driven them when I was high.

Wife: But sweetie, you don't know what you're doing sometimes. Even though you don't want to hurt them, you might. Last weekend on the camping trip you were nodding off all day in the van. *[Again, Mary is specific and stays on topic.]*

Addict: I was tired.

Wife: Oh, come on. Even Sarah knew you were using. She's only six, and she said you looked "funny" again.

Addict: Point well taken. I won't be around the kids if I'm using.

Wife: Rob, you've already promised me that a bunch of times. I guess I'm going to have to get the kids away from you if you're using. *[Mary tells Rob exactly what the consequence of his using will be.]*

Addict: Are you kidding? You can't take the kids away from me!

Wife: I'm not taking them away from you permanently, I'm just going to protect them while you're using. They can't see you that way. It scares them.

Addict: Where would you take them?

Wife: To my parents', I guess. When you're not using you're a great dad, but I think you're hurting the kids emotionally now by using around them, and you could hurt them physically if you try to drive them while you're high. I know you don't want that. *[Mary is empathetic but determined to protect their children.]*

Addict: I can't believe this. You think I'm dangerous to the kids?

Wife: Yes, I'm afraid I do. I can help you get to detox and then to treatment, and then we won't be so afraid anymore.

"I Can't Give You Any More Money"

Uncle: I need to talk to you, Rob.

Addict: A lot of people have been saying that to me lately, Uncle Billy.

Uncle: I know. Mary and I spoke this morning. I want you to know that I can't lend you any more money until you get some help. *[He warns Rob of a clear consequence.]*

Addict: Whoa! Get help for what?

Uncle: Come on, Rob. You know what I'm talking about. Mary and your friends tell me that you're spending a hundred bucks a day on heroin. I don't mind helping you out, but the money I've been giving you is supposed to be for the mortgage, not drugs.

Addict: You think I'm not using the money for the mortgage?

Uncle: No, I'm sure you are. But if you've got enough to spend that much on drugs, you shouldn't need any money to pay the mortgage. And I don't want to be supporting you using that stuff.

Addict: So you're going to put me, Mary, and the kids out on the street?

Uncle: Of course not. I want you to go to detox, like Mary and your friends do. We can't make you go, but we can at least not help you keep going back to the drugs. *[Billy stays on track with his message.]*

Addict: Fine. Keep your money. But you're not going to control me.

Uncle: Of course I'm not going to control you. But there's no way I'm going to give you that money if you go on using drugs.

Addict: Listen, I get it. I know you're trying to help me. Sorry I got mad. But I think I will handle this on my own and detox myself. In fact, I even started doing that this morning. Did you know I used half what I usually use in the morning when I got up today? I'm going to stop. Isn't that great?

Uncle: I'm glad you used less, Rob, but you've said that to your friends a hundred times before. They don't believe you can stop on your own, and I guess I don't either. *[Although Billy only suspected a drug problem, Mary and Rob's friends had told him about the severity of the problem, so Billy was not taken in by Rob's suggestion that his problem was under control.]*

Constructive Coercion by an Employer

But friends and family members are not the only ones who can use Constructive Coercion effectively. If you want to involve your loved one's employer in your plan, there are things he or she can do to help. It's something of a drastic step, but I've seen it work very well under the right conditions. The right conditions, in this case, are when the addict and his or her employer have a social relationship outside of the workplace, and/or the employer is a caring individual who wants to help. Of course, you need to be careful about something like this, because if the employer isn't sympathetic he or she may fire the addict.

I once worked with a man named Joseph who had a drinking problem. He had been told, separately, by both his wife and his boss—a former drinking buddy—that they were concerned about his health, but he basically ignored them. After he got drunk several times at business lunches, though, his boss sat him down and told him not to come to work until he got some help. The boss, in the meantime, contacted Joseph's wife to tell her what he'd done, so when Joseph got home she reinforced what the boss had told him. Hearing the same thing from both people, Joseph finally agreed to attend an AA meeting, although really just to placate them. At the meeting, though, when he heard other people talking about their drinking, it made him realize that he needed to do something about his own problem. Eventually he stopped drinking, and he credited it to his boss's help.

Here's an example of how an addict's employer can use Constructive Coercion to get him or her to enter a treatment program.

"I Need to Drink to Sell"

Addict: So what's up, Al? You wanted to talk to me?

Employer: I'm worried about you, Joe.

Addict: How come?

Employer: It's your drinking at lunch. It hasn't really changed since we talked about it last month.

Addict: Sure it has. I've cut down. It's exactly what we talked about.

Employer: Well, you may have cut down some, but you're still acting the same way. Just yesterday at lunch you were slurring your words, and you fell down on the way out of the restaurant. It's not good business, Joe. Everyone was looking at you. *[Al tells Joe the truth.]*

Addict: Oh, come on. We just had a few laughs. Those guys love us.

Employer: Not really. In fact, their head guy said they don't want you going on calls to their place anymore. He said it's bad for the junior people to see you that way. He even said you need help, which I agree with, by the way.

Addict: But there's no way I can totally stop drinking. It's what makes me who I am, what makes me able to be the life of the party. Otherwise I get nervous, the business lunches aren't any fun, and I don't sell a damn thing. I need to drink to sell!

Employer: Well, the alcohol's not helping you now. In fact, it's hurting you. Not only aren't you selling anything, they don't even want to give you the chance anymore.

Addict: It's okay. I'll go but I'll be cool.

Employer: Not good enough, Joe. I'm sorry to have to say this, but if you drink, you can't come to work. *[Al warns Joe of a clear, logical, and reasonable consequence.]* It's bad for everybody—you, me, and everyone else. But we can set you up with a therapist who knows about addiction.

Addict: Oh, great, now you're firing me?

Employer: Nope. I'm just saying that if you drink you can't come to work. And as your friend *and* your boss, I just want to see you get help and come back to work. *[Al stays on message and expresses his concern, both personally and professionally.]*

    If, however, you're thinking of enlisting the addict's employer in your efforts, there's one other thing you should remember. The Americans with Disabilities Act (ADA) prohibits employers from discriminating against anyone with physical or mental disabilities, including addiction. So neither people who are actively addicted to alcohol or to drugs can be discriminated against at work solely because of their disease. ADA protections evaporate, however, if the addict comes to work under the influence of the substance, or violates workplace rules regarding its use. If work is an issue for your addicted friend or loved one, it would be a good idea to consult a lawyer who's familiar with mental health law to find out how the ADA protects addicts.

Legal Coercion Exercised by a Judge

    As I've said, if you must use coercion to convince an addict to enter treatment, it's always best to use the mildest method possible. If, however, your own efforts, as well as those of the addict's other friends, family members, or employer, have failed to achieve your goal, the next step would be to go to the legal system. There are several ways that you can use the law to coerce addicts, including threatening the loss of visitation rights or custody of a child, threatening legal commitment, and, in those instances in which the addict has committed a crime, enabling him or her to enter treatment rather than go to jail.

Child Visitation or Custody Rights

I have, on occasion, worked with addicted parents who are going through a divorce, or who have been divorced and have child custody agreements in place. In situations like these, a judge can coerce an addict to go into treatment by denying even chaperoned visits with a child unless the addict not only enters a program but can document his or her sobriety. Once the addict has been sober for a specified period of time, the judge will usually allow, first, chaperoned visits, then overnights, and eventually return custody of the child to the recovering addict. Arrangements like these can be very helpful in maintaining long-term sobriety, as losing custody of a child is often the "bottom" that motivates addicted parents to finally seek treatment. I've served as a "monitor" for many patients who are trying to rid themselves of their addiction so they'll be able to visit with their children. And I've seen that, frequently, although they start working toward achieving a healthy lifestyle for the child's sake, they eventually want to do it for themselves.

Legal Commitment

Asking to have an addict committed to a facility is, at least in theory, another way in which friends or family can coerce him or her into treatment. As I mentioned in the last chapter, if there's a problem that makes it necessary for you to bring your addicted friend or loved one into an emergency room, and there's an immediate danger to his or her safety, hospital personnel can hold the addict, even against his or her will, until the danger has passed. However, this type of emergency commitment generally lasts only between forty-eight and seventy-two hours, or until the addict is no longer intoxicated. Ordering an addict into longer-term treatment is something that only a judge can do, and only in those states that have such commitment statutes. Even then, legal protections make it relatively uncommon for judges to issue such orders unless the addict has committed a crime. In fact, commitment for addiction treatment is so rare that I generally advise friends and family against expending any time or energy even looking into the possibility.

If, though, you feel that your loved one's addiction has progressed to the point where commitment seems like a reasonable option, I would strongly urge you to speak with a mental health attorney. He or she will be able to tell you, first, whether or not your state even has laws that enable addicts to be committed, and second, how likely it is that you'll be able to carry out any threats you may make about commitment. You should also bear in mind that, despite what the attorney may tell you, it's entirely possible that your request will be denied in court, and you should accordingly make plans for what you'll do if that happens. In my experience, when a request for commitment has failed, family members frequently find themselves in a position in which they can do nothing but wait for the next crisis in the addiction and hope they'll be able to intervene at that point.

Criminal Acts

Intoxication with a substance—referred to as "voluntary intoxication" in legal terms—is never accepted by the courts as an excuse for criminal acts. However, the legal system is finally beginning to understand that treating addicts is ultimately more effective than punishing them. So if the addict in your life has committed a nonviolent crime, it may be possible for him or her to be sent to a treatment program rather than to jail. In fact, although there are variations from state to state, many judges have several ways in which they can coerce an addict into treatment. They can release addicts without prosecution in exchange for entering a program, delay prosecution pending completion of a program, or offer a reduced sentence in exchange for completing treatment. Since, however, the laws are different from one state to another, if you find yourself faced with such a situation it's important for you to find an attorney who's familiar with the laws in your area.

Many states today also have special "drug courts"—a collaboration between the criminal justice and addiction treatment systems—that can be used to coerce addicts into treatment. The first of these courts was instituted in 1989 in Dade County, Florida. Frustrated by the number of drug-related cases flooding the courts, judges in the Eleventh Judicial District began experimenting with treatment-based alternatives to punishment for nonviolent drug offenders. The county was so successful in decreasing the rate of further offenses that it generated a nationwide interest in similar programs, and now every state has one.

Although, again, laws vary from state to state, all of these programs incorporate five basic elements. First, they enable local authorities to quickly identify addicts and get them into the system. Second, they provide community-based treatment supervised by a judge. Third, they require regularly scheduled hearings in which progress and program compliance are monitored. Fourth, they provide punishments as well as rewards that are tied to the addict's behavior. Finally, they require mandatory drug testing on a regular basis until the treatment has been completed. If you think that your friend or loved one might benefit from one of these drug courts, you can find out about local options by contacting a mental health attorney, a family court judge, or a local treatment center.

Although I know from experience that not every method of Constructive or Legal Coercion works with every addict, I also know that they can work when used appropriately. At the same time, I have to admit that, while using these methods may sound relatively easy on paper, confronting an addict like this can be both difficult and painful. The most important thing to remember when you do it is *why* you're doing it—that is, to avoid the potentially lethal alternative. Very few people like coercing others into doing things they don't want to do, but again, this is an extraordinary situation, and it may mean saving your friend or loved one's life.

When Nothing Else Works

- Every addict is coerced—in some way—into treatment.
- If you haven't been able to convince the addict to go into treatment, a professional addiction treater can provide assessment, suggestions, and referrals.
- The best coercion is the gentlest, and it's always preferable to tough love.
- A little extra effort from friends and family is sometimes all it takes.
- Formal Intervention can cause more problems than it solves.
- Constructive Coercion exercised by family and friends is more effective than Formal Intervention.
- Constructive Coercion exercised by an employer can be risky, but it can also work.
- Legal Coercion, though least desirable, can save the addict's life.

Now you've learned about what addiction is and how addicts try to avoid dealing with it, as well as what you and others can do to convince or coerce the addict in your life to start treatment. But exactly what is treatment, what should you be looking for if you're considering a treatment facility for your friend or loved one, what different types of treatment are available, and which of those are best to avoid? I'll start answering all those questions in the next chapter.

Part III

TREATMENT OPTIONS

Chapter Seven

WHAT TREATMENT IS

Up to this point I've been telling you about how important it is for your friend or loved one to get treatment for his or her addiction, and what you can do to help bring that about. In this chapter I'm going to tell you exactly what treatment is and what types of treatment are available. Of course, if you've already found a practitioner you're comfortable with, he or she may well have recommended a particular form of treatment. If you haven't, though, or if the practitioner has made several suggestions, this chapter will help you make a choice.

Treatment for drug addiction is basically a process designed to get an addict to change his or her behavior so he or she will stop, or at least slow down, the damage caused by the addiction. However, even before your loved one starts treatment, if he or she is exhibiting symptoms of withdrawal from an addictive substance, it may be necessary for him or her to go through the process of detoxification. These symptoms range from being merely uncomfortable to being both painful and dangerous, and can make rehabilitation difficult if not impossible. Even if the addict is only uncomfortable, he or she may find it hard to concentrate on treatment. And if the addict is in physical pain and/or danger as a result of withdrawing from the substance, there's literally no sense in even attempting rehabilitation without first going through detoxification.

I'll tell you more about this process in chapter 9, but for the moment all you need to know is that detoxification is essentially the process of taking care of an addict while the addictive substance comes out of his or her body, and that because different substances cause different types of withdrawal symptoms, the process varies depending on the type of addiction. Because the withdrawal symptoms for most addictive substances are not that severe, many, if not most, addicts have no need for a formal detoxification program and can start treatment immediately. If, however, your friend or loved one exhibits more severe symptoms, he or she should go through detoxification before starting treatment for the addiction itself.

There are several different kinds of treatment for addicts, but they all fall into one of two broad categories—inpatient or outpatient programs. At the most basic level, the difference between inpatient and outpatient programs is that in the first the patient lives in the facility while in the second he or she lives outside the facility. There are also, however, other very considerable differences between them, and if you hope to be successful in helping your friend or loved one free him- or herself of addiction, it's extremely important that you know what each kind of program offers and when it's most appropriate for an addict to enroll in one or the other. Making a choice between in- and outpatient programs is not necessarily, however, an either/or situation, as the addict in your life may well need both at different points in time. Even if, for example, an intensive inpatient program would be best for him or her right now, once he or she has been through that program, a less intensive outpatient one would in all likelihood be more appropriate.

I'm going to tell you more about the various types of inpatient and outpatient programs later, but for the moment, inpatient treatments include dual diagnosis programs, therapeutic communities, intensive inpatient programs, halfway houses, and sober living houses. Regardless of the specific type of program, however, these types of treatment can provide several benefits for your friend or family member. By removing the addict from his or her normal environment, they give him or her the opportunity to learn very quickly about addiction and relapse prevention.

They also keep him or her from the cues that normally set off substance use in the outside world. But this separation from the real world is a two-edged sword. While it's true that it protects addicts from experiencing these day-to-day cues, it does little to prepare them for their return to the real world, where these cues are present everywhere. The best inpatient facilities recognize this problem and create "step-down" procedures using passes out of the facility, halfway houses, and integrated after-discharge programs to remedy the problem. Even so, because I don't feel that removing addicts from the real world is ultimately beneficial, I recommend inpatient treatment only when outpatient rehabilitation has failed or appears likely to fail.

Outpatient treatments include day treatment programs, comprehensive outpatient addiction treatment programs, outpatient group therapy centers, and methadone programs. Groups like Alcoholics Anonymous also fall under the umbrella of outpatient treatment, even though what they offer is not actually considered treatment, because their programs are conducted by addicts in recovery rather than by professional addiction treaters. (The peer-led nature of AA's program is, however, actually one of its greatest strengths, and I'll tell you more about it in chapter 11.)

As I mentioned, I feel very strongly that outpatient programs are preferable to inpatient ones. To my mind, their primary benefit lies in the fact that rather than being cloistered in a treatment center and, accordingly, kept away from the day-to-day cues that set off their substance use, addicts in outpatient programs are exposed to those cues and, in the process, provided with an opportunity to learn how to manage them. On the other hand, if an addict is unable to attain and maintain sobriety in an outpatient program, an inpatient program would clearly be preferable. Like the decision to enter a regular medical hospital, the decision to enroll in an inpatient addiction treatment facility should not be taken lightly, but should not be avoided if necessary.

How to Decide on Inpatient Versus Outpatient Treatment

But exactly how do you decide whether inpatient or outpatient rehabilitation is the best choice for the addict you love? In general, inpatient care is a good idea when the addict has a psychiatric problem in addition to his or her addiction, has social problems (such as homelessness) that would make success in an outpatient program unlikely, or is unable to remain sober for any substantial period of time. In addition, those who have tried and failed to complete an outpatient program are usually best served by an inpatient program. One potential source of help in making this decision are the criteria developed for this purpose by the American Society of Addiction Medicine, published in *Principles of Addiction Medicine*, second edition, by A.W. Graham (American Society of Addiction Medicine, 1998). These criteria, which are often used by health insurance companies and others to decide what level of care is necessary for an addict, look at the question in terms of six different dimensions.

The first, which is the *Intoxication/Withdrawal* dimension, suggests that if the addict is intoxicated or suffering from severe withdrawal symptoms, he or she will most likely need an inpatient environment for his or her own safety. The second, the *Biomedical Complications* dimension, suggests that an addict who has severe health problems that might distract from treatment, such as heart disease, would also be better off in an inpatient environment where medical help is readily available. The third dimension, *Emotional Behavioral Complications*, which covers psychiatric problems, recommends outpatient treatment if the problems are mild, but inpatient care if they're on the more severe end of the spectrum. For example, an alcoholic who's upset and demoralized might be treated on an outpatient basis, but one whose depression has risen to the level of suicidal thoughts would require inpatient treatment.

Treatment Acceptance, the fourth dimension, concerns how accepting or resistant to treatment the addict is. Obviously, the more resistant he or she is, the more likely an inpatient program will be necessary to engage him or her (and the more likely the addict will try to avoid the treatment!). The fifth dimension, *Relapse,* considers the history and likelihood of the addict's relapsing and suggests that the more likely it is to happen, the more appropriate inpatient treatment would be. Finally, the *Recovery Environment* dimension, which assesses whether or not the addict has a "recovery-friendly" environment to return to, posits that the addict who comes home to a house full of other addicts—or even social users who refuse to stop—would be better served in an inpatient facility.

Although of course every addict's situation is different, these criteria do cover all the main areas of concern. So while no system like this is perfect, if you carefully consider each of the criteria included it should be very helpful in enabling you to make a decision regarding the most appropriate type of treatment for your friend or loved one.

I recall once working with an addict who was a perfect candidate for inpatient treatment. He'd failed to complete several outpatient rehabilitation programs, and although he was enrolled in one at the time, was extremely resistant to the whole idea of treatment. I tried on a number of occasions to convince him to try an inpatient program, but even though I couldn't get through to him, I was able to convince him to allow his mother and a close friend of his to talk with me. After I spoke with them, they went home and had this conversation with him.

"We Just Want You to Try Something Else"

Mother: Sean, I'm really concerned about your meth use. You look like you're sick! And the outpatient program doesn't seem to be helping. *[The addict's mother keeps to the facts rather than getting emotional.]*

Addict: Well, yeah. But I think I'm getting it now. I have a great sponsor. [He turns to his friend.] You even said so yourself, Ted.

Friend: I know I did, Sean, and I *do* think your sponsor is great. But I don't think he or your rehab program is really helping you. You're getting skinnier and skinnier every day. *[The friend doesn't denigrate the sponsor or the program but notes that they don't seem to be working.]*

Addict: Inpatient is too expensive.

Mother: It *is* expensive. But I'm sure we can find one that our insurance covers. We can't bet your life on an outpatient program that's not working! *[The mother focuses on priorities.]*

Friend: Right. And if your insurance runs out you can always apply for Medicaid. The program I went to was in a public hospital, and Medicaid paid for it. It wasn't very fancy, but I got treatment. And I'm still alive! *[Ted also focuses on priorities. Saving money can't be a rationale for dying from addiction.]*

Addict: And there's no guarantee it will work.

Friend: That's true. But it's a hell of a lot more likely to work than what you're doing now. We just want you to try something else.

Addict: Yeah, but even if I go in, when I get out things will be exactly the same. The dealers will still be calling me all the time, same as now. No inpatient place can stop that!

Friend: You're right, Sean. No rehab can change the outside world. But you can learn how to handle it when the dealers try to call you, like I did. I managed the cravings by calling buddies I had from rehab, and I got a new cell phone number so the dealers couldn't get in touch with me. Practical stuff like that. *[Ted acknowledges that rehab can't change anything external but also gives Sean the benefit of his own experience.]*

Addict: I can get a new cell phone now. I don't need rehab for that.

Mother: But Sean, if it was that simple you would already have done it. It looks to me like you just can't do it on your own now.

Addict: Okay, okay, I got the point. I guess I can look at a rehab place.

Sean did tour an inpatient facility, but he rejected it, he said, because he wouldn't be allowed to smoke except during certain hours of the day. Frustrated, his mother and Ted drove him home. But several weeks later he was arrested for possession of a small amount of methamphetamine. After he'd spent several hours in a jail cell, Ted picked him up and, seizing the opportunity, suggested that they drive back to the inpatient facility. Sean reluctantly agreed, and not only entered the program but stayed for a full twenty-eight days. I later congratulated Ted on his quick thinking, thanks to which, at least in part, Sean has now been sober for more than two years.

Inpatient Programs

Generally speaking, inpatient programs are programs where the addict lives and receives intensive treatment, usually consisting of group therapy, individual counseling, and psychiatric care as needed. As I said earlier, there are several different types of inpatient programs, including dual diagnosis programs, therapeutic communities, intensive inpatient programs, halfway houses, and sober living houses. Inpatient programs are the "big guns" of addiction treatment and should accordingly only be used when the severity of the problem justifies their expense in terms of time, money, and commitment.

Dual Diagnosis Programs

Dual diagnosis programs are for those addicts who, in addition to their addiction, have been diagnosed with a mental illness like schizophrenia, bipolar disorder, or major depression, and accordingly need complex and intensive treatment. For that reason, programs like these are generally conducted in a hospital setting and can last from a few days to many months, depending on the severity of the addict's symptoms. As with all rehabilitation programs, of course, addicts suffering from severe withdrawal symptoms may have to first go through detoxification even before treatment begins. Once the addict has gone through the detox process, treatment usually consists of a combination of medications, psychotherapy, group therapy, and peer-led support groups, all of which should be coordinated by a clinician, preferably an addiction psychiatrist.

Considering the special challenges that dually diagnosed addicts face, programs like these have several very important advantages. One of these is that they enable the treatment of the addiction problem and the psychiatric problem to take place simultaneously, which is the most effective way of doing it. Facilities that have to send addicts elsewhere for psychiatric treatment provide less coordinated and therefore less effective care. In addition, dual diagnosis programs not only can provide the structured services such patients need, they also have better access to outpatient dual diagnosis facilities as well as peer-led self-help groups for the dually diagnosed (sometime called "double trouble" meetings).

There are, however, also some disadvantages to programs like these. For one, they are often more expensive and longer lasting than those for the singly diagnosed. Also, addicts sometimes object to being recommended to such programs out of concern that they will be labeled "crazy." While this is certainly an understandable concern, any added, and certainly unfair, stigma attached to these programs is usually well worth the improved care they provide to the dually diagnosed individual. Interestingly, that same issue can actually work to your advantage. Both insurance companies and courts seem to consider dual diagnosis programs more legitimate than other types of programs, possibly because they see the mentally ill as somehow more deserving of treatment than those who are simply addicts. Regardless of the reason, though, if your friend or loved one is dually diagnosed, you should take advantage of whatever additional assistance insurance companies or courts are willing to provide.

Therapeutic Communities

Therapeutic communities (TCs), the best known of which are Phoenix House and Odyssey House, are intensive treatment facilities where addicts live for from twelve to twenty-four months. First developed to treat mental illness, and modified in the 1960s for use with narcotics addicts, these types of facilities are now used to help those suffering from any form of addiction. Although TCs do employ professional addiction treaters, unlike other rehabilitation programs, which stress the importance of those professionals, they emphasize the importance of pressure from the community in treating, reeducating, and rehabilitating addicts in order to reintegrate them into the sober world.

That treatment usually consists of intensive and well-orchestrated peer pressure designed to help the addict avoid substances, feel and show respect for others, and live a moral and productive life. All of this is enforced, in part, by a system of punishment and rewards that's based on the addict's behavior. If, for example, an addict comes late to a meeting, he or she might be required to clean the lunchroom after the noon meal. If, on the other hand, an addict consistently lives up to his or her responsibilities, he or she will be rewarded by promotion within the hierarchy of the TC. Such promotions lead to additional responsibilities, such as monitoring the behavior of new entrants into the program, as well as additional privileges like receiving passes to leave for short periods of time.

Like all inpatient programs, therapeutic communities are beneficial for addicts who've been unable to stay sober over a long period of time without supervision. Even more important, TCs can be particularly helpful for those addicts who have severe and ingrained personality problems related to their drug use. For example, an addict who's been lying and stealing in order to support his or her habit would benefit from the strict boundaries most TCs maintain as well as from the immediate confrontation of dishonest or even evasive behavior. Another advantage of TCs is their ability to foster a sense of group identity among addicts who have the opportunity to work with others toward a common cause. This group identity—and the pride it generates—can be extremely helpful, especially for an addict who's had little experience with a group of people who are on his or her side and want the best for him or her.

Of course, TCs also suffer from the same disadvantage as all treatment facilities—the addict is free to leave at any time. So if you feel that this kind of program would be advantageous for the addict in your life, it's important not only to convince him or her to enter the program but, perhaps even more important, to complete it. There are also, however, some additional disadvantages to these programs, including the relatively strict rules and regulations at TCs, which many addicts, not surprisingly, are likely to bristle at. For the addict who has at least some understanding of the damage addiction has done to him or her, and can get past his or her initial resistance, the TC model can be tremendously useful. However, for those addicts whose denial is too strong, or who can't get past their objections to all the rules, an early discharge is probably inevitable.

Intensive Inpatient Programs

For many years the best-known model for inpatient rehabilitation programs was the twenty-eight day "Minnesota Model" developed in the 1950s at Hazelden, the rehabilitation center in Center City, Minnesota. In fact, even though over the last ten years this model has become less popular—due to a lack of convincing evidence that it's any better than others, as well as to changes in insurance reimbursement—most intensive inpatient programs are still based on it. As a rule, these programs include group therapy, educational lectures, and psychiatric care, but also use AA or AA-like forums in which patients identify themselves as addicts, tell their stories, and get support from their peers. Many offer a "family day" in which family members can interact with addicts in a controlled environment and learn how they can (and can't) help in the future. However, while most intensive inpatient programs include all these elements, they often emphasize different aspects of the treatment. Some, for example, are less focused on AA, others are more family-oriented, and others concentrate more on psychiatric care. So if you're considering trying to convince a friend or loved one to enroll in one of these programs, you should ask the admissions staff what they're best at.

Like all forms of inpatient treatment, these programs provide addicts with a measure of safety that can't be attained in outpatient facilities. That is, the addict will be more closely observed for any psychiatric or medical problems and, for that reason, have a better chance of getting help quickly if and when he or she needs it. More important, though, they provide addicts with a great deal of vital information on addiction as well as relapse-prevention strategies that they can take with them when they leave the facility. They're also advantageous in that they're less time-consuming than therapeutic communities (although many such programs now base an addict's length of stay on his or her needs rather than on a preconceived notion of how long treatment should take). Another advantage of these programs is that they provide patients with the opportunity to live with others who are experiencing similar if not identical problems. As films like *28 Days* demonstrate, the connection with other addicts in these programs is as important as, if not more important than, the connection with clinicians.

There are also, however, some disadvantages to these programs, particularly their sequestered nature. Because the addict is (usually) not exposed to addictive substances inside the facility, he or she is likely to come away from it with an unrealistic perspective on the challenges he or she will face in the outside world. This problem can, however, be solved by arranging for "step-downs" in intensity of treatment once he or she leaves the facility, through halfway houses, sober living houses, and intensive outpatient programs.

Perhaps the biggest stumbling block in convincing an addict to enter any inpatient program is his or her desire to not be "locked up." Even though this is actually an unrealistic concern—since no program can deprive an individual of his or her liberty without a judge's order—the objection is still understandable and should be addressed. Here's an example of how the adult son of an addict dealt with it.

~~~~~~~~~~~~~~~~~~~~~~~~~~~~~~~~~~~

"I'm Not Going to Be Locked Up Like That"

Son: Dad, I really think the treatment place we found for you is a great idea. The staff seemed great when I spoke to them, and they could take you right away. *[The addict's son sees the situation optimistically and presents it that way.]*

Addict: No way, David. I'm not going to be locked up like that. I haven't committed a crime.

Son: Look, Dad, it's not a jail. You can leave anytime you want. I can see how you wouldn't want to live in a place like that for a month, but it's no worse than the apartment you've been staying in, and probably better! *[David reminds his father that he won't be locked up and that, while the facility isn't luxurious, it's at least as good as where he's been living.]*

Addict: It's a funny farm! I'm not doing it.

Son: But Dad, this cocaine thing is really hurting you. You haven't gone to any Cocaine Anonymous meetings at all, and you only went to the outpatient program we found for you a couple of times.

Addict: That's because I picked up. *[The father uses a slang expression for "had a relapse."]*

Son: That's exactly the point, Dad! Maybe an inpatient place would keep you from picking up like that.

Addict: If I'm not locked up, what's to prevent me from leaving?

Son: Nothing. You can leave whenever you want to. But the counselor I spoke to told me that just about everyone who's admitted finds something about the program that's helpful, whether it's one of the counselors, the groups, or even another patient. And there aren't any drugs there, so at least you won't be faced with that temptation.

Addict: Well, I'm not signing myself in for the full twenty-eight days. *[Although the addict is still raising objections, he's beginning to recognize that the program might be beneficial.]*

Son: You don't have to. The counselor said that when you're admitted they recommend the full twenty-eight days, but they don't ask or expect you to commit to it right away. *[The son recognizes that his father is starting to come around and is willing to meet him halfway.]*

Addict: I don't know, David. What about my job? They're certainly not going to give me a month to go and rest up at some spa! And I'll get fired if someone tells them I'm a cocaine addict!

Son: To tell you the truth, Dad, they probably already

know you've got a problem with cocaine, or at least with something. They could fire you now for all the days you've missed, and they may already be getting ready to do that. It seems to me that you're more likely to lose your job if you don't go into treatment. And if you do go into treatment, you've got a better chance of keeping it. I asked a lawyer about it, and she told me that you're probably protected by the Americans with Disabilities Act, at least as long as you don't show up to work while you're using.

Addict: Yeah, they have been hinting at letting me go. I guess it couldn't hurt to try the place out. When can you take me over there?

Halfway Houses

Halfway houses are supervised residences where addicts who have completed intensive inpatient treatment live for anywhere from a few weeks to over a year. As such, they essentially provide a bridge between the intensive treatment and the outside world, and are accordingly appropriate for addicts who are highly vulnerable to relapse if they return to their old environment. Making that transition can be extremely difficult, and a good halfway house can be of enormous value in helping your friend or loved one adjust to life on the outside. It can do this basically by providing an intermediate level of supervision between the 24/7 oversight of an inpatient facility and the complete absence of supervision in his or her own home. Many of my patients have told me that that transition provoked them into using again at exactly the moment when they were most vulnerable—when they were discharged from a more intense treatment program.

Unfortunately, not all halfway houses are of the same quality. In fact, they range from the spectacularly successful to the miserably unhelpful, so you have to be particularly careful in selecting one. If—or perhaps when—you're evaluating halfway houses for your friend or loved one, you should look for one that's connected to an inpatient program and that's had a long-term relationship with that program, as well as one that has an experienced staff to help the patients deal with the reentry to daily life. It should also have a competent staff, a clear list of obligations for the residents, and a decent physical environment. Of course, many addicts would prefer to return home as soon as their inpatient stay is over, and for many of them that's perfectly all right. But for the addict who's had problems on returning home in the past, or for whom problems seem likely, halfway houses are definitely the way to go.

Sober Living Houses

Sober living houses are usually the next-to-last step back into real life for the addict in recovery. After leaving a halfway house (or, occasionally, an intensive inpatient program), a group of patients gets together to rent an apartment to live in with the understanding that the apartment will be completely drug- and alcohol-free. Sometimes this step is facilitated by the halfway house or intensive inpatient program, and sometimes the addicts spontaneously decide to do it themselves. However it comes together, though, a sober living house, while not actually a program, can serve as the next logical step in the progression from inpatient treatment back to life in the real world.

Sober living houses vary widely in their formats and rules. Some, for example, have very strict requirements, while others are much more informal and have few if any rules. Of course, regardless of how structured a sober living house is, living with other addicts has its risks, the most obvious of which is the danger of one of them slipping back to drugs and bringing the others down with him or her. Much more often, though, I've seen how enormously helpful to their roommates the addicts in sober living houses can be as they struggle together to remain sober. In fact, although I can't offer any statistics to prove it, my experience certainly suggests that addicts who are dedicated enough to establish a sober living house are much more likely to do well than others. For that reason, when your friend or loved one is ready to leave an intensive inpatient program or a halfway house, I would do all I could to encourage him or her to find a sober living house.

Outpatient Programs

Generally speaking, outpatient rehabilitation programs are those in which treatment programs are provided at a facility but the addicts live elsewhere. Such programs have group and individual counseling of various intensities, and sometimes provide other services such as vocational help and medical treatment. As with inpatient treatment, there are several different types of programs, including day treatment programs, comprehensive outpatient addiction treatment programs, outpatient group therapy centers, and methadone programs. As I mentioned earlier, groups like Alcoholics Anonymous, while not actually forms of treatment, also fall into this category.

Day Treatment Programs

Among outpatient programs, day treatment programs, which are generally conducted in a facility near or at least associated with a hospital, are the most intensive. In fact, they're similar to inpatient dual diagnosis programs in that they're designed primarily to help individuals with psychiatric illnesses who also have addiction problems. Like dual diagnosis programs, day treatment programs offer patients full-day psychiatric care, group therapy, social work services, and sometimes even medical care in which addiction and psychiatric treatment are combined. Unlike inpatient dual diagnosis programs, however, day treatment programs send their patients home at the end of the day, whether that home is a group living situation or a private home.

Given the similarities between these two types of programs, it may be somewhat difficult for you to determine which would be more appropriate for your friend or loved one. As with virtually all the programs I've discussed, there are both advantages and disadvantages to both. As I mentioned earlier in this chapter, dual diagnosis programs are advantageous in that they provide addicts with intensive 24/7 treatment without the temptation of drugs or alcohol. Day treatment programs provide similarly intensive treatment but can also send patients back to the real world at the end of the day to practice the skills they've learned. So if the addict in your life is ready for that challenge, a day treatment program would make the most sense.

Comprehensive Outpatient Addiction Treatment Programs

Comprehensive outpatient addiction programs are less time-consuming than day treatment programs in that they only require patients to be present in the facility anywhere from a few hours a week to a few hours a day. Even so, some do offer a broad range of services. Providing treatment primarily in the form of group encounters and group therapy, this type of program is best for the individual who has just left an inpatient addiction treatment facility or one who needed but refused to enroll in such a program. With their structured schedule of group meetings, individual counseling, and urine toxicology tests to determine whether or not patients are using substances, these comprehensive programs can provide help to people who are addicted to a variety of substances as well as those who have been dually diagnosed but don't need the more intensive services of a dual diagnosis or day treatment program.

There are, as always, both advantages and disadvantages to these programs. Perhaps the great advantage is that they enable addicts to receive serious treatment while returning at least partly to school or work. On the other hand, there are also some disadvantages, the most significant of which is the lack of strong supervision, since staff frequently only see addicts for a few hours every week. In deciding whether or not a comprehensive program is appropriate for your friend or loved one, then, you should take into account how strong his or her recovery seems to be, any past experiences he or she has had with outpatient treatment, and whatever recommendations the staff of the program provide.

Outpatient Group Therapy Centers

Some programs simply offer group therapy for addiction. I've put these programs into a separate category because they don't offer the full array of services usually associated with other outpatient programs. In my experience, these centers work best for relatively high-functioning addicts who are already working with a good therapist, have a stable home environment, have a strong connection with AA or a similar group, and are either working or attending school. In such situations, the addict can use the outpatient therapy as a boost and a weekly check-in regarding his or her addiction.

Methadone Programs

Methadone clinics are often not thought of as outpatient rehabilitation programs both because they frequently serve as mere dispensaries for methadone and because they have reputations as unpleasant places where drug addicts congregate. But even though some facilities deserve this poor reputation, there are others that provide exemplary outpatient addiction treatment, particularly for addicts who have had several tries at avoiding opiates and haven't been able do so. Such clinics—which are usually publicly funded and attached to medical schools or public hospitals—offer their patients a wide array of addiction, psychiatric, medical, and vocational services, including psychiatric medications, tuberculosis treatment, HIV treatment, family counseling, and even job-training opportunities.

In fact, I think it's very unfortunate that, because of the generally negative attitude many people have toward methadone clinics, addicts as well as their friends and loved ones tend to shy away from even considering the possibility of enrolling in such programs. I'm going to tell you more about methadone treatment in chapter 9, but for the moment I'd simply ask you to keep an open mind about programs like these. In the meantime, if you are thinking about trying to convince the addict in your life to enroll in such a program, and are encountering resistance from him or her, the following dialogue may be helpful.

"Methadone Clinics Are Dangerous"

Sister: Howard, I'm so worried about your heroin use that I even found out about a methadone clinic you could go to.

Addict: Are you kidding me, Suzie? A methadone clinic? I wouldn't be caught dead in a place like that.

Sister: What have you heard about methadone clinics? *[Rather than jumping in with her own side of the argument, Suzie asks her brother a question, which is a much more effective tactic.]*

Addict: Methadone clinics are dangerous! They're drug hangouts! You can get anything you want there. In fact, that's exactly where to go if you want to buy.

Sister: I know that may be true of some clinics. But I went over to the one at the university hospital and it looked about the same as any other clinic there. And the counselor I talked to said that it's paid for by Medicaid, and that they can provide you with medical care and whatever other kind of help you need. They even have counselors who'll work with you if you need vocational services or help in getting back to school. You should at least go take a look at it. *[Suzie has the facts in hand.]*

Addict: Okay, okay. I get it. You went to see it and it looked fine. But you can't be seriously suggesting that I go to a methadone clinic for the rest of my life.

Sister: No, I'm not. The counselor said that they have both a thirty-day detoxification program, where you taper off the methadone, and a long-term maintenance program, if that's what you need.

Addict. I'm not putting that stuff in my body. They say it settles in your bones.

Sister: Please, Howard! You inject heroin that you buy out on the street every day. Plus, the counselor told me that it's not true that methadone settles in your bones. It does last longer in your body than heroin, but all that means is that you only have to take it once a day instead of shooting up three times a day.

Addict: It's just replacing one drug with another. I'm not interested.

Sister: I guess it is replacing one drug with another. But at least with methadone you can just take it orally once a day and then get on with your life, instead of spending your whole day looking for money and heroin. If you do the detoxification program you can be clear of it in a month, and with the maintenance program they say that you don't even notice the methadone, unless you forget to take it. *[Suzie confronts Howard about his unwillingness to take methadone even though he's apparently willing to take heroin.]*

Addict: Yeah, but you know, heroin's not the only problem I've got. I also feel depressed a lot of the time.

Sister: I know you do. And the counselor said they have treatment for all kinds of things there, even depression. Maybe you could finally see a psychiatrist and get some help for that.

Addict: They have that?

Sister: Yeah, they do. What do you say we go over there this afternoon?

Addict: Well, if they can deal with my depression too . . .

What Treatment Is

- Treatment is essentially a means of helping the addict stop or reduce his or her addictive, self-destructive behavior.
- If your loved one is exhibiting physical signs of withdrawal, he or she may require detoxification either before or during treatment for the addiction.

- Every program for addicts falls into either inpatient or outpatient treatment.
- Inpatient treatment includes dual diagnosis programs, therapeutic communities, intensive inpatient programs, halfway houses, and sober living houses.
- Outpatient treatment includes day treatment programs, comprehensive outpatient addiction treatment programs, outpatient group therapy centers, and methadone programs.
- Outpatient programs are preferable unless the addict's situation is such that he or she requires inpatient care.
- The addict with serious psychiatric or social problems usually needs to be treated on an inpatient basis.
- The addict who has failed several outpatient attempts should enroll in an inpatient program.
- Therapeutic communities are long-term treatment options.
- Halfway houses and sober living houses can serve as a bridge to the sober world.
- Intensive outpatient programs can provide not only addiction services but also psychiatric, medical, vocational, and social services.
- A good methadone clinic could be the right choice for your loved one.

Now that you have a clearer idea of exactly what treatment is, the difference between inpatient and outpatient programs, and know something about the various types of treatment that are available, I'm going to tell you about the kinds of things you should be looking for when considering a treatment facility for your friend or loved one—which is the subject of the next chapter.

Chapter Eight

WHAT TO LOOK FOR IN A TREATMENT FACILITY

Now that you have a better idea of what treatment is and the forms it takes, the obvious question to ask is, "How do I know which facility is likely to provide my friend or loved one with the best treatment?" Just as there are criteria for selecting the most appropriate practitioner to work with the addict in your life, there are criteria for choosing the most appropriate treatment facility. Although you might be able to get some idea of what a program has to offer by reading a brochure or looking at a website, as with selecting a practitioner, the best way to choose a facility is to visit it and speak with someone who can provide you with the information you need to make an intelligent decision. Depending on the facility, that person may be called an admissions counselor, intake worker, outreach coordinator, or something similar. Again, the best way to arrange for these meetings is to call the facility, determine the most appropriate person for you to speak with, explain your situation, and ask for an appointment.

When you do meet with the representative of the facility, in order to evaluate what it has to offer, there are six aspects of treatment that you should ask about: (1) How does the facility deal with life-threatening problems? (2) How does the facility handle the issue of confidentiality? (3) Do the practitioners in the facility understand—and have a structured approach to dealing with—addicts who go back to using substances after they've stopped? (4) Do all those who work in the facility continuously strive to help their patients attain and maintain abstinence? (5) How does the facility deal with "treatment fatigue," that is, the hopeless feeling that addicts, those who love them, and clinicians who treat them sometimes develop? (6) How do the facility's practitioners determine each addict's readiness to be discharged from the facility and go back to real life?

Dealing with Life-Threatening Problems

As a doctor, my primary goal is to preserve life. That, in fact, is the primary goal of all of us who treat addicts. And we demonstrate it, ultimately, by trying to help them escape the hold that addiction has on them. But the first step in attaining that goal is making sure that any addict under our care is treated—and immediately—for any life-threatening problems. Addiction can, of course, always be life-threatening, but the moment that an addict actually starts treatment is one of the most dangerous. That's because by the time an addict finally enrolls in a program, he or she is often at the end of his or her rope, that is, hopeless and, often, in agony. To make matters worse, the addict at this point also has to face the very treatment that he or she has been trying desperately to avoid. A good treatment facility, then, whether inpatient or outpatient, is one that puts the addict's safety first and expresses that by doing three things—recognizing the importance of safety, being able to evaluate and either provide or arrange for treatment for the physical manifestations of addiction, and demonstrating the knowledge and skills that are needed to treat self-destructive or suicidal behaviors.

If you're evaluating an inpatient facility, one way you can tell how concerned they are about safety is by asking how they handle addicts who are going through withdrawal. And you'll know that you've found an appropriate facility if its representative tells you that the staff is trained to recognize the symptoms of withdrawal and has a plan in place for treating any addicts who are experiencing it or for transferring them to a facility where they can be treated. Similarly, you can determine how good the facility is in evaluating and arranging treatment for addiction-related medical problems by asking how they would deal with a patient who appears to be ill and in need of medical attention. In this case, what you want to hear is that the patient receives a comprehensive evaluation by a licensed physician and, if necessary, is treated promptly for the problem. Finally, in order to learn about the extent of the staff's knowledge and skills in treating self-destructive or suicidal behaviors, the best question to ask is how they deal with depressed patients or those who express suicidal thoughts. The kind of answer you're looking for here is one that shows the facility has a serious and well-thought-out plan for assessing depressed or suicidal patients that includes assessment by a psychiatrist; regular, timed observation by staff; or even full-time one-on-one observation.

Since inpatient and outpatient programs are different, though, if you're considering an outpatient facility for your friend or loved one, when you meet with the facility's representative you should ask somewhat different questions. On the issue of safety, for example, you should ask how those in the facility would determine if a patient required more intensive treatment than they could provide and needed to be transferred to an inpatient program. The response you'd want to hear in this situation would be one that demonstrates the facility's ability to recognize when patients are medically or psychiatrically unstable or have persistent relapses, as well as its willingness to transfer such patients when appropriate. In regard to dealing with the physical manifestations of addiction, the best way to get a good sense of how a facility handles it is to simply ask how they deal with addicts in withdrawal. And you'll know you're on the right track if the representative tells you that the facility has a nurse or other health-care professional who's been trained to recognize withdrawal symptoms and to determine the appropriate kind of treatment. Finally, on the issue of dealing with self-destructive behaviors, you should ask the facility's representative how they would know if a patient is acting in a self-destructive way. In this instance, the answer you want to hear is that the staff holds regular meetings during which each patient is discussed, and that everyone in the program—whether staff or patient—is encouraged to bring up any concerns they may have about any individual's safety.

Dealing with Confidentiality Issues

Every type of addiction treatment uses some form of psychotherapy, and one extremely important element of all psychotherapy is confidentiality. In fact, it's even more important in addiction treatment than in other areas because of the stigma attached to addiction and the concern many addicts have about other people learning about their problem. At the same time, because of the nature of addiction, it's often advantageous for the addict to bring his or her friends or family into the process, and that can't be done without breaching confidentiality. Although, under the law, a clinician has to breach a patient's confidentiality under certain circumstances—such as if he or she believes that a child is being harmed or that the patient intends to harm someone else—it normally can't be done without the patient's permission. If, however, the clinician can get the addict to agree, it can make a significant difference.

I recall one middle-aged cocaine addict who had initially insisted on complete confidentiality in regard to his addiction problem, a request I was obligated to respect. But as we worked together it became clear to me that he couldn't possibly be telling me everything about his addiction, since he didn't know many of the details of what he did while he was intoxicated. When I finally convinced him to bring his wife in, we learned not only that his behavior when intoxicated was even more bizarre than he'd thought, but also that, because she put up with it, his wife's devotion to him was much greater then he realized. Although this was the only time his wife came into the therapy room, breaching confidentiality on that one occasion had a profound and life-altering effect on him.

Because breaking confidentiality in this way can be advantageous, when you meet with the representative of either an inpatient or outpatient facility, it's important that you ask how the facility approaches talking with friends and family about the addict. You could, for example, start out by asking if the facility has educational and/or therapy sessions that the family can attend, and to what extent you'll be allowed or encouraged to participate in the addict's care. Personally, I think that the more family participation the facility offers, the more successful the treatment will be. Of course, if the addict refuses to allow his or her clinicians to speak with you, they'll be obligated to respect that request, except, as I mentioned, in a few very rare instances. So you may have to accept silence from the facility at first, although as the addict gets away from the addictive substance he or she may have a change of heart and be willing to involve you and other friends and family in the process.

Whether you're considering an inpatient or an outpatient facility for your friend or loved one, however, if he or she is a minor, it's important to bear in mind that the law treats minors very differently than adults when it comes to confidentiality. Although, again, state laws differ, generally speaking a person under the age of eighteen has no right to have clinical information kept confidential from his or her parents. This can, of course, be a problem if your adolescent son or daughter sees the therapist simply as an extension of you and refuses to provide him or her with any information. For that reason you should ask anyone you're considering working with how they handle such situations.

Ideally, what they'll tell you is that, while they recognize and will fulfill their legal obligations, they'll also work with you to try to arrange a compromise under which your child can be assured of at least enough confidentiality that the therapy can go forward. Compromises like these usually consist of an agreement among the therapist, the addicted adolescent, and his or her parents that the therapist will call the parents only if the addict is engaging in some dangerous activity. It's not likely to satisfy everyone—in fact, it probably won't entirely satisfy anyone—but an arrangement like this will guarantee that you'll find out about dangerous or life-threatening behavior while, at the same time, enabling your child to move ahead with his or her treatment without having to worry that the therapist will report every misstep to you.

Dealing with Addicts Who Go Back to Using Substances After They've Stopped

In an ideal world, as soon as you expressed your concerns to the addict in your life, he or she would immediately stop using drugs or alcohol. Unfortunately, though, we don't live in an ideal world. And there's nothing more frustrating for an addict or those who love him or her than when he or she goes back to using an addictive substance. The fact is, though, that as addicts move toward treatment, as well as at every step in the treatment itself, slips, relapses, and binges are nearly inevitable. I'm not saying this because I'm hopeless, or because I expect addicts to fail, but because I'm aware of the usual course of events in addiction, and I don't want you to be surprised or to lose hope after a slip. In fact, I'm extremely hopeful about treating addiction—I wouldn't be able to continue doing it if I wasn't—but I'm also realistic about it. So while I hope that the addicts I work with don't go back to using, I know they probably will, and it's best to be prepared for it.

A "slip" is usually defined as a short return to using the abused substance, or any illicit substance. An addict who slips, then, may use the drug once or twice over the course of a day. "Relapses" and "binges," on the other hand, last longer. An addict who relapses or binges may, for example, use the drug many times over the course of a weekend. (To be honest, though, these definitions are a bit fluid and vary from practitioner to practitioner. The definitions I've given you are the ones I use myself to distinguish among the various types.) But since it's likely that, even after he or she has started treatment, your friend or loved one will go back to using the substance to at least some extent, it's essential that you ask the representative of whatever facility you're considering what their policy is in regard to such situations.

Ideally, he or she will tell you that the facility has three ways of dealing with these situations. First, that it has a mechanism in place for dealing with the cues that led to the relapse. This means that whenever an addict slips it will prompt the facility's staff to look for failures in the treatment and to find ways to improve it. Second, that it provides a means by which the addict can open up about a slip or relapse to other addicts and their treaters. That is, that when participating in either individual or group therapy sessions, the addict will be treated compassionately by both the clinician and the other addicts if he or she admits to slipping or relapsing. And, finally, that the attitude its staff takes toward addicts who slip is one of encouragement rather than criticism. In practice, this means that they see slips as a learning experience rather than as an indication of some kind of moral lapse on the addict's part. And this, in turn, enables the addict to "get back on the wagon" with a minimum of shame and embarrassment.

Unfortunately, despite their best efforts, treatment facilities sometimes have to discharge individuals who continue to relapse. Although this may seem punitive—and it almost always is—if facilities have to decide between what's best for one patient and what's best for all the addicts in their care, they frequently must choose the latter. When I was the director of an inpatient addiction ward at Bellevue Hospital, I occasionally had to discharge a patient because he or she had relapsed. Although I always knew that the discharge wasn't in the addict's best interests, I had to protect the other patients on the ward, and I knew that keeping the relapser there could have an adverse effect on them. In the best circumstances, if being discharged from a treatment facility makes your friend or loved one feel that he or she has hit "bottom," it can serve as an impetus to convince him or her to try again.

Striving for Abstinence

Most clinicians consider abstinence to be an important goal of treatment, but there's considerable difference of opinion on the best way to attain that goal. On one hand, there are facilities that concentrate on harm reduction, that is, trying to reduce the harm to the addict caused by the addictive substance and to find ways to minimize the amount of the substance used and the length of time it's used. On the other hand, some facilities insist that their patients commit immediately to long-term abstinence, in some cases from the very beginning of treatment. To my mind, though, neither of these extremes is particularly helpful to the addict, and it's accordingly important for you to find out how each facility you're considering handles this issue.

While it's true that whatever can be done to reduce the harm a substance does to an addict is a good thing, stressing harm reduction over abstinence can lead to problems. For one thing, harm reduction efforts don't always have the same effect that those who use them intend. For example, addicts sometimes use such efforts to justify behavior that, while less dangerous than their previous behavior, is still self-destructive. In practice this means that if a treatment facility provides addicts with clean needles in an effort to reduce the transmission of HIV, the addicts will often take this as tacit approval of the drug use itself. Similarly, clinics that are too understanding of slips can—however unintentionally—promote the idea that a relapse is somehow a good thing. At the other extreme, demanding that addicts maintain abstinence—particularly from the beginning of their treatment—can also present problems. If, for example, a newly sober alcoholic in a facility that insists on abstinence has a slip, he or she may be made to feel like a failure. And the last thing you want to do in a situation like this is to make the addict feel hopeless.

Generally speaking, practitioners who go to either one of these extremes have lost track of the fact that recovery from addiction takes time, and sometimes much more time than one would prefer. In order to make sure, then, that that hasn't happened in the facilities you're considering, it's important for you to ask those you speak to about their stance on the issue. Ideally, they will tell you that the facility starts by concentrating on reducing the damage from addiction while urging abstinence, and once the addict has gained a foothold, makes greater efforts to convince the addict to stop using the substance altogether. To my mind, this flexible approach makes the best sense, primarily because even though relapses are regrettable, over the years I've learned that each time an addict slips, he or she has the opportunity to learn something about how to keep it from happening in the future.

Dealing with Treatment Fatigue

Another issue you should concern yourself with in selecting a facility for your friend or loved one is the phenomenon that clinicians themselves call treatment fatigue, which affects addicts, their friends and families, and even clinicians. There are several reasons that this happens, the most important of which is probably that addicts themselves, almost by definition, generally feel hopeless about ever getting better. And, unfortunately, that feeling is often contagious and can affect those around them. Another reason is that people—addicts, their families, and clinicians alike—sometimes misunderstand the essential nature of addiction. They don't recognize that relapses are to be expected, so when relapses occur, which they often do, they tend to feel hopeless about the addict's ever freeing him- or herself of the addiction. And a third reason is that because our society stigmatizes addiction, addicts—as well as those who treat them—can be made to feel like pariahs, which, not surprisingly, makes it more difficult for them to remain hopeful.

It's at best unfortunate if the addict in your life and/or you have this feeling of hopelessness, but the last thing you want is to have him or her enroll in a program in which the staff feels that way. Any clinician who's lost hope is unlikely to be of much help to addicts simply because he or she is less likely than a hopeful clinician to act aggressively in treating the problem. The real issue, then, is how you determine whether or not the staff of the facilities you're considering are suffering from treatment fatigue. One of the best ways to do that is to ask how they deal with patients who relapse during treatment and how they feel about the "revolving door" phenomenon in which addicts go in and out of treatment. Hopefully, what you'll hear is something like, "Well, relapses do happen, but that's no reason to give up. Addicts also sometimes have to go through treatment several times before they're able to attain stable sobriety. And we see that as a challenge to find the right treatment for that individual. We're also actually encouraged when an addict we've worked with comes back to treatment. It means he or she still wants help, even if there's been another slip. . . ." The point is that, while no addiction therapist can tell what the future holds, it's essential that he or she remain aggressive and optimistic about an eventual recovery. The answer to the question, "When do you give up on an addict?" is, "Never."

Determining When the Addict Is Ready to Go Back to Real Life

While it's obviously essential for your friend or loved one to get the treatment he or she needs, it's also important for all those involved in that treatment to remember that the ultimate goal is to get the individual back to the life he or she had before becoming an addict. And that means returning him or her as quickly as possible to those things that provide structure in almost everyone's life—school or work and relationships with others. However, since what each addict returns to is different, it's important that the staff of any treatment facility be aware of those differences and not send the addict back to the real world until he or she is ready to handle it. And even though it might seem premature at this point to ask how the staff of a facility decides when an addict should leave the program and what kind of recommendations they make regarding care for the addict afterward, doing so can provide you with some valuable insight into the way the facility operates.

If you're talking to a representative of an inpatient facility, what you will want to hear is that before the addict is discharged, clinicians from different disciplines will get together to discuss it, and that in making that decision they'll take into account a variety of factors. One of these should be what the addict is likely to find when he or she gets home. If, for example, an addict has a difficult relationship with his or her spouse, going back to that individual may only serve to present problems. But if he or she is returning to a loving, supportive significant other, going home is likely to only help him or her continue on the road to recovery. Another factor that should be considered is what kind of job the addict would be returning to. It would not, for example, be advisable for an addict to leave a facility to return to the same high-stress job that contributed to his or her addiction in the first place. On the other hand, if the addict's job is one that's not likely to be a source of anxiety, returning to it can be very beneficial.

Another factor they should take into account is the addict's connection with AA or other peer-led groups. The addict who's been to at least a few AA meetings and obtained a sponsor while in treatment is much more likely to be able to stay sober on the outside than one who has yet to make that kind of connection. You would also want to hear that those making the decision about discharging your friend or loved one will take into consideration how confident he or she feels about remaining sober. While no one can guarantee sobriety, when an addict has both a high degree of confidence in succeeding and a specific, concrete plan for doing so, he or she is much more likely to remain sober over the long term.

Finally, you should ask about the kind of recommendations the staff usually makes regarding follow-up care when a patient is discharged. Ideally, the facility's representative will tell you that the staff recognizes that discharged patients must be given the opportunity to continue to receive care, through AA groups, addiction-knowledgeable therapists, and/or "step-down" programs like halfway and sober living houses, and that they make appropriate recommendations and/or arrangements for them to do so.

Even if the facility you're considering for your friend or loved one is an outpatient one, it's advisable to ask whoever you speak to what happens after the addict has completed the program. What you want to hear in this situation is that they always provide patients with a discharge plan that includes peer-led groups like AA, individual counseling, and psychiatric care as necessary, as well as some follow-up visits. But even if the discharge plan only recommends AA meetings, you can check on the seriousness of the recommendations by asking if the facility has the addict try out AA meetings before discharge, recommends specific AA meetings, or helps the addict get a sponsor.

What to Look for in a Treatment Facility

- A treatment facility should be able to diagnose a life-threatening problem and either provide or arrange for treatment immediately.
- Confidentiality is an important aspect of therapy, and a facility should make its policies clear.
- Addicts often slip during treatment, and a good facility handles it by using those slips as much as possible as learning experiences.
- Striving for abstinence is always a good goal, but the best way to achieve it is by using a flexible approach to recovery.
- A good facility doesn't keep addiction treaters who are suffering from treatment fatigue on staff.
- Recovering addicts must return to live in the world again, and the best facilities take great care in determining when it's most appropriate for them to do so and what kind of treatment they will need afterward.

Now that you have a better idea of what treatment is, and what you should be looking for in a treatment facility, the next thing you have to know about is the step that many addicts must take even before starting treatment—detoxification, which is the subject of the next chapter.

Chapter Nine

DETOXIFICATION AND MEDICATIONS

Even before your friend or loved one starts treatment, if he or she is exhibiting symptoms of withdrawal from the addictive substance it may be necessary for him or her to go through a process of detoxification. Depending on which substance he or she is using, these symptoms can range from relatively harmless and mildly uncomfortable to seriously dangerous and extremely painful, and can make rehabilitation not only difficult but, sometimes, impossible. Detoxification allows an addict to eliminate the substance from his or her body and, in the process, alleviate the withdrawal symptoms so that he or she can go forward with treatment. However, because different substances cause different symptoms, the program your friend or loved one goes through has to be appropriate for his or her specific type of addiction. In this chapter I'm going to tell you about those various types of programs, who they're for, and how they work. I'm also going to tell you about how addiction treaters use medication in both the detoxification process and in the longer-term treatment of addicts.

The first question you have to ask yourself, though, is, "Does my loved one even need to go through detoxification?" The answer to this question depends on the type of substance he or she is using, and, accordingly, how the addict reacts when he or she stops using it. As you'll remember from the discussion of the various kinds of addictive substances in chapter 2, there are basically four types. First there are the central nervous system depressants, including alcohol, barbiturates, benzodiazepines, and opiates. Second are the central nervous system stimulants, which include amphetamine, caffeine, cocaine, and methamphetamine. The third type includes hallucinogens like LSD, marijuana, MDMA, mescaline, and mushrooms, and the fourth includes other substances such as anabolic androgenic steroids, inhalants, and PCP.

Withdrawal symptoms from the third and fourth categories can include depression, anxiety, and physical lethargy, all of which are usually uncomfortable but not serious. (Although some of these drugs, particularly steroids, can cause both devastating depression and suicidal behavior in heavy users.) The first two categories, however, commonly cause painful and sometimes dangerous withdrawal symptoms. Withdrawal from central nervous system depressants including alcohol, barbiturates, and benzodiazepines is extremely dangerous and can, in some cases, even result in death. Withdrawal from opiates like heroin, morphine, Percodan, and others, on the other hand, isn't particularly dangerous but can be very painful. Finally, withdrawal from central nervous system stimulants such as cocaine, amphetamine, and methamphetamine, which causes unpleasant but not dangerous side effects, can nevertheless lead to dangerous situations. So if your loved one has been using any of these substances, he or she will have to go through detoxification either before or at the same time that treatment begins.

Fear of these withdrawal symptoms may, in fact, be one of the reasons that your addicted friend or loved one is reluctant to go into treatment. He or she may have heard horror stories of agonizing "detox" experiences, and, not surprisingly, wants to stay as far away from the process as possible. The truth is, though, that modern medical technology can now provide relatively quick and comfortable detoxification from most substances of abuse, and it's important that you make the addict aware of that. At the same time, if you're having difficulty convincing your loved one to seek help for his or her problem, you should stress the benefits that he or she will gain from going through detoxification as well as treatment, that is, returning to physical and emotional health, or, to put it another way, getting his or her life back.

Again, though, it's important to remember that detoxification isn't treatment in itself and it won't prevent an addict from using the substance in the future. It is, at best, a first step toward treatment and rehabilitation. If, however, your loved one recognizes that he or she has a need for detoxification, you may be able to use that to encourage him or her to go on to treatment once the detox process is over. Let's say, for example, that your loved one is withdrawing from alcohol and experiencing the painful and dangerous shakes it can cause. If you can convince him or her to enter a detoxification program to alleviate those symptoms, you can be sure that the clinicians in the program will offer more definitive treatment once the immediate problem has been dealt with. Perhaps even more important—and I know this from experience—once an addict gets the substance out of his or her system, and begins to feel more like his or her old self, he or she is much more likely to be willing to go on to treatment.

Assuming that the addict does have to go through detoxification, the other question you need to ask is, "Would he or she be better off in an inpatient or outpatient facility?" This question, unfortunately, isn't quite as easy to answer. Although, as I said earlier, I generally feel that outpatient facilities are preferable to inpatient ones for rehabilitation treatment, when it comes to detoxification there are several situations in which I think inpatient programs can be better. If, for example, your loved one is withdrawing from alcohol, which is the most difficult of all, or even hints at suicide, it would make more sense to get him or her into an inpatient facility where he or she can be monitored both medically and psychiatrically.

But even when there's no such obvious need for inpatient care, there are other situations in which it may be advantageous. For example, if your loved one is being treated in a doctor's office, regardless of how experienced the doctor is or how much of an effort he or she makes, the addict may simply be unable to stop his or her use. In a situation like this, inpatient detoxification can be more effective because a hospital can use more aggressive medications than an outpatient doctor can, and the addict can be subjected to a more intensive program of individual and group psychotherapy to treat his or her craving for the substance. I've also heard from many addicts that just having the four walls of a hospital around them can alleviate some of the desire to return to using drugs.

Another situation in which inpatient care would be beneficial is if your loved one has tried on several occasions to detoxify him- or herself outside of a program but hasn't been successful. Rather than continuing a cycle of failed attempts at outpatient detoxification, getting the addict into an inpatient facility can enable him or her to make a quick and effective transition into treatment and, ultimately, sobriety. To be fair, I have to admit that inpatient care is no cure-all and often has to be repeated many times before the addict finally agrees to treatment. It can, however, represent the turning point in the addict's battle against addiction.

If you do choose an inpatient facility for your loved one to undergo detoxification, I strongly suggest that you find one that discharges its patients into a rehabilitation facility that's physically connected or nearby rather than one that sends its patients elsewhere for treatment. The "interface" between detoxification and rehabilitation is where many addicts get lost and return to their substance abuse, and without this sort of connection, detox can lead to a "revolving door"—an endless cycle of addiction, detox, and addiction that can ultimately end only in death.

Detoxification from Alcohol, Barbiturates, and Benzodiazepines

Withdrawal from central nervous system depressants like alcohol, barbiturates, and the Valium-like drugs called benzodiazepines produces the most serious symptoms, including tremors, agitation, fever, hallucinations, and seizures. If not treated immediately, these can progress to delirium tremens (DTs) and, eventually, death. If your friend or loved one has been using one of these kinds of drugs, he or she will have to be treated by a physician who will in all likelihood treat him or her by administering benzodiazepines like Librium, Valium, or Ativan, which prevent or reduce most of the withdrawal symptoms. Over a period of several days the practitioner will give him or her increasingly smaller doses of the medication until all the symptoms are gone.

This sort of detoxification treatment can take from a few days to several weeks, with an average of about five days, and can be done either on an inpatient or outpatient basis. However, since both alcohol and sedative withdrawal can kill if not treated appropriately, I strongly recommend that you either have your loved one treated in an inpatient facility or find a clinician and facility that are well versed in outpatient detoxification and will be able to monitor him or her every day at the beginning of the process. Of course, before any detoxification process can even begin, the addict has to agree to do it. Here's an example of how such a conversation might go.

"Are You Saying You'll Get Some Help?"

Addict: Look, I know this has been a long time coming, but I just want to tell both of you that I know I can't keep using this much Percocet. It slows me down, I have to lie to doctors to get it, and I feel like it's out of control. I know I have to cut down. *[The addict starts by offering to decrease her use.]*

Husband: Cut down? You've got to be kidding, Laura! You've lost your job. You've lost most of your friends. Your addiction is killing you, and it's killing our marriage, and you're talking about cutting down? That's crazy! *[Laura's husband is understandably frustrated by her apparent failure to see the seriousness of her addiction.]*

Addict: Okay, okay, maybe I need to stop. But I need to cut down first, don't I? I can think about everything else after I'm using less. *[A "lifetime commitment" is too much for Laura to consider at this point.]*

Husband: Oh, please, Laura, that's what we've been hearing all along. You've got to make a commitment to stop using the damn Percocet. And to never use it again. Do it for me and the kids.

Sister: Wait a minute, Jim. Let's listen to Laura. [She turns to her sister.] Are you saying you'll get some help for this? *[Laura's sister stresses the positive aspect of Laura's first offer.]*

Addict: Of course I am, Gwen. I *want* help!

Sister: Well then, look, Jim, if Laura says she wants to get some help, why don't we find a detox center and see if they can do something?

Husband: I suppose it's better than nothing. *[Jim sees the point.]*

Addict: It's a start, Jim. . . .

Detoxification from Heroin and Other Opiates

Withdrawal from heroin and other opioid drugs like Percodan, Vicodin, and morphine, although quite painful, is usually not physically dangerous. If the addict in your life is withdrawing from one of these drugs, you can expect him or her to exhibit symptoms like sweating, anxiety, goose bumps, runny nose, muscle cramping, and diarrhea. Unfortunately, one of the cruel facts of withdrawal from these substances is that the symptoms they cause can be almost immediately eased by using more of the substance. In fact, once most people have used these drugs for more than a few months, they're more likely to continue using them just to feel "normal" than to get intoxicated. In my practice I've seen many heroin addicts who are caught in this bind. In order to act, feel, and appear well, they have to use heroin every eight hours or so, and as long as they do, no one notices anything unusual about them. It's only when they stop using it that their obvious discomfort and physical illness make those around them aware that they're addicted.

As is the case with other central nervous system depressants, however, if your friend or loved one is withdrawing from one of these opioids, a physician can significantly, though not entirely, alleviate the withdrawal symptoms through the use of medications. Among the most frequently used of these medications are two other opioids, methadone and buprenorphine, the latter marketed under the brand names Suboxone and Subutex. (Suboxone is buprenorphine with a tiny amount of naloxone mixed in to prevent illicit injection of the medication. Subutex is pure buprenorphine.) Methadone is given to addicts as a liquid and buprenorphine is given in tablet form. Both, however, are provided in increasingly smaller doses until the addict is no longer exhibiting symptoms of withdrawal. The process usually takes between five and twelve days to complete, depending on the substance and the extent of use. Methadone can be administered only in a hospital or a federally licensed methadone clinic, but Suboxone and Subutex can be administered in specially licensed doctors' offices on an outpatient basis. Both types of medication are also sometimes used as a replacement for the substance of abuse, in which case an addict can use it over a much longer period of time.

Detoxification from these substances can be done on an in- or outpatient basis and at the same time that the addict starts treatment for the addiction itself. However, while the main symptoms of opioid withdrawal disappear within a few days, longer-lasting effects like sleeplessness or craving for the substance can last for weeks or even months. And these residual symptoms often cause detoxified addicts to go back to using the substance. That's why ongoing treatment and/or attendance at peer-led groups like Narcotics Anonymous are essential if the addict is to eventually attain sobriety.

A counselor at a detoxification center can be very helpful in letting an addict—as well as his or her friends and family—know how detoxification works and why it's beneficial. Here's an example of the kind of conversation a counselor might have with an addict.

"We Have Plenty to Offer You"

Counselor: What brings you in tonight, Laura?

Addict: My husband brings me in, actually.

Counselor: Well, I see you still have your sense of humor. Why did your husband bring you in?

Addict: Jim thinks I use too much Percocet. But I just use it for headaches. *[Laura minimizes her drug use.]*

Husband: She's groggy all day, most days. It can't be just for headaches.

Addict: But I can't stop. [Laura's eyes start to tear up.] I feel like shit when I do. I get all jumpy, my nose runs, and I can't concentrate on anything.

Counselor: Goose bumps?

Addict: Of course.

Counselor: Can't sleep?

Addict: That too. Guess you've seen this before.

Counselor: All the time. And I know some good ways to help, too. We can get you off the cycle of using the Percocet. We've got plenty to offer you here. *[The counselor encourages Laura.]*

Addict: But my headaches will come back.

Counselor: I guess the Percocet takes care of the headaches, at least, huh?

Addict: Sure does.

Counselor: Okay, I can understand that. Opioids like Percocet are great painkillers, so they do work for headaches. *[The counselor empathizes with an "upside" of Laura's use.]* But I know we can get you evaluated by a neurologist who can find you another treatment for those headaches.

Addict: Nothing else works.

Husband: But you have to stop the Percocet.

Counselor: Okay, okay, let's slow down. I understand that the Percocet has good effects and bad effects. But in detox we can slowly taper you off with other medications, so it's not so painful. You don't have to suffer like this! *[The counselor displays her understanding of the problem's complexity and offers a program for helping.]*

Addict: I guess it's worth a try. . . .

Detoxification from Cocaine and Similar Drugs

Compared to other substances, withdrawal from central nervous system stimulants like cocaine, amphetamine, and methamphetamine is relatively easy. So if your friend or loved one is withdrawing from one of these drugs, you can expect him or her to be uncomfortable but rarely in any kind of physical danger. Immediate symptoms usually include insomnia, anxiety, fatigue, extreme hunger, sadness verging on depression, and craving for the drug. Although none of these symptoms are dangerous in themselves, they can lead to dangerous situations. Withdrawal-induced depression, for example, can lead to suicidal thoughts as well as self-destructive acts. In addition, even though this initial period only lasts for about three days, for several weeks afterward the addict can suffer from lowered mood and energy, as well as a continuing craving for the substance. Since this can lead to his or her starting to take the drug again, it's important that the addict be treated.

Fortunately, some of the symptoms of withdrawal from cocaine and similar drugs—including insomnia, restlessness, and anxiety—can be treated with nonaddictive medications such as trazodone (Desyrel) and buspirone (Buspar). Unfortunately, however, no medications have been developed that combat the craving for the drug itself. For that reason, the most effective way of treating addicts withdrawing from these kinds of drugs is through what's usually referred to as "supportive care." This kind of regimen generally includes keeping the addict comfortable by providing him or her with a quiet, dark place to rest, plenty of liquids, and medical treatment of any other drug or psychiatric problems. In situations like these, it's also essential that treaters, friends, and loved ones encourage the addict by assuring him or her that things will get better.

Detoxification from these drugs can take place at the same time as treatment for the addiction itself. However, since this type of withdrawal often causes depression and lethargy, neither of which is fully relieved by treatment, it usually takes several days before the treatment begins to take effect. Although outpatient treatment, as usual, is preferable, inpatient treatment is necessary if the depression progresses to the point at which the addict becomes suicidal.

Once an addict has gone through the detoxification process, he or she is very likely to feel physically better. However, he or she is also likely to feel unrealistically confident about his or her ability to avoid using in the future. Here's an example of the kind of conversation such an addict might have with her husband and her addiction counselor.

"I Feel a Lot Better!"

Addict: I feel so much better now. Jim and I are so grateful that you convinced us to stay last week. You were right! The headaches are gone, too.

Husband: That's right. She looks and feels a hundred times better.

Counselor: I'm so glad to see that you're feeling better and those headaches are gone. You *do* look like a million bucks!

Addict: So when do I get out?

Counselor: Well, what did you think of the aftercare plan we put together?

Addict: You mean the plan you wrote out for me. [Laura laughs.]

Counselor: Well, you didn't sound too eager to help me set it up!

Addict: To be honest, I don't think I need it much. This has been one unpleasant experience, but I think I've learned my lesson. *[Laura feels she's been "scared straight," a notoriously ineffective way of staying sober.]*

Counselor: I know you're feeling great, but I think you could use some help in staying clean.

Husband: What kind of help do you mean? Laura didn't mention this to me. *[Laura hadn't told Jim of the counselor's recommendations. It's a good thing Jim is attending the meeting.]*

Counselor: I really think that you have a lot of work to do to keep that Percocet out of your system, Laura. I think you need some backup for yourself.

Addict: Please. You don't have to worry about me going back to one of those quacks who gave me the Percocet. It'll be that easy. *[Laura minimizes the problem.]*

Husband: It makes sense to me, Laura. Remember all those times you quit and then went back to using? *[Jim reminds Laura of the reality of her addictive use.]*

Counselor: That's right, Laura. And there are certainly going to be things that come up that might push you back to the drugs. I think the group therapy I told you about, as well as Narcotics Anonymous, would be really helpful for you. You should at least give it a try.

Husband: That makes a lot of sense to me. I guess we should set that up. *[Jim supports the professional's recommendations.]*

Addict: I don't know. I don't really think it's necessary, but I guess it won't hurt to give it a try.

Taking the Next Step: Making the Transition to Treatment

It's important to remember that detoxification doesn't stop an addict from using a substance or prevent him or her from using it in the future. That's what treatment and rehabilitation are for. Unfortunately, as you've seen, after going through detoxification some addicts feel so much better that they don't think they need any further treatment. I remember a patient of mine, a young lawyer, who was addicted to crack cocaine. Working together, his family, his girlfriend, and I were able to convince him to go through the detoxification process. Once he had, though, he felt so well that he didn't think it was necessary to continue with treatment for the addiction itself, and not long afterward he went back to using cocaine every day. We all used every technique we could think of to get him to go into a hospital where he could be treated, but although he continued seeing me several times a month, he refused to recognize the seriousness of his problem. Finally, out of frustration, in an attempt to shake him up I decided to "fire" him as a patient. On the day I'd planned to do it, though, he came into my office looking pale, tremulous, and agitated, and before I uttered a word, said, "Oh, all right, Doc, I'll go to the hospital today." He subsequently entered a detoxification program and had many years of stable sobriety.

What can you and other friends and family members do to keep your loved one from having to go through something like this? Although, as with many questions concerning addiction, the answer to this one has to be determined on a case-by-case basis, there are some general guidelines you can follow. First, you should applaud the addict for having gone through the detox process and getting him- or herself back to good physical health. It's a hard thing to do under any circumstances, and he or she deserves to be congratulated. At the same time, though, you also need to "plant the seed" that he or she will probably need more treatment, and that since the clinician who recommended it has had a lot of experience working with addicts, what he or she said is worth considering seriously. In other words, you should maintain your Creative Engagement by continuing to exert pressure on the addict as long as it seems to be useful and effective. That is, you should push as hard as you can without pushing him or her away. How far you should go is, of course, always subjective, but as with any life-threatening illness, there's always value in trying.

Medications Used for Longer-Term Treatment of the Addict

As I mentioned earlier, in addition to being used in the detoxification process, some medications are also used to help addicts over longer periods of time. Some of these medications deter the use of substances, some block the effects they have, and others serve as substitutes. One of those that acts as a deterrent, for example, is disulfiram (Antabuse), which is used in the treatment of alcohol dependence. If someone taking this medication drinks any alcohol, he or she will experience a headache, nausea, and dizziness. While some addicts just take a tablet every morning, some carry one in their pocket in case they should find themselves in a situation in which they might be tempted to take a drink, such as during a work-related "happy hour."

An example of a medication that blocks the effects of a substance is naltrexone (ReVia), which can be used in the longer-term treatment of opiate dependence. This medication acts as a preventive measure in that even if someone taking it uses an opiate, he or she can't feel the opiate's effects. And an addict who knows that he or she won't get high if he or she uses an illicit drug is much less likely to do it. ReVia has also been shown to decrease the craving for and use of alcohol, as has acamprosate (Campral).

Finally, there are those medications, like methadone and buprenorphine (Suboxone and Subutex), that are sometimes used as substitutes for addictive substances. The idea of providing an addict with a potentially addictive but relatively "safe" drug may go against some people's philosophies of treatment, but as far as I'm concerned it's still much better than contracting HIV or hepatitis C, or having one's life destroyed by illicit opioid use. It's important to remember, though, that a maintenance program like this should be just part of a comprehensive addiction treatment program that's designed for the addict's particular needs.

Detoxification and Medications

- Detoxification is necessary if an addict is exhibiting withdrawal symptoms.
- Detoxification is a bridge to treatment of addiction, not treatment itself.
- A detoxification program should be linked to a treatment program.
- Medications that reduce or eliminate withdrawal symptoms can be prescribed by practitioners to help addicts through the process.
- Withdrawal from central nervous system depressants like alcohol, barbiturates, and benzodiazepines can be treated with medications like Librium and Valium.
- Withdrawal from heroin and similar drugs is treated with other opioids like methadone and buprenorphine, which can also be used as relatively safe substitutes for the addictive substances.
- Addicts withdrawing from cocaine, amphetamine, and methamphetamine can be treated for some of their symptoms with supportive care, but there are no medications that have been proven to combat the craving for the drugs themselves.

Now that you know about the various forms of detoxification and the medications practitioners use to help addicts work their way through the process, the next thing you need to know about is one of the integral elements of all forms of treatment—psychotherapy, which is the subject of the next chapter.

Chapter Ten

PSYCHOTHERAPY

Whether conducted on an inpatient or outpatient basis, every type of addiction treatment uses psychotherapy in one form or another, including individual, group, couples, family, and Network Therapy. Although all of these forms take somewhat different tacks, they're similar in that they all focus on the addict and his or her problem, and in that most of them use social pressure to try to get the addict to change his or her behavior—or at least begin to think about the consequences of that behavior. All of these pathways to treatment have proven to be helpful for some individuals, but it's important to remember that no one method is best for every addict. Since most treatment facilities offer a particular type of therapy, or some variation on one of them, in order to make an informed decision about which would be most appropriate for the addict in your life, you should know about all the different types. In this chapter I'll accordingly tell you something about each one.

Individual Therapy

Individual therapy essentially consists of a patient and a therapist meeting on a regular basis, usually from one to three times a week, to enable the patient to understand his or her problems and move toward solving them. The therapist—a psychiatrist, psychologist, social worker, or other trained clinician—will usually use one or more of several different methods to achieve his or her goal. The method that most people are familiar with is psychoanalysis, in which the patient free-associates and the therapist analyzes what the patient says or fantasizes about, in an attempt to gain an understanding of his or her feelings and behavior. Another frequently used type of individual therapy is cognitive-behavioral therapy, which focuses instead on what the patient says and on his or her way of thinking. A third common type of individual therapy is supportive psychotherapy, in which the therapist concentrates on helping the patient deal with the world, partly by supporting the patient's adaptive behaviors and providing him or her with a warm and trusting relationship. Although each of these types of therapy is different, most therapists combine elements of all of them to provide each of their patients with whatever he or she needs.

When used to help convince addicts to enter treatment, or as a part of the treatment itself, individual therapy can be very beneficial as it can provide a place where the addicts can focus on their own needs, as well as an environment in which they can open up about whatever demons may be troubling them. However, this type of therapy alone is not a very effective way of treating addiction and has to be used in conjunction with other methods such as twelve-step programs, group therapy, family meetings, or medication. This is because addicts are very likely to minimize, distract from, or just plain lie about their substance use. And unless there are people other than the therapist involved in the process who can "call them" on any conscious or unconscious evasions, the therapist won't be able to get a true picture of the problem. The fact is that addiction festers in secrecy, so the more that can be done to eliminate even the possibility of secrecy, the more likely the addict will be able to attain sobriety.

Individual therapy can, however, be used very effectively to coordinate the various efforts that the addict should be making to address his or her problem. In my own practice, for example, although I may only see patients once a week, I may also make sure they attend AA meetings four times a week, go to a professional group therapy session once a week, see a couples therapist every two weeks, and have their medications monitored by their spouses. Individual therapy, then, is very appropriate for the addict who wants to use it for this purpose and who's able to develop a trusting relationship with the therapist. On the other hand, it's less likely to be effective in helping an addict who's agreed to see a therapist only to placate others—such as a spouse or parent—and isn't really interested in ridding him- or herself of the addiction.

Ideally, once the addict has attained sobriety, he or she will be able to start working on whatever problems there may have been in his or her life even if there'd been no addiction problem. Working through the developmental stages of leaving our parents and our homes, building intimate relationships with others, and grappling with educational and work stresses are things we all have to deal with. And the addict who's come through the crisis of addiction with the help of a therapist has the advantage of having already developed a relationship that will help him or her to effectively handle these issues.

Individual therapy sessions, of course, vary from patient to patient, but to give you an idea of how such sessions work, here's an example of how an addict and her therapist might talk about peer pressure and alcohol.

"They Can All Drink and Nothing Bad Happens to Them"

Addict: So, once again everyone went out drinking on Saturday night.

Therapist: Again, huh? *[The therapist stays open-ended.]*

Addict: Yeah, and I didn't go, but it was really rough. They didn't even invite me this time.

Therapist: Hard to know what's worse, being invited and not being able to go, or just not being invited.

Addict: It's really depressing. Sometimes I think I'd be better off just drinking and having fun.

Therapist: Do you think so? *[The therapist explores the addict's thinking about this all-important subject.]*

Addict: Well, at least I'd be with my friends.

Therapist: Yeah, that's right. Anything else? *[The therapist presses for a full consideration of the consequences.]*

Addict: I'd probably end up drunk again. That happens every time. And I just can't get past the image of myself being tossed into a cab by my boyfriend again. Embarrassing! And then I'd have the headache the next day, and have to miss work again . . .

Therapist: Sounds like you think that would be inevitable. *[The therapist underlines the addict's own understanding of the consequences.]*

Addict: But at least it would be fun!

Therapist: Didn't sound like that much fun when you described it. In fact, you had a look on your face that said "yuck!"

Addict: Well, for a little while it would be fun.

Therapist: So why haven't you done it yet? *[The therapist avoids the position of being the "spoilsport" who's telling the addict not to drink and makes the point that the addict herself has made that decision.]*

Addict: I guess I just don't want the problems that always hit me when I drink.

Therapist: Guess not. That's a tough decision, but one you should be proud of. *[The therapist supports the addict's decision and behavior.]*

Addict: But it's not fair. They can all drink and nothing bad happens to them.

Therapist: You're right. It's not fair. *[The therapist agrees and supports the addict in her feelings.]* But you've got to take care of yourself.

Addict: I know I do. It's just hard sometimes. . . .

Group Therapy

The basic purpose of group therapy is to enable members of the group to learn how they function with other people and then to improve on it. Such groups typically consist of people who have no connection outside the group and are led by professionals—usually clinicians trained in group therapy—who can and do direct the group toward profitable discussions and away from unhelpful ones. One of the most common types of group therapy is the social skills group, in which members can get feedback on their own skills and compare other people's perceptions to their own—often very different—perceptions.

When used specifically to help addicts, groups focus primarily on how their members' lives have been affected by addiction and on how they can learn from and support each other. This type of therapy can play a major role in getting an addict to begin—and stick to—treatment. It's particularly effective in the early stages, before the addict has accepted the fact that he or she even needs treatment. That's because hearing other addicts tell their stories, which are usually very similar, is frequently an eye-opening experience that can lead an addict to appreciate the fact that he or she is not alone in the addiction and, perhaps more important, that other addicts may have something to offer in the way of practical advice and emotional support. It's also very helpful for those who are very deep into recovery and either need or want a "refresher course," because hearing the stories of newly sober individuals can remind the experienced person of his or her own potential problems with substances.

There are also, however, several other benefits to this kind of therapy. One of the most important of these is that the group's leader helps participants understand and deal with the emotional roadblocks to recovery that even the most intelligent people face. And this understanding, along with the knowledge that change is possible, helps addicts see that there's a way out of their misery, and that once they've shed their addictions they can go on to have productive and fulfilling lives. In addition to this message of hope, group therapy enables recovering addicts to recognize that they have to be vigilant in guarding against the return of the addiction and helps them in their efforts to maintain that vigilance. Finally, group members benefit from the presence of a therapist who can diagnose and then treat or refer addicts who have mental illnesses or difficulty maintaining relationships, as well as help them build up their social self-confidence in a relatively protected environment.

There are, though, some addicts for whom this method is

unlikely to be very helpful. For example, an addict who is overly suspicious of others—whether due to the substance use itself or a psychiatric illness—will not be able to function well, if at all, in a group. Similarly, addicts who suffer from profound social anxiety generally don't respond well to group therapy because of the necessity for social interaction. While it would probably be advantageous for such people to address their social anxiety at some point, it's best for them not to do so while in the throes of an active addiction. There are, of course, also many people, whether they're addicts or not, who are reluctant to talk about their most intimate problems in a room full of strangers. But an addict may be particularly concerned about confidentiality and as a result be unable to bring him- or herself to share his or her thoughts and feelings with a group. While I certainly understand this reluctance, I find the process so helpful that I encourage every addict I work with to at least try attending a group therapy session.

If individual therapy sessions vary from one patient to another, group therapy sessions are even more varied. There are any number of subjects that come up in such meetings, but one of the most frequently talked about is how to deal with friends who still use drugs or alcohol. Here's an example of how such a conversation might go.

"You Just Have to Bail Out"

Facilitator: So, who wants to start tonight?

Billy: Yeah, I really need to talk about this. Last night I went out with the guys from work, and they were really getting to me. I almost used—I probably would have used—but I didn't want to face y'all here tonight. [He laughs.] But those guys weren't right. I mean, they were sniffing cocaine right in front of me, and they know I have a problem. Seriously, I was so pissed at them. *[Billy blames "the guys" for his temptation.]*

Roger: So you didn't use?

Billy: Nope. But those guys were really tempting me!

Andrew: Well, it's great you didn't use, anyway. *[Andrew offers appropriate congratulations.]*

Billy: Thanks.

Roger: I second that motion. Strong work. I don't know if *I* could have held out with people sniffing cocaine right in front of me.

Andrew: Me, either. No way I could resist that. *[He gets some good reality testing.]*

Facilitator: So you didn't use, but you were really close. Right, Billy?

Billy: That's right. If it weren't for those guys ruining my night, I would have had a great dinner out.

Facilitator: It sounds like you were really close. So close that most people in this room wouldn't have made it.

Eddie: I wouldn't have made it. In fact, I know that I just can't go to those kinds of dinners anymore. Too much stress. *[Eddie tells the others about his own strategy: he doesn't put himself in bad situations.]*

Billy: But I gotta go to them. It's part of the job.

Eddie: That's what I used to think. But since I stopped going no one said anything. I don't think they noticed.

Andrew: Yeah, I guess that's right. If you hadn't been at the dinner, you wouldn't have been tempted by those guys. *[Andrew confronts Billy's attempt to blame his coworkers.]*

Roger: Maybe you could avoid those dinners out. *[Roger makes a concrete suggestion.]*

Facilitator: Sounds like that's a consensus.

Billy: But totally impossible! These guys don't have a problem with cocaine—they only use when we go out, once a month or so. I don't want to insult them by refusing to go out with them.

Andrew: Do they know what cocaine does to you?

Billy: I guess not.

Roger: I doubt they'd be insulted. They probably don't pay as much attention to you as you think. But even if you did insult them, even if you lost your job, that would be better than if you go on another binge.

Andrew: The last one almost killed you, man! *[Andrew points out a clear consequence.]*

Facilitator: Sounds like the group thinks you just have to bail out on any more dinners with these guys.

Billy: I hate to admit it, but I guess you guys are right. . . .

Couples Therapy

The purpose of couples therapy is essentially to enable couples to function better together, usually by helping them communicate in a more effective and loving way. This kind of therapy is normally conducted by a therapist—a psychiatrist, psychologist, or social worker—specially trained in this process. When used to help addicts recover, however, couples therapy usually focuses on helping the addict stay sober while preserving the relationship and allowing the couple to be more honest with each other, particularly about the addiction. Honesty is obviously important in any relationship, but when an addict in a relationship lies about the addiction, that in itself can become the problem that leads to the relationship failing. So unless the addict is honest about his or her addiction, there can't be any progress in either the treatment of the addiction or in the effort to help the couple heal.

Because of the nature of the relationship between the people involved, couples therapy presents several special advantages— as well as disadvantages—that don't present themselves in other forms of therapy. Among the advantages of couples therapy for addicts is the fact that addicts often consider their relationships the one thing they're not willing to lose because of the addiction. And, in fact, I've counseled many couples who came to me because the addicted partner was determined to shake his or her addiction in order to save the relationship. Ultimately, of course, it's important for an addict to want to stay sober for his or her own sake, but if the desire to maintain a relationship serves as an impetus to start treatment, I consider that a golden opportunity that shouldn't be passed up.

The most common disadvantage that couples therapy presents in dealing with addiction lies in the fact that the addiction and the relationship are often bound up together. More often than not, the couple met while using drugs and/or alcohol, and the substance use was central to the romantic and passionate "rule breaking" at the beginning of the relationship. That is, having sex while intoxicated, the use of the illegal drugs themselves, and the flouting of societal norms served—and continue to serve—the couple as an aphrodisiac. As a result, the couple may not even know how to interact without the use of drugs or alcohol.

In a situation like this, the relationship itself can interfere with the addict's recovery. If, for example, one of the partners is an addict and the other is not, they tend to have very different perspectives. The nonaddicted partner can't understand why the addict doesn't just cut down on the substance use and is likely to think that the addict's inability or unwillingness to do so means that he or she doesn't care about the relationship. At the same time, particularly when the relationship is based in part on the substance abuse, the addicted partner may be afraid that ending the addiction will end the relationship, and will accordingly do whatever he or she can to keep that from happening.

Another situation in which the relationship can interfere with the recovery process occurs when the couple is accustomed to using substances when having sex. Especially if the relationship began with the use of alcohol and/or drugs, the couple may feel that they can have no sexual life together without the addictive substance. It's not unusual, for example, for couples who smoke marijuana to say that they need it to "relax" or "unwind" or "get comfortable." For that reason, one of the therapist's tasks may be to reassure the addict that abstinence from addictive substances will not doom him or her to a life without intimacy or sexuality. Of course, a sober relationship can actually be *more* intimate because the substance-induced haze between the two people has been removed. When one of my patients told her boyfriend that their sex life was better with cocaine, he laughed out loud and said, "Are you nuts? When we have sex and we're using cocaine I don't feel anything!"

The relationship between the couple can have a negative impact on the recovery process in other ways as well. Sometimes, when the addicted partner can't stop the problematic substance use, the nonaddicted partner finds comfort in devoting him- or herself to caring for the obviously troubled lover—a classic example of codependence. At other times, the nonaddicted partner may become addicted by following his or her partner's lead. The writer Caroline Knapp, in her book *Drinking: A Love Story,* referred to one partner drinking heavily to prevent the other from drinking all the alcohol in the house as "defensive drinking."

As with all the other methods, couples therapy is more appropriate for some addicts than others. People most likely to be helped by this method include addicts who are involved in what is still, despite the addiction, a loving relationship, and those whose commitment to their partners is still stronger than the pull of the substance. Perhaps not surprisingly, however, couples therapy is unlikely to be particularly valuable when both partners are addicts. One drowning person can't save another, and the only possible path to recovery for a couple who are both addicted is for both partners to get treatment, preferably separately, with plenty of support from nonaddicted friends and family outside of the relationship. Others who are not likely to be particularly aided by couples therapy include couples where one partner cannot contain his or her anger, or couples where one or both partners have "one foot out the door."

As with group therapy, conversations in couples therapy can range over a wide area. However, one of the most frequent topics of conversation in such therapy is how addiction can affect trust in a relationship. Here's an example of how such a conversation might go.

"You Lied to Her About It in the Past"

Therapist: So, welcome back. What's on your minds today?

Addict: She's on my case all the time. She just doesn't let up!

Therapist: Tell me about it.

Addict: It gets crazy sometimes. I went out last week to get some cigarettes and she accused me of using pills when I was out. No way. I can't live like this, with this constant suspicion!

Wife: Well, I thought you might be using.

Therapist: What made you think so?

Wife: He was gone for half an hour, plenty of time to hook up with the dealer and use! *[Barbara expresses a reasonable suspicion.]*

Addict: Well, I didn't!

Therapist: Alan, have you used at all in the last week?

Addict: Nope. But if she keeps this up, I just might.

Therapist: So Barbara will be to blame if you use? *[The therapist confronts Alan's unreasonable blame laying.]*

Addict: No, not really. But she really pisses me off.

Therapist: Can you tell Barbara what pisses you off?

Addict: Sure I can. [He turns to face Barbara.] It's your constant suspicion, even when I'm not doing anything. I can't take it. *[He expresses his frustration.]*

Wife: But Alan, that's exactly when you would use—when you were going out to get cigarettes.

Therapist: Okay, I think I'm starting to understand. Barbara, did you have any other reason to suspect Alan had used? Did he look high?

Wife: No. But I saw the pattern.

Therapist: Me, too. And I can understand your suspicions, Barbara. [He turns to Alan.] Do you see what Barbara was concerned about?

Addict: Yeah. But I wasn't doing anything.

Therapist: I know you weren't. But I guess we can both see Barbara's point. When you went out for cigarettes, that's when you did use, and you lied to her about it in the past. Right?

Addict: Yeah, but this time I wasn't.

> Therapist: Right. But I think it'll take a while to rebuild that trust, and you may have to endure her suspicions for some time to come. Probably anyone would have them. *[The therapist agrees that both Alan and Barbara have good points.]*
>
> Addict: I guess. But I wish she'd back off.
>
> Therapist: Well, I think that Barbara may have to let herself trust you a little bit more each day, especially in situations where you've messed up in the past. Can you do that, Barbara?
>
> Wife: I can try. But it's going to be hard.
>
> Therapist: Both of you have difficult tasks here, but we can work on it together. *[The therapist has assigned Alan to be more patient with his wife's understandable concerns and has assigned Barbara to make a change and let herself trust Alan more and more every day.]*

Family Therapy

Generally speaking, family therapy focuses on the relationships between family members, how those relationships developed, and how they can be improved. It's usually conducted by a specially trained therapist on a weekly basis. It can, however, also be very effective in helping an addict overcome his or her addiction. When there's an addict in the family, even though the therapist continues to focus on the family overall rather than on any individual—including the addict—he or she is able to treat the addict in the context of his or her family relationships, educate the family about addiction, and ultimately help the family help the addict free him- or herself of the addiction.

As with couples therapy, because of the nature of the relationship of those involved, this method presents both advantages and disadvantages that don't otherwise present themselves. One of the most important advantages lies in the bond that exists among family members. Even in those families where patience and emotional energy are exhausted, these bonds can be used to foster the use of Creative Engagement to enable family members to recognize what they can realistically do to help, support the addict without enabling use of a substance, and use whatever leverage they have to encourage the addict to go into treatment. In addition, by providing family members with a better understanding of addiction, this type of therapy can help stabilize the family, improve its relationships, and enable it to focus on the addiction without losing track of other, sometimes unrelated, problems.

Family therapy also, however, has some disadvantages that don't present themselves in other types of therapy. One of the greatest of these is the complex nature of the family system itself and the conflicting priorities it can sometimes cause. Each member of the family brings his or her own problems to the table, many if not most of which are unrelated to the addict's use of substances. And while it's important that the family therapist brings to light how each member contributes to the family's problems, the addict's immediate—and possibly life-threatening—problem can get lost in the mix.

Another problem that's likely to come up when there's an addict in the family is codependence. A good definition of codependence is "any suffering and/or dysfunction that is associated with or results from focusing on the needs and behaviors of others." This problem occurs when a family member or members abandon their own legitimate needs in order to help the addict.

An example might be a mother who gives up her social life, financial stability, and job in order to help a grown-up child who's an addict. Of course, addicts need the love and support of their families to help them through the recovery process. But when anyone, despite his or her good intentions, becomes so involved that he or she loses all sense of proportion and balance, it creates problems for others, and neither the addict nor other members of the family benefit.

As with the other methods, there are some addicts for whom family therapy is likely to be particularly beneficial, and some for whom it would not be as appropriate. Among the first are those addicts who have deep and powerful family bonds, and those whose family members have generally positive feelings toward each other. Those in the second group would, obviously, include addicts whose family members do not feel particularly close to each other, but also those addicts who can't restrain their anger and/or who—either legitimately or not—blame their families for their addiction. In fact, because of the difficulties inherent in this type of therapy when addiction is involved, only a family therapist with experience in treating addiction should even attempt to work with a family that has an addicted member.

The nature of the dynamics within a family sometimes tends to make family therapy more contentious than other forms of therapy. One of the most difficult subjects for families to tackle is a family member's emotional "protection" of the addict and his or her addiction. Here's an example of how such a conversation might go.

"You Girls Are Exaggerating"

Therapist: It's nice to meet all of you. What are we meeting about?

Wife: Well, you certainly get to the point. [She laughs.]

Therapist: Yes, I guess I do.

Wife: Well, our daughters asked us to come in because they're concerned about their father's cocktails. But honestly, I don't see much of a problem. *[This sounds plausible.]*

Sandy: Oh, please, Mom. He's drunk every night! *[One of the daughters offers a contrary opinion.]*

Addict: That's not true, sweetie. I have a few cocktails before dinner and that's it.

Ellen: Dad, I must say, you do get a bit loopy most nights. *[The other daughter agrees with her sister.]*

Wife: You girls are really overreacting here. Dad's always had a drink when he gets home from work.

Ellen: And he always gets loopy!

Addict: Oh, please, that's not true. I enjoy my cocktails as a way to relax, but that's it. My liver is fine. I just had my checkup and the doc said everything checked out. *[Bob tries to deflect his daughters' attention from the problem— they're not worried about his liver.]*

Wife: That's right. I was right there with him. Doc asked him how much he drank, and Dad told him two or three cocktails after work. That's it. It's not like he's driving or anything.

Sandy: Dad, are you still having your cocktails in the water glass?

Addict: Yes . . .

Sandy: And you fill it to the top, right?

Addict: Mom fills it.

Sandy: Whatever. And it's straight vodka, right? No ice? No juice?

Addict: I guess . . .

Ellen: Those aren't cocktails, Dad. Those are huge quantities of pure liquor. No wonder you fall asleep on the couch every night. *[Ellen confronts her father with the truth rather than letting him pretend that he just drinks elegant little cocktails.]*

Wife: He likes it that way. *[She is still defending her husband's alcoholism.]*

Ellen: Does he like it when his grandkids can't wake him up for dinner?

Wife: That only happened once! You girls are exaggerating.

Ellen: Mom, it only happened once because that's the only time they bothered trying to wake him up. They usually just assume he's going to stay passed out on the couch and miss dinner, because that's what he always does.

Wife: He's taking a nap.

Sandy: [She raises her voice.] It's not a nap, it's a blackout!

Addict: Can I say something here?

Therapist: Please do.

Addict: I think this is all a big mistake. I have a few drinks after work, in my own house, and you girls are all up in arms. *[He's still minimizing the problem.]*

Therapist: Wow. It sounds like there are two very distinct perspectives on Bob's drinking. Let me try to understand what the concerns are. . . . *[The therapist will go on to point out the mother's attempt to defend her husband's behavior, which is clearly harmful to him.]*

Network Therapy

Network Therapy, which was developed in the mid-1980s by Dr. Marc Galanter, was designed specifically to bring family and friends together to help an addict achieve and maintain sobriety. In this method, working with a therapist, between three and seven concerned family members and friends form a group—a network—that meets every week, beginning as soon as the addict enters treatment and continuing for a year or so after the addict has achieved sobriety. In addition to attending these network meetings, the addict also meets alone with the therapist once a week.

At the weekly meetings, network members focus on the positive changes the addict is trying to make and, acting as a team, support each other and the addict, encourage him or her to maintain abstinence, and help the addict weather stresses in his or her daily life. These themes are echoed during the individual sessions the addict has with the therapist, although these individual sessions also provide an opportunity for the addict and the therapist to work on any issues other than addiction that are present in the addict's life.

One advantage of Network Therapy is that the therapist can provide network members with ongoing advice about the best ways to respond if the addict should fall back into his or her old addictive behavior. So if—and/or when—that happens, they're better able to deal with it and can provide a supportive, protective network for the addict as he or she goes through the recovery process. Another benefit of this method is that, because it provides friends and family members with a sophisticated understanding of addiction, they will be able to recognize addictive behavior even after formal therapy has ended.

As with the other methods, some addicts are more likely to benefit from this type of therapy than others. These include individuals who, despite their addiction, have remained connected to their friends and family members, as well as those whose friends and family are both willing and able to come to the therapist's office on a regular basis. In fact, I've often been surprised at how easy it is to recruit network members, even (or especially) for those addicts who have burned a lot of bridges. Most caring people will jump at the chance to help an addicted loved one if they can do so without being taken advantage of. On the other hand, addicts who have few or very weak social relationships are less likely to find this form of therapy particularly helpful.

As you can see, there are several forms of therapy—including individual, couples, family, and Network Therapy—that can be a powerful force for sobriety. However, since each of these types has both advantages and disadvantages, it's important that you choose the therapy—and the therapist—that's most likely to be beneficial for the addict in your life.

~~~~~~~~

Psychotherapy

- Every type of addiction treatment uses some form of psychotherapy, including individual, group, couples, family, and Network Therapy.
- Not every type of therapy is right for every addict.
- Individual therapy is best when used to coordinate the various efforts an addict should be making to address his or her problem.
- Group therapy is most effective when it focuses on particular addiction problems.
- Couples therapy, when properly conducted, can stabilize the addict's sobriety.
- Family therapy can be very helpful when there's an addict in the family but must be conducted by a family therapist who's experienced in addiction treatment.
- Network Therapy is similar to family therapy but sometimes preferable because it focuses on the addict and his problem, rather than other family dynamics.

Now that you've learned what treatment is, what to look for in a treatment facility, and the various types of treatments that are available from professionals, there's one further type of help that you need to learn about. That type is Alcoholics Anonymous and other peer-led groups, and it's the subject of the next chapter.

Chapter Eleven

ALCOHOLICS ANONYMOUS AND OTHER PEER-LED GROUPS

Although Alcoholics Anonymous is an organization rather than a treatment for addicts, it can be very helpful for your friend or loved one if he or she is an alcoholic, or even if he or she is addicted to some other substance. Founded in Cleveland in 1935 by a New York stockbroker known as Bill W. and an Ohio doctor known as Bob S., both of whom had been "hopeless" alcoholics, AA offers an inspirational, nondenominational faith-based program of peer support for sobriety from alcohol addiction. The organization—which has over 2,000,000 members in more than 100,000 groups in 150 different countries—defines itself as "a fellowship of men and women who share their experience, strength and hope with each other that they may solve their common problem and help others to recover from alcoholism. The only requirement for membership," they say, "is a desire to stop drinking," noting that, "Our primary purpose is to stay sober and help other alcoholics to achieve sobriety."

Interestingly enough, despite how long AA has been in existence and how many addicts it's helped, there are still a lot of people who don't understand how the organization works. There was one addict I worked with who had that problem even though his brother had been a member of the organization for several years. And the addict's brother only discovered it when he suggested to the addict that he try AA himself. My patient later recounted their conversation.

~~~~~~~~~~~~~~~~~~~~~~

"I'm Not Joining Any Kind of Cult!"

Brother: Jerry, I really think you should check out an AA meeting. At least take a look at it!

Addict: That is so not happening, Al. I'm not joining any kind of cult. *[The addict expresses a common misconception about AA.]*

Brother: Look, Jerry, I've been a member for four years, and I haven't seen anything to make me think it's a cult. No one's ever asked me for money. And no one's ever told me I had to believe in anything. In fact, what they have told me is that I should question anything I have doubts about. They even have a sign on the wall that says, "Take What You Need, Leave the Rest." *[Al tries to explain the organization's philosophy by telling his brother about one of its slogans.]*

Addict: I don't even believe in God, Al.

Brother: A lot of AA members don't. And you don't have to. They just ask that you believe that there's some power in the universe that's greater than you. Some people call it God, others call it Mother Nature. Some people even see AA itself as the higher power. The main thing is that you understand you're not in control of everything.

Addict: I already know that. . . .

Brother: I know you do. But sometimes it's important for somebody to remind you.

Addict: I understand that, too. But I also don't like the idea of having to listen to someone try to convince me that I should stop drinking.

Brother: You don't have to do that, either. In fact, when you come to an AA meeting they make it a point not to intrude on your personal space. Most likely someone will just introduce himself and offer you a cup of coffee. If you want to talk, fine. If not, that's fine, too.

Addict: Well, I don't want anyone to see me at the meeting. They'll know I have a drinking problem.

Brother: So? *[Al opens up a discussion rather than responding immediately.]*

Addict: So I'll lose my job! And Andrea might leave me. Those people at AA can't be expected to really keep it a secret!

Brother: Jerry, believe me, everyone around you already knows you've got an issue with alcohol. It's a little hard to miss, bro. *[Al gives his brother a reality check.]*

Addict: Very funny. But those AA bums will spread it all around to people I don't even know.

Brother: I doubt it. That never happened to me, and I've been going to meetings for a long time. I guess it could happen, but if someone does blab, it'll just prove that you're getting help for a problem, nothing else. The way I see it, though, the way things are going now you're already in danger of losing your job and your wife!

Addict: You really think it's okay?

Brother: Look at me, Al. You can see how much AA's helped me.

Addict: Well, I guess it wouldn't hurt to attend one meeting. . . .

The Twelve Steps

The basic tenets of AA's program are encompassed in the now well-known twelve steps of recovery that were developed by Bill W. and first published in his book, *Alcoholics Anonymous,* in 1939. These steps describe the experiences of the first members of the organization and are meant to serve as a guide for those who want to attain and maintain sobriety. AA does not, however, consider acceptance of the twelve steps to be mandatory, so while some AA groups refer to them frequently and encourage members to complete them in order, others treat them as incidental to the business of helping each other with sobriety.

The Twelve Steps of Alcoholics Anonymous

1. We admitted we were powerless over alcohol— that our lives had become unmanageable.

2. Came to believe that a Power greater than ourselves could restore us to sanity.

3. Made a decision to turn our will and our lives over to the care of God *as we understood Him.*

4. Made a searching and fearless moral inventory of ourselves.

5. Admitted to God, to ourselves and to another human being the exact nature of our wrongs.

6. Were entirely ready to have God remove all these defects of character.

7. Humbly asked Him to remove our shortcomings.

8. Made a list of all persons we had harmed, and became willing to make amends to them all.

9. Made direct amends to such people wherever possible, except when to do so would injure them or others.

10. Continued to take personal inventory and when we were wrong promptly admitted it.

11. Sought through prayer and meditation to improve our conscious contact with God, *as we understood Him,* praying only for knowledge of His will for us and the power to carry that out.

12. Having had a spiritual awakening as the result of these steps, we tried to carry this message to alcoholics, and to practice these principles in all our affairs.

As you can see, the steps have several recurring themes. One of these, as my patient's brother explained to him, is the idea of surrender to a "power greater than ourselves." Although this symbolic surrender is sometimes misinterpreted as implying helplessness on the part of alcoholics, admitting an inability to drink in moderation can actually empower your loved one to find ways to avoid all alcohol and, ultimately, reclaim his or her life. Recognizing the existence of God—as the steps put it, "as we understood Him"—and seeking His help in attaining sobriety can help in the addict's recovery because doing so reminds him or her that he or she isn't all-powerful and therefore can't control everything in his or her life. If, for example, an AA member complains about his or her spouse, boss, or friends being a bad influence, another member will remind him or her that he or she can't control other people. And acknowledging that lack of control forces the addict into figuring out how to respond to other people's behavior, even if that behavior might provoke him or her to drink.

Another theme concerns the importance of alcoholics taking and continuing to take inventory of themselves. AA urges its members to do this so they can recognize the damage drinking has done to them as well as others, and, wherever possible, make amends. Finally, there's a third theme that concerns helping other alcoholics. Once an AA member has attained sobriety, he or she is encouraged to reach out to help others who have yet to do so. This kind of effort is designed not only to help those who have not yet stopped drinking but also to strengthen the member's commitment to maintaining his or her own sobriety.

How Alcoholics Anonymous Works

Although the twelve steps lay out the basic tenets of AA's program, the organization's primary means of achieving its goals is through its regularly scheduled meetings. These meetings are held throughout the day in places like church basements, community halls, or hospital meeting rooms, and are either open or closed to the public.

Open Meeting

Open meetings can be attended by anyone who wants to come, including those who think they may need AA, those who have friends or family members who might benefit from the organization, and health-care professionals who want to simply observe and learn. This means that even if your friend or loved one isn't sure that he or she wants or needs to stop drinking, he or she can come to a meeting, test the waters, and reach out for help if and when he or she is ready. Although no one is required to participate during meetings, anyone who wants to may do so. In keeping with the organization's primary goal of helping its members achieve sobriety, however, if and when anyone starts going into detail about personal problems, the group usually directs the conversation toward drinking as a likely cause of whatever those problems may be.

Actually, there are two kinds of open meetings—open *speaker* and open *discussion* meetings. During open speaker meetings, members "tell their stories," that is, describe their experiences with alcohol, explain how they came to join the organization, and talk about how their lives have changed because of it. A typical speaker might tell a story like this.

"But I've Got Sobriety, and I've Got Hope"

Speaker: Hi, everyone, my name is Samuel, and I'm an alcoholic and an addict.

AA members: Hi, Samuel.

Speaker: I'm the speaker for tonight, and I'm going to tell you the story of my addiction and of how I got to sobriety. I drank a little in high school, but just a few beers on Friday night with the guys. Never had a problem with it. In college, too, I don't think I drank much more than anyone else. We'd drink at football games and at frat parties. I had a few bleary-eyed mornings, but that was it. And I did great in school—got a 3.70 GPA. It wasn't until after I started working that the trouble started. I had an entry-level job in investment banking, and after work we'd all go out for a few beers, to wind down, you know. But it wasn't exactly social drinking, it was partly business. The senior guys were all there on Thursday nights, and you damn sure went if you wanted to get to know them and be buddies. At first, I was doing fine, both in my work and in the socializing aspect of the job. I worked hard and played hard, too. But pretty soon I noticed that the nights weren't ending up so well for me. I'd make an ass of myself with some comment about a girl or something, and pretty soon the guys weren't laughing with me, they were laughing at me. And when I'd get to work the next day I wouldn't remember what the hell I'd done, and I noticed that people would avoid me. But did that stop me? No! I decided that I just had to pace myself. Great strategy. I ended up pacing myself into a drunk-driving beef that I managed to elevate to resisting arrest because I shoved the cop. Coming back into work after a day and a half in jail wasn't pretty. They all knew where I had been, and that was the final straw on that job. They let me stay on a few weeks but then let me go. Even then I didn't quite make the connection between alcohol and losing my job. I just figured I'd "overdone it" one night and then been unlucky enough to have a bunch of spoilsports with me in the office. Of course, when I got fired, my girlfriend, Annie, wasn't too happy. She tried to help by suggesting that we only drink at home and only during football games, which was one of my favorite times to drink. Problem was, it wasn't only Sunday football. There were college games on Saturdays, and I couldn't miss Monday Night Football. And since I wasn't going out anymore, those Thursday night games starting looking pretty good, too. I ended up drinking more than I ever had, and alone, since Annie left me. Can't say I blame her. It was only when I actually ran out of money that I went to an AA meeting. Didn't even have a dollar for the coffee fund. But you all took me in. So now I'm standing in front of you, 128 days sober. I got a sponsor. (Hi, Bobby!) I got this 120-day chip. I haven't got a job, and I haven't got a girlfriend, at least not yet. But I've got my sobriety, and I've got hope. Thanks for listening.

AA has people tell their stories this way because doing so benefits both the addict and those listening to him or her. When alcoholics tell their stories, often making fun of their own inability to recognize the seriousness of the problem, they remind themselves as well as their listeners of the grave consequences of drinking. By laughing at his or her own foibles and weaknesses, the alcoholic lays them out for the rest of the group to see and, in the process, makes them less secret and less scary. The alcoholic also makes the point that he or she remains hopeful because he or she is attending AA meetings and working through the twelve steps to recovery. Finally, by describing his or her inability in the past to recognize the warning signs of relapsing, the speaker reminds everyone in the group of what they have to be on the lookout for.

During open discussion meetings, on the other hand, one member speaks briefly about his or her experiences and then leads a discussion about an alcohol-related problem, such as a particular stress that alcoholics face or a strategy for dealing with relapse. The kind of discussion that takes place in such a meeting might sound like this.

Cravings and AA

Group leader: So now that I've told you a little bit of my own story, what we're going to talk about tonight are cravings and AA. Who wants to start?

Chuck: I'll start. I'm afraid I'm an expert on cravings. I have them right here, and all the time. I listen to you people tell your war stories and, to tell you the truth, it makes me want to drink. Honestly, it sounds like fun when you people go on and on about the parties you used to go to. So here's what I do. When I feel like drinking, I try to remind myself that it's my own Stinking Thinking, just my addiction talking, and that my addiction is clever, and it's just waiting for me to let my guard down. Sometimes that works. But sometimes it doesn't. Times like that I just remind myself that I'm only going one day at a time and that I don't have to make any lifetime commitment. That's what I do.

Andrea: That doesn't work for me. If I have a craving, I have to *do* something, not just think about it. And what I do is tell another alcoholic about my craving, as soon as possible. If I'm here, I tell you people about it. If I'm not here, I have a list of names and numbers of people I can call. Sometimes I have to go five or six people down the list before I find someone who picks up the phone. But it's okay, because just doing that helps keep me from taking a drink until I can get hold of someone.

Group leader: Two great strategies, reminding yourself about Stinking Thinking, and telling another alcoholic. Both of them stop the clock.

Regina: Can I say something?

Group leader: Of course.

Regina: Those strategies don't work for me, and I think the AA meetings might be bad for me anyway. We're all a bunch of drunks here, and what good can you do me? Two weeks ago I went out drinking with a guy I met here! Which is exactly what my mom said would happen if I got involved with AA!

Andrea: Regina, I know that was a bummer, but what you should have done in that situation was . . .

Group leader: Hold it, Andrea, you know we've got a rule against cross talking here. Talk about your own experience. *[Cross talking is what AA members call giving direct advice or making comments about another alcoholic's problem, and it's banned at most AA meetings.]*

Andrea: Yeah, right. I forgot that. But I had a similar situation. The first time I came to an AA meeting, I hooked up with a guy and we got high for a few days afterward. I blamed AA, of course, and I didn't come back. But then I met a girl at school who I used with all the time, and then I hung out with a dealer I met at the laundromat, and I realized that I could meet someone to use with anywhere, including AA. But at least at AA almost everyone is trying to do what I'm trying to do, which is to stay sober. Now I'm careful who I hang out with, regardless of where I meet them. And I don't blame AA if I make an unhealthy choice. Most of you knuckleheads don't want to use anyway.

Brad: Yeah, I was just thinking about meeting people to use with at meetings. I haven't done that, at least not yet, but I've sure had cravings at meetings. In fact, that's why I stopped coming last month—I stopped believing in AA. I figured that if I could have cravings even in these rooms, how could I ever be sober outside of them? But then this earthling *[i.e., nonaddict]* set me straight. When I told him why I'd been avoiding AA, he asked me if I had to believe in AA for it to work, and then I remembered the saying, "Bring the body, the head will follow." So I just came back, and no more cravings. Don't quite know why.

Group leader: Does anyone else want to speak?

Just as telling and listening to personal stories help the speaker and his or her listeners at open speaker meetings, open discussion meetings are helpful to both the group leader and those participating in the conversation. Not only do they enable people to share their experiences, which helps reinforce their commitment to sobriety, they also make it possible for others to learn from those experiences and apply what they've learned in their own efforts to remain sober.

Closed Meetings

Closed meetings are attended only by official members of the group, their guests, and prospective members, to make sure that everyone's anonymity is protected. Anonymity is, however, respected in both open and closed meetings. This was an extremely important aspect of the organization during its early years because there was such as stigma attached to the word "alcoholic" that members didn't want to be identified as such. Although being labeled an alcoholic isn't as much of a problem as it once was, AA maintains the tradition of anonymity for two reasons. First, because members recognize that those who need help might be reluctant to admit it if they knew their problem might be discussed in public. Second, because anonymity has a spiritual significance to the organization in that it discourages members from seeking, as they put it, the kind of "personal recognition, power, prestige, or profit that have caused difficulties in some societies."

As with open meetings, there are two types of closed meetings. One of these is the closed *discussion* meeting, which is conducted in the same way as the open discussion meeting but is attended only by members and prospective members of the organization. The other kind is a *step* meeting (which is usually, although not always, closed), during which members talk about one of the twelve steps. At these meetings, AA members talk about the meaning of the step as well as about their progress toward completing it. The conversation during one of these meetings might sound like this.

Step 9

Rhonda: So, welcome, everybody. Today is our step meeting, and we're going to be working on Step 9. Peter, could you read it off the wall mural?

Peter: Sure. "Step 9. Made direct amends to such people wherever possible, except when to do so would injure them or others."

Rhonda: Okay. "Such people" are the ones we listed in Step 8 as having harmed and to whom we're willing to make amends.

Sarah: Anyone who doesn't have a long list doesn't belong in this room. [There's laughter in the room.]

Rhonda: Okay, seriously, does anyone want to share their Step 9 with us?

Harold: I can. And Sarah's right, I guess I have a long list and I really belong here. The one I hurt most was my mother, but I have no idea how to make amends to her. I lied to her and stole from her, and I just didn't give a damn about her at all. There's no way to make amends for all that.

Rhonda: I guess not totally.

Peter: I paid back a few people I'd stolen from.

Harold: I could pay my mother back for what I stole from her. But it's not the money that's the hard part. I blamed her for my drinking. She nagged me about it, but not in the right way. She was pissed off and she said horrible things to me, so much that I went and drank to get her out of my head.

Peter: Well, do you know how much you stole from her?

Harold: I can estimate, but that's really not the issue. She doesn't care about the money.

> Peter: The money is at least one way you can pay people back. It's not much, but at least it's something. And they appreciate that it's a solid, real thing that you're doing.
>
> Harold: I guess so. But should I tell her that she made me drink?
>
> Rhonda: Is that even true?
>
> Harold: No. I drank because I'm an alcoholic. She just gave me the reason.
>
> Rhonda. You mean that day.
>
> Harold: Yeah, that day. But I could always find a reason. *[Harold is repeating something that's often said in AA meetings about an alcoholic drinking simply because he or she is an alcoholic, and that the "reasons" they give for drinking are usually just efforts to cover up that fact.]* So maybe I'll just hold back on the fact that I blamed her for my drinking and that I don't blame her now.
>
> Peter: Sounds like a good idea. There's no reason to hurt her more. . . .

As with the other types of conversations that take place at AA meetings, those that occur during step meetings are designed to benefit everyone involved. Like the conversations that take place during discussion meetings, by allowing people to share their experiences they enable others to learn from them and to strengthen their desire to remain sober.

How Alcoholics Anonymous Helps Addicts

As I've already mentioned, although AA is not a form of treatment, it can be very effective in helping your loved one reach and maintain sobriety. It does so essentially by using a combination of peer support, spirituality, and psychological strategy. Support from a community of recovering alcoholics is central to AA's program. This community, in fact, comes to virtually replace the alcoholic's previous social circle, which is very beneficial because the alcoholic's drinking buddies are usually, at best, reluctant to lose a comrade and, at worst, don't want the alcoholic to stop because it would only make their own problems more obvious. Of course, neither you nor the alcoholic's other friends or family members are to blame for his or her drinking. Nevertheless, you have in all likelihood come to identify him or her as a "drunk," "intoxicated," or an otherwise "sick" member of your group. By defining the alcoholic differently, as someone who wants to recover from addiction, and by emotionally supporting that new identity, AA groups can have a profound and sometimes immediate impact on your friend's or loved one's behavior.

One of the ways the group does this is through the use of sponsorship, which is essentially an experienced AA member serving as a mentor for a newcomer to the group. Soon after your friend or loved one starts attending AA meetings, he or she will be offered sponsorship or request it from a member who has at least a year of sobriety and is willing to undertake the task. A sponsor will typically help the addict clear his or her home of alcohol, plan strategies for breaking the news about his or her alcoholism to the new member's family, and, perhaps most important, be available at all times to help the alcoholic overcome any temptation he or she may feel to have a drink. Sponsorship benefits not only the newcomer and the sponsor but the group itself. By helping a new member, an established member not only strengthens his or her own sobriety but symbolically repays AA and his or her own sponsor for the help he or she has received.

The group also fosters this sense of community by encouraging members to speak with each other after meetings. By providing addicts with a place where they can build a social life without addiction, AA can be enormously helpful for those who have to change the "people, places, and things" associated with their addiction. AA parties are always joyful occasions with all the fun of any other party, except, of course, without drugs or alcohol.

Finally, by putting an end to the secrecy with which he or she has hidden his or her alcoholism, your friend or loved one will receive support from a group of dedicated, recovering alcoholics who have the best of motives for helping him or her achieve sobriety. This support, and the genuinely empathetic nature of the group, is usually very obvious to the newcomer and contributes to his or her desire to stop drinking. It can, in fact, enable the addict to develop hope and start seeing him- or herself as a sober, productive, and contented individual.

The spiritual aspect of AA's program can be equally important in helping your friend or loved one attain and maintain sobriety, particularly if he or she has only recently become sober. Most alcoholics experience a period of euphoria immediately after they've stopped drinking, but once that euphoria wears off they may awaken to the reality of shattered marriages, dim job prospects, and the emotional wreckage of years of chronic alcohol abuse. And the fact is that recovery is a long-term process that can be achieved only with patience and courage. AA's founders, and its current members, believe that recognizing that there is a "power greater than ourselves" can be instrumental in enabling the newly sober alcoholic to develop the courage that he or she will need to face these difficulties.

This aspect of AA's program, however, often provokes resistance in potential new members. "Why," they sometimes ask, "should I join a religion I have no interest in just because I want to stop drinking?" But even though AA encourages its members to recognize a greater power, it isn't a religion. In fact, long-term AA members say that that "power" can be almost anything—the traditional image of God with a long flowing beard, Mother Nature, Buddha, even the AA fellowship. In other words, it can be anything but the alcoholic him- or herself. AA believes that accepting the existence of an entity more powerful than oneself is essentially admitting one's inability to control life's ups and downs. And that until an alcoholic gives up the idea that he or she has the power to control the use of alcohol, he or she will never "recover" from alcoholism. Of course, the alcoholic is considered to be in control until he or she takes the first drink. It's only afterward that he or she loses it. That's why AA concentrates on the strategies necessary to avoid taking that first drink. As one of its more memorable aphorisms has it, "First the drinker takes the drink, then the drink takes the drinker."

AA can also help the addict in your life change his or her behavior by using several sophisticated psychological strategies. The first of these is confronting the addict's denial of his or her addiction. As I've already discussed, denial is the first line of defense for all addicts, and I've seen people deny their alcoholism to such an extent that it's literally mind-boggling. I remember one alcoholic whose alcohol-laden breath I could smell from my waiting room but who, nonetheless, insisted not only that no one knew about his alcoholism but that I was simply making up my observation about his breath because his wife had called me earlier to tell me about it. AA members help alcoholics like these by pointing out their alcohol-laden breath, slurred speech, and poor personal hygiene in an honest but empathetic way that helps them accept truths that they would immediately reject if they came from family, friends, or coworkers.

Another psychological strategy AA uses is encouraging alcoholics to be dependent on the organization itself. Alcoholics are, by definition, people who depend on alcohol for comfort, for emotional support, and as a means of escaping from the inevitable uncomfortable moments of life. However, if your loved one's dependence on alcohol is replaced by dependence on a supportive group of people who are focused on sobriety, he or she can begin to feel emotionally safe without having to resort to the immediate—but temporary—gratification of alcohol. To be fair, I must admit that there are some alcoholics and their families who believe that one can become too dependent on AA. In my mind, though, in the presence of a life-stealing disease like alcoholism, dependence on something healthy like AA is a perfectly reasonable way of breaking the addiction. After the addiction is treated and the individual is sober, the dependence on AA can, if necessary, be addressed.

The third psychological strategy AA uses is fostering the addict's identification with individual AA members and with the AA philosophy of abstinence and clean living. It does this by asking each member to identify him- or herself as an "addict" or an "alcoholic," and by providing them with the opportunity to see long-term members who are leading happy, productive, and sober lives. This, in turn, enables addicts to break free of their self-identification as active alcoholics and to develop new identities as nonpracticing addicts who are now in recovery. In fact, the addict's membership in a large group of people who believe in abstinence itself fosters the feeling of being part of something larger than him- or herself, which can both increase self-esteem and help protect the addict against self-reproach and relapse to alcohol.

One thing Alcoholics Anonymous does not take a position on, however, is the use of psychiatric medications such as Prozac and other antidepressants in the treatment of alcoholics. The organization doesn't address this issue for the very good reason that, although the newly sober alcoholic is at grave risk for becoming addicted to other substances—including not only depressants like marijuana and heroin but also some medications prescribed by doctors—it recognizes that such medications are often necessary. And, in fact, the majority of psychiatric medications are nonaddicting, necessary for the psychological stability of those who take them, and helpful in keeping those individuals from drugs of abuse. So even though individual AA members are free to give their own opinions about medications, and sometimes do, AA officially says that since its members do not practice medicine, the organization takes no official position on the use of these medications.

Nontraditional AA Groups and Similar Organizations

Most AA groups are made up of people with a variety of backgrounds and interests who can empathize with each other about their problems with alcohol. However, in large urban areas, AA meetings are also frequently attended by people who are addicted to alcohol as well as other drugs, and some who are addicted to drugs other than alcohol. It's also not uncommon to find groups in urban areas that are attended by people who have more in common than just their alcoholism. There are, for example, nonsmoking groups, groups for women, college students, lesbians, gay men, and affluent alcoholics, as well as "double trouble" groups for those with both mental illness and addiction. This separation of groups by gender, sexual orientation, or socioeconomic level isn't done to discriminate against anyone but, rather, to help the members understand each others' troubles in dealing with alcoholism.

There are also, however, groups for those who are uncomfortable with the central tenets of AA itself. In New York City, for example, there's a group called "We Humanists," which is made up of people who don't like the spiritual side of the typical AA group. (This group used to be called "We Atheists," but a minister who hosted the group suggested the name change.) This group has deleted all references to God from its meetings and concentrates instead on the peer support and psychological aspects of AA's program. By creatively changing the structure of their meeting without losing the guiding principle—the quest for abstinence—this group's members have modified AA so it's helpful even for some who don't like AA. Other groups have simply replaced the word "God" with "Higher Power" and kept all the central AA concepts, including the spiritual element.

The success of Alcoholics Anonymous has also spawned the development of many similar groups. Offshoots like Narcotics Anonymous, Cocaine Anonymous, and Pills Anonymous concentrate more on addictions to those particular substances. Although the addictive process is similar, some of those who are addicted to these substances are more comfortable with such groups because the psychological effects are slightly different. Beyond the addiction to various substances, groups like Gamblers Anonymous, Overeaters Anonymous, and Sexual Compulsives Anonymous also use the twelve-step philosophy developed by the founders of AA to help group members deal with their compulsive, self-damaging behaviors.

How to Find an AA Group

If you're curious about how and why AA works, the best thing to do is attend a few local meetings and see for yourself. Newcomers are usually welcomed into the group as much as they want to be and get as much instruction in the principles of AA as they request. Contrary to some stereotypes about AA, members hardly ever proselytize in an intrusive way. Although offers to sponsor an alcoholic aren't usually made until after he or she has attended a few meetings, your friend or loved one will probably be given the phone numbers of several AA members to call for advice, help, and support. He or she will also be advised of AA's first two rules: (1) Don't drink, and (2) Go to meetings. These basic rules keep the focus on abstinence and remind the alcoholic that in order to gain the full benefit of AA's program, it's necessary to come to meetings. As he or she attends more meetings and moves toward sobriety, older members provide him or her with more information about AA's tenets.

Finding a meeting to attend is usually very easy. Anyone involved in addiction treatment can provide you with information about AA groups in your area. Most major cities also have an "Intergroup" number that will direct you to the nearest AA meeting or help you find a suitable one. (You can find these Intergroup numbers on AA's website.) If you can't find a group through these means, however, you can always look in the telephone book. Most directories have a listing for Alcoholics Anonymous, usually at the beginning of the White Pages.

There are, though, two schools of thought on selecting an AA group. The most common one suggests that the alcoholic should simply find the nearest group and join in, regardless of the gender, socioeconomic class, or other background of its members. There is, though, a second school of thought that suggests a prospective member should look for a group of people with whom he or she feels comfortable, so that he or she will be able to concentrate on dealing with the alcoholism without having to be concerned about other issues. And, as I mentioned, there are AA groups—at least in urban areas—made up of people who feel comfortable together because they share some specific trait or background other than their alcoholism. However the alcoholic chooses his or her AA group, though, the most important thing is to go and not to worry about which group is best. Although "shopping" for an AA group might enable the addict to come up with a better fit, he or she should avoid an irrationally obsessive search for the perfect group. You can help with this by encouraging him or her to "just go" to a meeting and not obsess about it, or by going *with* him or her the first time or two.

Al-Anon and Alateen

Al-Anon and Alateen, organizations that sprang from AA, are designed specifically to help people like you, the friends and family members of addicts, understand addiction on an emotional level, which can, in turn, better enable you to help the addict. Al-Anon is for any member of an alcoholic's family and Alateen is specifically for their teenage children or siblings. Lois W., AA cofounder Bill W.'s wife, began Al-Anon in 1951 and published a book about it, *The Al-Anon Family Groups,* in 1955. Thanks to newspaper advice columnist Ann Landers's praise of the group's commonsense approach to dealing with alcoholics and other addicts, the organization grew very rapidly. Today there are some 30,000 groups worldwide.

Rather than adopting AA's focus on the addict, these groups concentrate on the addict's friends and family. They teach that even the most concerned friend or family member can't make the addict stop using, and that the best course to follow is one of detachment. According to the group's philosophy, this kind of detachment is "the first step to a happier and more manageable life" for members of the addict's family. It's also, though, a very effective way to help the addict in your life, because the frustration and resentment that can build up in a burned-out caregiver can lead to abandonment or even physical violence toward the individual who's ill. You may have experienced some of this frustration yourself. By attending Al-Anon or Alateen meetings, you'll have the opportunity to meet others who have faced the same kind of problems that you have, to learn from them, and, ultimately, to get your life and your "self" back as you struggle to help the addict the best way you can.

The ideas promoted by Al-Anon and Alateen are, however, sometimes taken to an unreasonable extreme. As with tough love, those ideas can be misinterpreted as calling for abandoning helpless individuals to their fates. But the real strength of the program lies in its interfamily supportiveness, not in its encouragement to disengage from the addict. (In fact, in my experience as a therapist, I've found that when friends and family use Creative Engagement rather that disengaging themselves, the addict is much more likely to achieve—and maintain—sobriety.) Of course, as with any peer-led group, anyone in Al-Anon or Alateen can say anything they want, and occasionally bad advice is given along with the good. Overall, though, if you're interested in helping the addict in your life, I would strongly urge you to attend at least one of these groups' meetings to determine for yourself whether or not joining would be beneficial.

Although, again, Alcoholics Anonymous is not a treatment, many people have found that when combined with professional treatment like counseling or psychotherapy it can be extremely helpful. In situations like these, the counselor or therapist should be told that the alcoholic is going to AA so he or she can cooperate with the alcoholic's working through the twelve steps and encourage the relationship with a sponsor. Together, AA and treatment provide complementary strategies in the struggle for recovery from alcoholism.

Alcoholics Anonymous and Other Peer-Led Groups

- The first of AA's twelve steps—admitting powerlessness over alcohol—actually empowers the alcoholic to reclaim his or her life.
- Anyone can attend an open AA meeting.
- AA helps addicts by using peer support, spirituality, and various psychological strategies.
- AA helps addicts break the secrecy they build up around their addiction.
- AA offers itself as an emotional support for addicts.
- AA discourages denial by asking each addict to identify him- or herself as an addict or an alcoholic.
- AA takes no official opinion on appropriately prescribed medications.
- Al-Anon and Alateen, while not forms of therapy themselves, can help friends and family members of addicts address their common problems.

Now that I've told you what treatment is, and about the various types of treatment and other programs that I recommend for your friend or loved one, I want to tell you about some of the forms of treatment that I don't recommend, which are, accordingly, the subject of the next chapter.

Chapter Twelve

STRATEGIES TO AVOID

All the methods I've discussed so far, with the exception of tough love and Formal Intervention, are strategies I've seen work with many—if not all—addicts, and that I wholeheartedly recommend. There are, however, several other methods that, although they have their advocates, I feel it's best to avoid. None of these strategies are illegal or immoral, nor do they constitute medical malpractice. However, they're not generally accepted among addiction treaters, for reasons that I'll explain in this chapter. This isn't to say that these methods never work or that you should never try them. In the final analysis, almost any method that might work should be used to help an addict. In my opinion, though, these methods should be used, literally, only when and if all other efforts have failed.

Going It Alone

As I mentioned earlier, because addiction festers in secrecy, one of the most important ways you can help the addict in your life is by drawing him or her out of that secret world. And one of the reasons it's so hard to do that is that keeping the addiction a secret protects the addict in several important ways. If no one else knows about it, the addict is—at least in theory—safe from the stigma associated with addiction, safe from the possibility of losing the love of his or her friends or family, and safe from the possibility of losing his or her job. Perhaps even more important, by not telling anyone about his or her problem, the addict can avoid having to confront the shame that many addicts feel about being addicted. And feeling shame, that is, believing that you're inherently a bad person, destroys the will to change and repair whatever damage you may have done. To make matters worse, trying to get an addict to recognize that he or she has a problem and to deal with it often increases his or her shame and, accordingly, his or her resistance to treatment.

So even if the addict in your life is interested in getting treatment, he or she may prefer trying to deal with it him- or herself instead of involving others. If that's the case, you do of course have to respect the addict's privacy and let him or her make the decision about who's going to be told about the problem. At the same time, though, since starting treatment and attaining and maintaining sobriety is virtually impossible without emotional support from others, it's essential that the addict not try to "go it alone." That's why, as someone who cares about the addict, you have to make it clear that it's actually in his or her best interests to be as open as possible with others about the addiction.

In discussing it with the addict—and you should discuss it with him or her—there are a couple of points it's important for you to bring up. The first of these is that addiction, as I explained earlier, is a disease rather than a character flaw, and that it should accordingly be addressed just as any other medical problem would be. The second is that while admitting the addiction and getting it treated might seem humiliating or potentially damaging to the addict's reputation, it's nothing compared to the continuing damage that not treating the addiction can cause. And the truth is that by the time most addicts have reached the stage at which they're considering admitting their addiction, although they may not be aware of it, virtually everyone in their lives already knows or will soon know about it.

Of course, the approach you take in discussing this with the addict is extremely important. One family I worked with started the conversation with their addicted son by telling him that, despite the fact that they were angry with him, they would always love him and support him. They urged him to go into a detoxi- fication program and assured him that they would help him fi- nancially if he lost his job in a bookstore because he'd joined the program. Knowing how his family felt, I'd already told him that they would probably help him, but having his parents and siblings look him in the face and say so made all the difference. Embold- ened by his family's support, the young man went to work that afternoon and told his boss that he was going to be out for about a month in order to "get a drug problem taken care of." Much to his surprise, the boss not only wished him well but promised that his job would be waiting for him when he returned. This story obviously worked out well, but even if the young man had lost his job, he was better off getting his addiction treated than he would have been if he'd continued down the road he was on.

Just to give you a better idea of how you might approach your addicted friend or family member, here's an example of how such a conversation might go.

"I Can Do This on My Own"

Wife: Stan, I'm so worried about the way you've been using those Percocets. I think you should get some help for it.

Addict: To tell you the truth, I'm getting worried about it, too. I know how to detox from this stuff, and I'm going to do it. I really need to, I know.

Wife: I'm so happy to hear that! You're so much happier when you're off that stuff. *[The wife rightfully supports the addict's intention to stop.]*

Addict: I know, Deb. So you're going to have to bear with me for the next three or four days. You know that withdrawal really sucks. . . .

Wife: Yeah, I know. Maybe this time you could get some professional help to make it easier. *[The wife reacts to her husband's immediate concern—withdrawal—and proposes a remedy.]*

Addict: Nah. No need. I don't want to go to detox.

Wife: Well, if you don't want to call a professional, why don't we call your brother? He loves you, and I know he'd do whatever he could to help.

Addict: No way! I don't want to drag him into this.

Wife: How come?

Addict: Because it's not his problem. He's got his own life.

Wife: That's true, but you could use support from people who care about you, and he and I are numbers one and two on that list.

Addict: No! I can do this on my own! Why do you have to involve my family?

Wife: Stan, the family's already involved. We all care about you and want what's best for you. And every other time you've tried this on your own you've relapsed within a few days. Why not try something different this time? *[The wife confronts the addict about his repetitive relapses.]*

Addict: I said, no! I don't want to hang out my dirty laundry in front of everybody.

Wife: Well, I think they already know that you're back to using because you missed Susie's christening. For such a family-oriented guy, that was pretty unusual, and I'm sure they figured out what was going on.

Addict: Did you tell them?

Wife: Nope. But I didn't have to. They've been suffering along with you for the last year, and they knew that unless you got hit by a truck, nothing but a relapse would have kept you from that christening.

Addict: So, what, you want to announce this on the evening news?

Wife: No, Stan. I just want to invite your brother over here so he can help us get through this.

Addict: You really want him to come?

Wife: Yeah, I do.

Addict: Fine, call him if you want to.

Wife: Okay, I will. *[The wife chooses not to confront her husband about the fact that he seems to be putting all the responsibility on her shoulders. But she keeps her priorities in order, the first of which is to help her husband get sober, and agrees to make the call herself.]*

When and how the addict chooses to make his or her addiction public will of course vary from one person to the next. Some alcoholics, for example, choose to do so during an AA meeting by getting up in front of the group and saying, "My name is Joe, and I'm an alcoholic." By saying these words aloud to a group of recovering alcoholics, the addict is identifying him- or herself as a person in need of help and, simply by doing so, makes it more difficult for him or her to go back to denying the problem. Others, however, find this kind of public display humiliating and may prefer to admit their addiction in a more private way by just telling their friends and family about it. Regardless of how the addict in your life chooses to make his or her addiction known, though, it's essential that you and the addict's other friends and family be supportive. Again, this is what Creative Engagement is about.

Moderation Management

Moderation Management (MM) is an organization that calls itself "a behavioral change program and national support group network for people concerned about their drinking . . . who desire to make positive lifestyle changes." The program, they say, "empowers individuals to accept personal responsibility for choosing and maintaining their own path, whether moderation or abstinence," and "promotes early self-recognition of risky drinking behavior, when moderate drinking is a more easily achievable goal." The group is, accordingly, similar to Alcoholics Anonymous in that it urges behavior modification for problem drinkers and provides support to help its members. It's different, however, in that MM distinguishes between problem drinkers and alcoholics, and because instead of urging abstinence as the ultimate goal, it allows its members to determine on their own how much of a problem their drinking is and to modify it only if they consider it necessary.

The organization tries to help people make this determination by requiring new members to complete thirty days of abstinence from alcohol, during which time they're expected to attend meetings, examine how much they drink and how drinking has affected their lives, learn the organization's guidelines and limits for moderate drinking, and, if necessary, set moderate drinking limits and start working toward achieving "balance and moderation in other areas" in their lives. After this thirty-day period, they're expected to adhere to the following.

The MM Limits

- Strictly obey local laws regarding drinking and driving.
- Do not drink in situations that would endanger yourself or others.
- Do not drink every day. MM suggests that you abstain from drinking alcohol at least 3 or 4 days per week.
- Women who drink more than 3 drinks on any day, and more than 9 drinks per week, may be drinking at harmful levels.
- Men who drink more than 4 drinks on any day, and more than 14 drinks per week, may be drinking at harmful levels.

To a certain extent, it's difficult to fault an organization that argues that people should take personal responsibility for their drinking, and I'm sure there are some people who could benefit from the group's work. People who, for example, are relatively light drinkers and don't actually have an addiction problem would probably find the group helpful. There are, after all, some people who don't have diagnosable drinking problems but do occasionally have issues with alcohol. However, to my mind, MM's philosophy is nevertheless problematic because of its underlying assumptions. The first of these is the assumption that an individual can determine on his or her own exactly how serious a drinking problem he or she may have. Based on my experience, it's simply not possible for people to do that, and I consider even making the effort a waste of valuable time that could instead be expended in finding real help. The second assumption is that it's possible to set drinking limits that are appropriate for everyone. The problem with this is that everyone reacts to alcohol differently. Some individuals could drink double—or even triple—what MM recommends and have no problems with their relationships, work lives, or physical health. On the other hand, some people could drink half of what MM recommends as a limit and consistently cause themselves and others severe problems.

It's true that, in advocating total abstinence, AA as well as all mainstream addiction treatments may "overtreat" some people who really only need to cut down on their substance use. But aiming for total abstinence has the benefit of avoiding potentially tragic mistakes. In addition, even if someone who's an alcoholic can control his or her drinking for a time, it doesn't prove that moderate drinking is safe. In fact, more often than not, attempts at moderation lead to disaster. That's why I advise addicts I'm treating not to attempt the moderation strategy—not because I know that it's *doomed* to failure, but because I think it's very likely to *lead* to failure. If, however, an addict I'm treating wants to pursue this strategy, I continue to try to help him or her in any way I can.

Ultra-Rapid Opioid Detoxification (UROD)

Ultra-Rapid Opioid Detoxification (UROD) is a method that was first used in 1990 and is now being widely advertised on the

Internet as a "quick fix" for addiction to opiates. When an opiate addict undergoes this procedure, he or she is put under a general anesthetic, as if he or she was going to be operated on, and then given a high intravenous dose of an opiate-blocking medication like naltrexone. The medication knocks all the opioid molecules (like heroin) off the opioid receptors in the addict's body and then blocks them from returning, in effect instantaneously detoxifying him or her.

There are actually two very real benefits to this method. The most obvious one is that it's quick and, at least as long as the addict is anesthetized, painless. Rather than going through the four or five days of muscle cramps, agitation, and diarrhea that addicts typically experience with more conventional forms of detoxification, the opiate addict who undergoes UROD goes under general anesthesia for several hours and is then revived and sent on his or her way. The other benefit is that, due to the nature of the process itself, once the addict starts going through it, he or she can't change his or her mind. Perhaps not surprisingly, then, this kind of instant gratification is very appealing to most opioid addicts.

However, like most addiction treaters, I believe that the potential risks of UROD far outweigh its benefits. To start with, general anesthesia itself carries a risk of harming or killing even otherwise healthy patients, which is why it's only used for surgery when absolutely necessary. And since those who have this procedure done—heroin addicts—are rarely very healthy, their risk of dying under general anesthesia is even higher than the norm. In addition, recovery from general anesthesia can not only be quite painful, it can also result in dizziness, nausea, and lethargy for up to twenty-four hours. To make matters worse, when an individual has undergone UROD, that recovery period often takes place outside of a hospital setting, where there's no immediate medical support. Finally, and perhaps even more important, six- and twelve-month follow-up studies have shown that addicts who underwent UROD were no more likely to still be sober at those points than those who had gone through the conventional detoxification process.

Ibogaine Treatment

Use of a plant-based substance called ibogaine has, like UROD, been touted as a "quick fix" for addiction and is accordingly very appealing to addicts who would like to avoid the conventional forms of treatment. Its first documented use was as a hallucinogen in African religious rites in the nineteenth century, and it was first suggested as a cure for addiction in the late 1980s. Its proponents claim that it can alleviate the symptoms of withdrawal as well as decrease or eliminate the craving for opioids like heroin. The addict takes a single dose of the substance and within an hour experiences visual hallucinations that advocates claim help break the hold of addiction on his or her mind. He or she is supposedly also able to review his or her entire life and assess whatever decisions he or she has made.

However, the few research studies that have been done on ibogaine are, at best, inconclusive. In one, on its use in heroin withdrawal, twenty-five out of thirty-three heroin users reported that their withdrawal symptoms stopped within twenty-four hours of taking it. One of the thirty-three subjects died, however, reportedly from hidden heroin use, which suggests a dangerous interaction between heroin and ibogaine. In another study, which looked at the effects of a single dose of ibogaine on seven opiate addicts, after thirty-eight hours none of the subjects displayed any withdrawal symptoms. However, a follow-up done fourteen weeks later showed that only three of the seven were still opiate free, which suggests that the method is no more effective than more conventional ones. Overall, the fact that a patient died in one of these studies, combined with the lack of convincing data proving its effectiveness, suggest that ibogaine is not the solution to addiction that its advocates claim it to be. It is possible, however, that future studies will show that it can be a safe and effective way of helping addicts.

Untrained Counselors

Something else I think it's advisable to avoid are counselors who lack formal training and supervised experience in treating addiction. Such counselors may, in fact, hinder more than help your loved one in his or her search for effective treatment. The best, most experienced addiction treaters possess a strong understanding of addiction and a broad knowledge of the various treatments and peer-led support groups that are available. Armed with this knowledge, they can recommend those treatments that are best suited to the addict in your life and save the addict from wasting his or her time and energy on those that are unsuitable. An inexperienced counselor, by contrast, is likely to lack the resources and background he or she needs to provide the addict with the best and most useful advice.

This does *not* mean, however, that the addiction treater must have a professional degree to be effective. In fact, just because someone has a degree in medicine or psychology doesn't necessarily mean that he or she has any more than a basic knowledge of addiction. On the other hand, some counselors without formal degrees have educated themselves extremely well and are very knowledgeable about the range of treatment available. When interviewing potential treaters, then, it's important that you focus on their knowledge, training, and experience in the field rather than on the degrees they hold.

Medications Alone

As I explained in chapter 9, medications like naltrexone and disulfiram can be used effectively to both help your friend or loved one stop abusing a substance and to help him or her after he or she has stopped. But such medications alone can't enable the addict to achieve and maintain sobriety. Because there's a psychological as well as a biological component to addiction, it's essential that the addict be treated for both. And the best way to do that is to make sure that he or she is involved in a program that includes not just drug treatment but also psychological counseling and membership in a peer-led support group.

Substitution

Finally, I would advise you to do whatever you can to keep the addict in your life from substituting one illicit addictive substance for another—even if the second substance appears to be better in some way. What I'm talking about, for example, is the cocaine addict who thinks that, since she's never had a problem with drinking, switching to alcohol makes sense because it enables her to quell her craving with a substance that's safe, legal, and relatively inexpensive. Or the intravenous heroin addict who switches to smoking marijuana because he figures it's both easier to get and safer to use. Although making such substitutions might seem like a good idea, the problem is that someone who's addicted to any substance is extremely vulnerable to becoming addicted to others, a phenomenon often referred to as "cross-addiction." So the cocaine addict who starts drinking instead becomes an alcoholic, and the heroin addict who gives up the needle for the joint gets hooked on marijuana. That's why it's important that you make it clear to your friend or loved one that however much "better" one illicit substance may be than another, the best substance to use is always none at all.

It's important to remember, though, that using psychiatric medications to help an addict recover is not the same thing as using other addictive substances. As I discussed in chapter 9, medications like Librium and Valium can be used effectively to decrease the dangerous or uncomfortable effects of withdrawal from illicit drugs, while medications like Prozac can be used to treat the underlying psychiatric conditions that sometimes contribute to addiction. So while it's true that when used in this way such medications are being substituted for illicit substances, they can contribute to an addict's long-standing sobriety, and on that account fall outside the range of medications that should not be taken.

Two other addictive substances that also fall outside this area are the opioids methadone and buprenorphine. As I explained earlier, doctors sometimes prescribe these for heroin addicts—as well as users of some other substances of abuse—as a substitute for the illicit drugs. Methadone is available only in hospitals and federally licensed clinics, but buprenorphine can also be prescribed by specially licensed physicians, and taking maintenance doses of either can provide addicts with some very real benefits. Both can be taken orally once a day and can be provided in a dosage that doesn't cause side effects, and neither generates the vicious cycle of intoxication and craving that heroin does. As I've said, abstinence should always be the ultimate goal. However, if your friend or loved one is addicted to heroin or other substances that could be replaced with methadone or buprenorphine, you might want to consider the possibility of getting him or her into a carefully managed maintenance program.

Strategies to Avoid

- Always encourage your loved one to *not* go it alone.
- Moderation Management doesn't work for most addicts.
- Ultra-Rapid Opioid Detoxification (UROD) isn't worth the risk.
- Medications alone are rarely effective for addiction treatment.
- Substituting one addictive substance for another can result in cross-addiction.
- Methadone or buprenorphine maintenance treatment is legal and should be carefully considered.

Up to this point, everything I've told you about addiction applies to virtually all addicts. There are, however, certain types of addicts who present special situations, including teenagers, older people, addicts with mental illnesses (dually diagnosed addicts), addicts with medical illnesses, and pregnant addicts, and they're the subject of the next chapter.

Part IV

WHEN ADDICTION IS JUST ONE OF THE PROBLEMS

Chapter Thirteen

SPECIAL SITUATIONS

I hope the information in this book has helped you to learn more about addiction and about how you can help your friend or loved one rid him- or herself of it. In all the discussions I've presented, though, I've talked about addicts in a fairly general way. That is, I've provided information and advice on how to deal with most addicts. There are, however, certain situations that need to be approached and handled somewhat differently. These include situations that involve teenagers, older people, addicts with mental illnesses (dually diagnosed addicts), addicts with medical illnesses, and pregnant addicts. Because addressing such issues as how to determine if these individuals are addicted, how to get them to acknowledge their addiction, and how to get them to enter treatment are not necessarily the same as for other addicts, in this chapter I'm going to provide you with the information you need to deal with these special situations.

Addicted Teenagers

Although illicit drug use among teenagers has decreased slightly in recent years, the numbers remain frighteningly high. In a recent nationwide school survey, nearly 15 percent of eighth graders and more than 28 percent of twelfth graders acknowledged that they'd used some illicit drug other than marijuana over the past year. The same survey showed that about 30 percent of teenagers drink excessively more than once a month. Unfortunately, the real numbers are probably even higher, since those who are heavy users aren't likely to be found at school diligently filling out surveys. And that's not even taking into account what's generally understood to be the very widespread use of marijuana among teenagers.

Teenage substance abusers represent a special situation for several reasons. One of these is that, if the teen is your child and under the age of eighteen, you have some legal control over him or her. Another is that, because of their status as minors, teenagers aren't entitled to the same guarantees of confidentiality that adults are. Perhaps most important, though, is the fact that the emotional pain of seeing a child you love afflicted with addiction can be much harder to bear than the pain you feel when dealing with an adult addict. And for that reason, trying to convince a teenager to enroll in a treatment program can be significantly more compli-cated than doing the same with an adult.

If you're concerned that a teenager in your life may be us-ing drugs, there are several things you can do. The first of these is to be nosy. It's your job as an adult—particularly if it's your child—and if you don't do it, the chances are no one else will. Second, if what you see suggests that there is a problem, you should ask the teenager about it. Of course, teenagers can be dif-ficult to talk to, so how you even raise the question is important. (There's a dialogue that follows that should help give you an idea of how to handle this.) Third, if you don't get a satisfactory answer to your questions—that is, if the teenager denies using drugs but you still feel he or she might be—you should ask his or her teachers, coaches, doctor, friends, and friends' parents about it. And, finally, if you still feel that there's a problem, you should arrange for him or her to be professionally evaluated for addiction.

Even if, though, you discover that a teenager in your life has used addictive substances, it's important that you not overreact to it. First of all, you have to recognize that there's a difference between simple experimentation and ongoing addictive use of a substance. Onetime use doesn't make someone an addict, and a teenager's experimentation with marijuana or alcohol, however unwise, doesn't mean that he or she necessarily needs treatment. Also, although parents and guardians should prohibit the use of any potentially dangerous substance, you need to remember that there's a big difference between occasional use of marijuana and, for example, shooting up with heroin on a regular basis. So before you get excited about a teen's drug use, you should find out more about what substance he or she is using, how relatively dangerous his or her situation is—was he or she, for example, drinking and driving?—and how likely he or she is to continue using the substance in the future.

Here's an example of a father using Creative Engagement by asking his teenage son about his drug use.

"Are You Using Drugs?"

Father: Billy, I need to talk to you about what happened last night.

Teenager: What do you mean? Nothing happened last night.

Father: Well, when you and the guys came in the back door, you all smelled like marijuana. *[The father starts with a simple observation.]*

Teenager: Not me.

Father: Well, I couldn't tell who it was, but I'd like to know what's going on. Are you using drugs?

Teenager: Nope.

Father: Listen, Billy, I'm not out to harass you on this. But Mom and I care about you, we're responsible for you, and we need to know if you're using marijuana. We want to figure out if it's hurting you in any way.

Teenager: You're not mad?

Father: Worried would be a better description. You're almost seventeen now, and we know that you'll be making all your own decisions soon. But for now we want to know what you're doing with drugs. *[The father concentrates on his concern—and his responsibility—for his son.]*

Teenager: Promise you won't be mad?

Father: I can't really promise that . . . but I do want to help in any way I can.

Teenager: Well, sometimes I do smoke pot with the guys after practice.

Father: Do you feel like it's doing you any harm? *[The father's question frames the whole discussion by emphasizing the main point—the drug's possible harm to Billy—while respecting his son's autonomy by asking for his opinion on the subject.]*

Teenager: I don't think so.

Father: Any ways it might? *[Rather than cross-examining*

Billy, his father stays open-ended and interested in Billy's thoughts on the subject.]

Teenager: Well, the only way I can think of is when I'm running. Sometimes, after I've smoked, I get out of breath more easily.

Father: Does your track coach notice?

Teenager: No. But he said that if he finds out that anyone on the team is using drugs or alcohol—or even smoking cigarettes—he's going to throw them off the team.

Father: That would be bad. I know how much you love competing. *[The father wisely underlines a consequence that would matter to Billy.]*

Teenager: I do. But I don't think it's done any harm. I only smoke once in a while on weekends.

Father: Ever drive when you've smoked?

Teenager: Are you kidding? I don't want to end up getting busted or smashing the car. I'd never get the car again.

Father: [He smiles.] Well, you're right about that. But I was more worried about you or your friends hurting yourselves in a car—any car.

Teenager: We're not stupid, Dad. You know I did make the honor roll again last semester.

Father: I know you're not stupid—far from it. I just want

to make sure that you don't put yourself in danger. What about other drugs? How much do you drink at parties? *[The father asks a difficult and intrusive but probably necessary question.]*

Teenager: I never use anything else. That seems too weird to me. I guess I drink a few beers at parties, but we watch out for each other. And someone gets to be the designated driver every time.

Father: I'm glad to hear you guys think along those lines. And I'm proud of how mature you're being about it. *[The father again underlines Billy's sensible behavior, even when he does use substances.]*

Teenager: You know, Dad, I'm doing great in school and track this year. So what's the harm in smoking pot every once in a while on weekends?

Father: Do you see any harm? *[The father waits for Billy himself to recognize whatever harm there may be.]*

Teenager: Like I said, coach would boot me off the team if he found out. And I'd hate to get busted by the police.

Father: Yeah. I guess those are potential problems with marijuana. But you also said it affects your breathing when you run.

Teenager: I guess. Are you going to tell me I can't use it?

Father: I'm going to tell you it's a bad idea to use it, but I'm not going to say that you may not use it. I think marijuana at your age has the potential for hurting you, in exactly the ways you said—your ability to run and possible trouble with the police. I think it could also hurt your ability to study if you use more.

Teenager: I won't.

Father: Well, I appreciate your honesty on this, son. I hope you and I can continue talking about this. And I hope you'll come to me if you see any signs of trouble. *[The father decides that Billy's use hasn't risen to a high enough degree of danger to warrant further action. He decides to try to encourage communication about the marijuana use.]*

Teenager: Okay, Dad. And thanks for treating me like an adult. . . .

In this situation, the teenager doesn't seem to have an ongoing problem with marijuana. However, if on the basis of your conversations with your own teenager, his teachers, his friends, and/or his friends' parents, it appears that he or she is at risk for continued or dangerous use of a substance, I would strongly advise you to contact an addiction-knowledgeable clinician who can provide a comprehensive evaluation of the situation. Of course, suggesting that a teenager go for an evaluation and actually getting him or her to do it isn't necessarily the same thing. If the teen is unwilling to go on his or her own, though, I'd suggest that you consider using more coercive measures, such as threatening the loss of important privileges like using the family car, participating in after-school activities, or going out with his or her friends. At the same time, though, be sure to let the teen know that you're employing these coercive measures only because you're concerned about him or her and not as a punishment.

"We're Going to Get You an Evaluation"

Mother: Samantha, Dad and I want to talk to you about something.

Teenager: What?

Father: Come on in and sit down. We've been really worried about your drinking, and we're going to get you an evaluation.

Teenager: Why? There's nothing wrong with me. I just drink with my friends sometimes.

Mother: But we're worried about your safety. How did you get home last night, for instance? *[The mother asks a fair and reasonable question.]*

Teenager: Becky drove me . . . I think.

Father: I guess you're not exactly sure how you got home, then?

Teenager: Well, I'm here, aren't I?

Mother: Yes. But only by luck. I don't think Becky drinks any less than you do.

Teenager: So how come I have to get an evaluation and Becky doesn't? I don't have a problem.

Father: This isn't about Becky. Your grades have fallen off, and you smell like alcohol most evenings now. Mom and I just don't know how to handle this.

Teenager: You have no right to judge me!

Father: We're not judging you, we're worried about you, so we want an expert to see you.

Teenager: You drank when you were a senior in high school! Why can't I?

Mother: I also broke my ankle when I was a senior in high school. That doesn't mean you should do the same thing!

Teenager: Well, what if I don't go? You can't make me see a shrink.

Mother: This is important, Samantha. We're not really giving you a choice on this. *[The parents are worried enough to insist that Samantha have an evaluation.]*

Teenager: Dad! I can't believe you, of all people, are doing this to me! Don't you trust me? I don't want to do this.

Father: I'm sorry, but we don't really trust you at this point, sweetheart. You say you don't have a problem, but you don't tell us the truth about your drinking. That's why we've decided to have you see an expert and let that person figure it out. *[The parents had agreed beforehand on what they would tell their daughter.]*

Teenager: I can't believe you're making me do this.

> **Mother: I know this isn't pleasant. But we'll see what the expert says about it . . . .**

If the evaluation indicates that the teen is addicted to a substance, you should obviously do all you can to convince him or her to go into treatment. Unfortunately, in addition to using many of the same tactics adults do to resist treatment, teenagers use some special tactics of their own. As this young woman did, for example, teens can try to play one parent against the other or play on their parents' guilt for having used substances when they were younger. For that reason, if you're trying to convince your teenager to enroll in a program, before you do so, you and your spouse or significant other should have a plan in place. That plan should include both what you're going to say to him or her and what you're going to do if he or she refuses treatment.

Surprisingly, sometimes just insisting on your recommendations carries the day with teenagers. I have, though, worked with many families who have had to use various forms of coercion to get their children into programs. If, despite your own efforts, the teenager still won't cooperate, you should consider working with his or her school. Guidance counselors in many schools have the authority to keep an addicted student out of school until he or she has been treated. This is a good example of using Constructive Coercion; rather than cutting the student off—as would be the case with tough love—it provides him or her with an incentive to get help. If even that doesn't work, though, you could also look into the possibility of going to court to have the teen sent to a treatment facility. Although it's best when an addict enters treatment voluntarily, regardless of his or her age, you should never hesitate to coerce him or her into treatment. This is a life-or-death issue, and you should always do whatever you can to get your child the help he or she needs.

Older Addicts

Although it's seldom talked about, there are 2.5 million adults over sixty-five in the United States who have alcohol-related problems. Some of these individuals were moderate drinkers whose drinking increased as they grew older, and some developed the addiction later in life. In fact, alcoholism is the most common addiction among the elderly, followed by prescription drugs and nicotine. Complicating matters is the fact that, as the average age of the U.S. population rises, more and more addiction problems are found in the elderly. Unfortunately, since many of these people no longer have significant roles as employees, breadwinners, or parents of young children, their addictions can continue, and their ability to function deteriorates, well beyond the point at which a younger person would have been confronted by friends or loved ones. Particularly at risk are those who are lonely, have lost family members, have multiple health problems, and/or frequently visit doctors and pharmacies.

Older addicts present a special situation for several reasons. One of these is that addiction in older people isn't always recognized as such. What are actually signs of addiction are often misinterpreted or attributed to problems of old age, such as medical illness, loneliness, or dementia. For example, the "pseudodementia" caused by alcoholism can be mistakenly attributed to Alzheimer's disease. And even when the addiction problems are recognized for what they are, because of their age, elders don't always get the kind of care they should. One reason for this is that trying to convince an elderly mother or father to go into treatment presents an uncomfortable role reversal for an addict's adult children, as a result of which they're sometimes inclined to simply ignore the problem. Another is the idea that "at his age, Grandpa should be able to enjoy himself," which is also often a way for adult children to avoid dealing with the issue. And the sad fact is that if Grandpa is addicted, he probably isn't having much fun.

If, then, you have any reason to think that an older person you love is having a problem with drugs or alcohol, it's essential that you pay close attention to both his or her behavior and his or her medical condition. If, for example, you notice that he or she is becoming depressed, missing social events, or even becoming confused, you should ask about drug or alcohol use. In addition, since, as the AA adage puts it, "There is no problem that alcohol can't make worse," if your loved one's high blood pressure or diabetes worsens, you shouldn't hesitate to ask if he or she has been drinking. I understand that it may be difficult to ask someone who's considerably older than you personal questions like these, but it can be done in a loving and empathetic way. Here's an example of how an addict's adult daughter talked with her about it.

"You Don't Have to Suffer Like This"

Daughter: Mom, I was really worried about what Dr. Jones said when we were at his office.

Addict: What? He said my hip is fine.

Daughter: Yes, but he also said that you had alcohol withdrawal when you were in the hospital and that they had to give you medicine to treat it.

Addict: He said that?

Daughter: Yes. He also said that your memory problems and sadness might be getting worse because of how much you drink. *[This is a common problem.]*

Addict: But I don't drink that much. I only have my two

glasses of wine before dinner. I'm just getting old, that's why I get forgetful, and why I can't go out to see my friends anymore.

Daughter: He said that even just drinking that much might give you withdrawal and that you could die from it. And I know how much you enjoy being with your friends. Maybe if you stopped drinking you could join them again. You don't have to suffer like this. *[The daughter addresses what's important to her mother, or at least has been important in the past.]*

Addict: That doesn't make sense. I never had withdrawal before.

Daughter: You've never been away from your wine, either, at least not in the last twenty years. I think we should go see that counselor Dr. Jones recommended.

Addict: I don't think I need that, sweetheart. I'll just go on the way I was before. I don't intend to have to go to the hospital again.

Daughter: But, Mom, the doctor also said your liver isn't breaking down alcohol like it did when you were younger and that you'll probably have problems with alcohol even if you don't get hospitalized again. Don't you remember him saying that?

Addict: No, I don't. And this is none of your business, anyway. I'm a grown woman and you're my daughter. You shouldn't interfere like this.

Daughter: Oh, Mom, helping you with this is just like my

helping you when you had a problem with your hip. And that worked out all right, didn't it?

Addict: I guess so.

Daughter: Good. So I'll make an appointment for you with the counselor, and I'll drive you over there. *[The daughter takes a specific, assertive action.]*

Addict: You're a pushy one, aren't you!

Daughter: Only because I love you, Mom. . . .

Addicts with Mental Illnesses (Dually Diagnosed Addicts)

As I've already discussed, individuals who suffer from both addiction and mental illness are referred to as "dually diagnosed." A frequently seen example of this is the alcoholic who also has clinical depression. The term "dual diagnosis," however, encompasses a virtually endless list of combinations, from the anxious individual who smokes marijuana to the schizophrenic who uses crack cocaine. And, unfortunately, there are many more individuals who suffer from this problem than most people realize. In fact, a recent nationwide survey found that 37 percent of those who'd been diagnosed with alcohol dependence/abuse also had another mental illness, as did 53 percent of those with a drug abuse/dependence problem.

Dually diagnosed addicts, of course, present a special situation because they require considerably more complex treatment than those who suffer from addiction alone. Not surprisingly, suffering from two diseases can be confusing, not only for the addict

and his or her friends and family but for addiction treaters as well, primarily because symptoms of addiction and other mental illnesses can mimic each other. For example, sadness, lethargy, and impaired sleep are commonly found not only among clinically depressed people but also among alcoholics. To further complicate matters, addicts who have been diagnosed with mental illness also typically take medications that can interact with the addictive substances in their bodies and/or be affected by intoxication or withdrawal. So not only is treating a dually diagnosed addict more complex, getting one to enroll in a treatment program can also be more complex.

Because of the similarities between some addictions and some mental illnesses, even determining whether someone is suffering from either or both afflictions can be very difficult. If you suspect that your friend or loved one may be in this situation, the best thing to do is try to convince him or her to be examined by a psychiatrist who's experienced in dual diagnosis. Under the circumstances, however, it might be difficult to get the addict to do so. In that case, if he or she appears to be in any immediate danger, I'd advise you to call 911. If, for example, the individual doesn't seem to be making any sense when he or she speaks, or says something about being better off dead, you should call an ambulance immediately. If, on the other hand, there doesn't seem to be any immediate danger but he or she won't agree to be examined, you might consider meeting on your own with a psychiatrist who can help you find ways to convince him or her to do so.

Even after your friend or loved one has been dually diagnosed, however, the nature of his or her problem may make it particularly difficult for you to convince him or her to enroll in a treatment program. One thing that may help is if you focus—and act—on the behaviors associated with the problem rather than on the diagnosis itself. If, for example, you have a son who's an alcoholic and he's rampaging through the house, it's entirely appropriate for you to call the police. Although a night in jail is no treatment plan, it might be just what he needs to make him realize that he needs treatment. Even if it doesn't, though, involving the police might serve as a way of getting him into legally mandated treatment. Whatever the result, you'll have protected the addict, yourself, and anyone else in the house from harm.

But making use of the addict's behavior doesn't necessarily have to be so dramatic. If, for instance, your cocaine-addicted daughter cares about succeeding in the future but is failing at school because of her substance abuse, you can use that failure as a way of goading her into treatment. In fact, if you exert steady, insistent pressure on objective issues like school or work failure, you'll have a much better chance of succeeding than you will by dramatically confronting the addict about the "wrongness" of drug use. Here's an example of how the wife and mother of a dually diagnosed man used this technique.

"The Cocaine Is Making Things Worse"

Wife: Ben, your mom and I have been worried about you for a while.

Addict: What, my wife and my mother are both worried about me? What have you two gals been chatting about?

Mother: It's not funny, Benny. Sarah says your mood swings are getting worse at home, and every time you come over to the house Dad says the same thing. It seems like you're either flying sky-high or so depressed that you look like you want to shoot yourself.

Addict: Hey, I've been going through a rough patch. It's nothing a little relaxation wouldn't help.

Wife: But, honey, I know you've been spending more money on cocaine, and I'm worried about the message we're giving to the kids. They know what you're doing up in the bedroom after you come home from work.

Addict: No they don't. They're little kids. They can't possibly know what cocaine is.

Wife: Well, they know what you act like. When you come home from work you're totally morose, and then when you come downstairs you're all giggly and energetic. Timmy asked me last week what was wrong with you. *[Sarah tells her husband the sad truth that even though they can't identify it, the children suspect there's something wrong with him.]*

Addict: So tell him I'm a manic depressive. It'd be the truth. At least that's what I think it is.

Mother: Now you think you're manic depressive? Like your uncle? Maybe you should be taking lithium like he did. *[Whenever there's a family history of psychiatric illness it makes it more likely that an individual might have it.]*

Addict: Maybe I should.

Wife: You're not manic depressive. It's the cocaine that does it to you.

Addict: Maybe, but I don't think so. I felt just as bad when

I wasn't using cocaine. In fact, that's why I started using it. *[Self-medication is common among the dually diagnosed.]*

Mother: So why don't you just cut out the cocaine, then we'll find out.

Addict: Actually, that's just what I was thinking.

Wife: Except you've tried that six or seven times in the last year, and you can't stop for more than a day or two. It looks to me like you're hooked.

Addict: So give me another chance. I'll quit tomorrow.

Wife: I think this is outside of your control, Ben. Whatever you have, whether it's manic depression or something else, it seems to be getting more painful for you. And the cocaine is making things worse. Your mom and I found a doctor who specializes in treating people with addiction and psychiatric conditions, and I made an appointment for you to see him.

Addict: I don't think I need all that. Like I said, I can just quit the cocaine.

Mother: Benny, I think Sarah's right. You haven't been able to quit the cocaine, and that makes it impossible to figure out if you've got manic depression or something else. *[The mother gets to the crux of the problem.]*

Addict: So you think I should just start taking lithium? That stuff's just like cocaine, they're both mind-altering drugs. I'm trying to stay away from that.

Wife: I don't even know what the doctor would prescribe for you, Ben. But if he does think lithium is the right thing, presumably it would help your mood swings rather than worsen them. That's a pretty big difference.

Addict: I guess. But I don't want to just substitute one addiction for another. *[This is a common concern among addicts, and one that should be encouraged, since the addict should be careful about what he or she puts into his or her body. But equating psychiatric medications with illicit drugs is inaccurate.]*

Wife: Me, either. And I'm glad that you're thinking that way, because you certainly need to be careful about what you take. But the doctor we spoke to said he was very cautious about using medications, and that he would talk to you about whatever medications he's thinking about prescribing. *[Sarah supports Ben's caution about taking in any substance.]* In fact, he says he sees this kind of thing a lot.

Addict: Mood swings and cocaine?

Wife: Yeah.

Addict: Well, I suppose I could give it a try.

Mother: Great! I'm sure this will help you feel better. *[The mother offers the addict encouragement.]*

The important thing to remember about a dual diagnosis is that both the diagnosis itself and its eventual treatment will be more complicated than it would be with addiction alone. This is because even after the addictive substance is totally out of the addict's body, he or she will still suffer from psychiatric symptoms that have to be treated. Assessing and treating someone who has been dually diagnosed might seem daunting—even overwhelming at times—but it provides the best hope of bringing about long-lasting results. Such treatment usually includes a combination of appropriate medications, psychotherapy, group therapy, and peer-led support groups, and should be coordinated by a clinician—most likely an addiction psychiatrist—who's familiar with the integrated treatment of addiction and mental illness.

Ironically, although a dual diagnosis is more difficult to treat than just addiction, there's actually something of an upside to it. If your friend or loved one has been dually diagnosed, it may actually be *easier* for him or her to get help. That's because the need for immediate treatment of mental illness—as opposed to addiction—is still more widely recognized and accepted in our society and in our legal system. Let's say, for example, that your father is an alcoholic who's trying to stop drinking. One of the effects of alcohol withdrawal, along with tremors and agitation, is a profound, biologically based sadness. When combined with the feeling of hopelessness about ever recovering that many alcoholics feel, this sadness could lead to suicidal behavior.

However, unless he actually attempts suicide, it would probably be very difficult for you to get a judge to have him involuntarily hospitalized. If, though, he were also diagnosed as suffering from clinical depression, because of the wider acceptance of mental illness, it would be relatively easy for you to get a court to hospitalize him if he so much as *hints* at committing suicide. In fact, on a practical level, as a result of this bias, you would probably find that psychiatrists who treat mental illness are more familiar with the laws and protocols for mandating treatment than counselors who treat addiction.

Addicts with Medical Illnesses

The addict who's suffering from a medical illness in addition to his or her addiction presents a special situation in that the illness provides his or her friends and family with a unique opportunity to help him or her throw off the addiction—whether the illness is related to the addiction or not. In those instances in which it is, such as gastric bleeding from alcohol or nasal problems due to cocaine use, the doctor or nurse who treats the illness will almost surely recognize that the illness is a result of addiction and will accordingly make recommendations for treatment. There are also, however, instances in which a medical problem can actually cause an addiction, such as when someone with a legitimate pain management problem becomes addicted to painkillers, which is often called "medical addiction." Here's an example of two women trying to convince their friend to get treatment for just such a problem.

"I Need the Pills for My Headaches"

Jill: Andrea, Beth and I want to talk to you about the pain pills you take.

Addict: What about them?

Jill: We're—well, we're worried about you. When you take them they seem to make you sleepy and kind of weird, and when you don't you get really nasty. *[Both of Andrea's friends have recognized a common pattern in opiate addiction.]*

Addict: I can't help that. I need the pills for my headaches.

Beth: I agree with Jill. A lot of people have asked us what's wrong with you. You seem so out of it a lot of the time. It's not like you. *[Beth communicates that she and Jill aren't the only ones who have noticed and are concerned.]*

Addict: Well, you guys don't understand. I take those pills because of the migraine headaches I get. It's not like it's illegal or anything. A doctor prescribes them!

Jill: But you go to a couple of doctors a week, right?

Addict: Yeah, sometimes.

Jill: And your getting fired had something to do with your not being on the ball at work, right? *[Jill doesn't let Andrea minimize the problem.]*

Addict: Okay, okay. I know the pills cause problems. But if I stop taking them the headaches come back, plus I get diarrhea and muscle cramps, and my mood gets really nasty. I can't stop taking them.

Beth: We know all about that. We looked it up on the Internet, and we found out that most of that is withdrawal from the pills. That's what happens to everyone when they stop taking them. And the headaches, well, the pills are probably actually making them worse. The website said that they're called "rebound headaches," and they're pretty common when someone uses these kinds of painkillers. *[Jill and Beth have done their research.]*

Addict: So what you're telling me is that I'm stuck with this?

> Jill: No, not at all. We researched what you could do. You could find a better medication for the headaches and taper off the painkillers.
>
> Addict: But I'd be scared to stop the painkillers. I'd feel terrible, and the headaches would come back.
>
> Jill: That's just the thing. We spoke to a neurologist who said there are plenty of nonaddictive medications for migraines, and ones that actually work better than what you're taking now. And she said that she knows how to detox you from the painkillers, too.
>
> Addict: That sounds like a dream. . . . You guys are great friends!

In this case, of course, the connection between the medical problem and the addiction is very clear. However, even medical conditions that aren't directly linked to addiction can serve as springboards to treatment. For example, if your alcoholic friend or loved one has diabetes, you can emphasize how much the extra carbohydrates from excessive drinking will harm his or her chances of recovery. Similarly, if the addict in your life suffers from heart disease, you can point out that the physical stress on the heart that occurs with cocaine use can make his heart condition worse. In fact, any time the addict interacts with the health-care system is a good opportunity to use Creative Engagement to underscore the addictive problem and push the addict toward seeking treatment for the addiction. Even if the addict rejects help on the basis that he or she "has enough to deal with right now," you should still use the opportunity to press him or her to get help.

Pregnant Addicts

Since crack cocaine came on the scene in the late 1980s, increasing attention has been focused on pregnant women and the effect of the drug on their children. Although research dollars and clinical strategies have lagged behind the public concern about this problem, legal responses have sprung up nationwide. Many states now prosecute women who use drugs during pregnancy, and even more states are requiring that positive maternal and neonatal drug test results be reported to either government agencies, like child services departments and health departments, or to the criminal justice system.

If your addicted friend or loved one is pregnant, it's obviously not only in her best interests but also in her child's for you to do whatever you can to convince her to enroll in a treatment program. Here's an example of how you might present such an argument.

"I Don't Need Any More Stress Right Now"

Friend: Annie, I've been really worried about your drinking. It seems to me that you might be endangering the baby.

Addict: You've got to be kidding me, Cece. I don't drink any more than I used to.

Friend: I know, but that's the thing. I read that even if all you drink is a couple of glasses of wine every night it could cause fetal alcohol syndrome.

Addict: I don't think so. You have to drink hard liquor, and a lot of it. *[Annie expresses a common misconception.]*

Friend: Actually, that's not true. Wine does have less alcohol, but if you drink enough you can match the alcohol in liquor. The article I read did say that a small amount of alcohol won't hurt a fetus, but they don't know where exactly the cutoff is. That's why they recommend no drinking at all—just to be safe.

Addict: Okay, I've got the idea, but I don't need any more stress right now. I really look forward to having that wine in the evening, and I don't think I could make it without it.

Friend: I know, but I can help you with that. I even went to a women-only AA meeting last night, and I talked to somebody who said they could help. I know you're feeling kind of stressed out, but the woman I spoke to said that the alcohol is probably making it worse. *[For a pregnant addict, women-only AA meetings can be an excellent choice.]*

Addict: You went to an AA meeting? For me?

Friend: Yeah. I'm that worried about you.

Addict: Wow . . .

Friend: Aren't you worried about it?

Addict: I guess I am. But I'm also worried that if I go for treatment I'll get arrested. For hurting my baby, you know. *[Some states require hospitals to report pregnant women who have positive urine toxicology tests for drugs or alcohol.]*

Friend: No, you don't have to worry about that. The woman at the meeting told me that in this state, hospitals and doctors don't report women who are addicted to something if they come for medical care. In fact, the hospital has to respect your confidentiality on this.

Addict: I guess you're right. I'm just so scared.

Friend: Don't worry. I'll go with you. The women at the AA meeting said I was welcome to come back with you anytime. Let's go tonight.

Addict: Okay . . .

Special Situations

- Be nosy about your teenager's use of drugs and alcohol but remember that not all drug use is addiction.
- Because of their standing in the family, and their legal status as minors, teenagers can be more readily coerced into treatment than adults.
- Older adults are as vulnerable to addiction as other people, but the signs aren't always as easy to read.
- Addicts who also have mental illnesses are both more difficult to diagnose and more difficult to treat.
- Medical illnesses and pregnancy provide friends and family with good opportunities to address addiction.

Conclusion

Several years ago the parents of a college-age man came to me for advice on how to help him with his addiction to heroin. They were essentially at the end of their rope. They'd already tried helping in a number of ways, including taking him to see several addiction treaters, paying for his treatment at a very expensive rehabilitation facility, and even cutting off all contact with him, but nothing had worked. The young man himself refused to meet with me, but I was able to help his parents formulate a plan that made it possible for them to stay in contact with him without in any way contributing to his use of heroin.

At my suggestion, they told him that even though they were terribly worried about him, they would't give him any money because they felt that doing so would be supporting his addiction. At the same time, they offered to help him get into an outpatient drug treatment program and to find out when their local Narcotics Anonymous (NA) group held its meetings. In addition, they told him that while he would be welcome in their apartment as long as he wasn't intoxicated, none of his drug-using friends could come to the apartment under any circumstances, and they would call the police if they felt endangered in any way. As it happened, the family did have to refuse him entry on several occasions, but while this was difficult—even heartbreaking—for them, they stuck by the rules they'd established.

Through their own individual therapies, the addict's mother and father were able to let go of the guilt feelings that were, I believe, leading them to continue to support their son financially. Working together, we were also able to build a plan that would allow them to both support their son emotionally and pay for a decent—although not luxurious—addiction treatment facility. Although the young man initially chafed at the idea of attending a less-than-posh treatment facility, he eventually agreed. While there, he met several other heroin addicts who not only gave him excellent advice on staying sober, but also convinced him to start attending NA meetings with them.

Unable to shake his addiction despite the meetings, the young man cycled in and out of treatment for several months. It was a difficult time for both him and his family, but because they never gave up on him, he began to realize not only that they had his best interests in mind but also, and more important, that he could trust them. Eventually—or perhaps inevitably—the young man suffered a heroin overdose. And because even his drug-using friends knew how committed his family was to helping him, the first ones they called were his parents. The overdose was bottom for the young man, and as his family continued to be there for him, both physically and emotionally, they were finally able to get him into a detoxification program and, eventually, to a competent outpatient psychiatrist who treated his addiction.

As I'm sure you can see, this story provides examples of both Creative Engagement and Constructive Coercion at their best. Not only did the addict's parents try to convince their son to get help, but even when that failed they stayed engaged, used several different forms of coercion to get him into treatment, and kept at it until, at last, he was ready to accept help. Although they didn't allow themselves to be taken advantage of, they continued to focus on the addict and his problems rather than their own. And most important, they didn't abandon him. Of course, I can't promise that if you practice these strategies with the addict in your life your story will have an equally happy ending. What I can tell you, though, is that I really believe in these strategies because I've used them in my practice for many years and have seen them work time and time again, even when those who loved the addict were beginning to give up on him or her.

In fact, if I could convey only one message to you it would be this: don't give up! Keep trying until you find a strategy that works. That means that if you suggest that your loved one join AA and it doesn't work, find a good detoxification program. And if that doesn't work, try to coerce him or her into getting help by withdrawing your financial support. And if even that doesn't work, call the addict's friends to get their support in getting him or her into treatment. Remember that giving up on an addict never solved anyone's problems—not the addict's and not those of the people who care about him or her.

Is all this effort going to be difficult? Yes, it is. Is it going to be worth it? When you see your child, your parent, your spouse, or your friend finally free of the horrors of addiction, you'll know that it was!

Where to Find Help

Organization	Address	Phone	Web Address/E-mail
Adult Children of Alcoholics	PO Box 3216 Torrance, CA 90510	1-310-534-1815 (messages only)	www.adultchildren .org info@adultchildren .org
Al-Anon/Alateen Family Groups	1600 Corporate Landing Parkway Virginia Beach, VA 23454	1-888-4AL-ANON 1-757-563-1600 1-757-563-1655 (fax)	www.al-anon .alateen.org wSO@al-anon.org
Alcoholics Anonymous	PO Box 459 Grand Central Station New York, NY 10163	1-212-870-3400 (check phone book for local listings)	www.alcoholics -anonymous.org
American Academy of Addiction Psychiatry (AAAP)	1010 Vermont Ave. NW Suite 710 Washington, DC 20005	1-202-393-4484 (phone) 1-202-393-4419 (fax)	www.aaap.org
American Society of Addiction Medicine (ASAM)	4601 N. Park Ave. Upper Arcade #101 Chevy Chase, MD 20815	1-301-656-3920 (phone) 1-301-656-3815 (fax)	www.asam.org email@asam.org
BACCHUS Peer Education Network and GAMMA	PO Box 100043 Denver, CO 80250	1-303-871-3068 (M–F 8–4:30 MST)	www .bacchusgamma.org bacgam@aol.com
Chemically Dependent Anonymous	CDA Communications, Inc. PO Box 423 Severna Park, MD 21146	1-888-CDA-HOPE	www.cdaweb.org

Organization	Address	Phone	Web Address/E-mail
Cocaine Anonymous	3740 Overland Ave. Suite C Los Angeles, CA 90034 PO Box 2000 Los Angeles, CA 90049	1-310-559-5833	www.ca.org cawso@ca.org
Families Anonymous	PO Box 3475 Culver City, CA 90231	1-800-736-9805 (referrals only) (M–Th 10–4, F 10–2 PST)	www .familiesanonymous .org famanon@ familiesanonymous. org
Marijuana Anonymous	PO Box 2912 Van Nuys, CA 91404	1-800-766-6779	www.marijuana-anonymous.org office@marijuana-anonymous.org
National Association of Addiction Treatment Providers (NAATP)	313 W. Liberty St. Suite 129 Lancaster, PA 17603	1-717-392-8480 (phone) 1-717-392-8481 (fax)	www.naatp.org
The Association for Addiction Professionals (NAADAC)	901 N. Washington St. Suite 600 Alexandria, VA 22314	1-800-548-0497 (phone) 1-800-377-1136 (fax)	http://naadac.org
National Clearinghouse for Alcohol and Drug Information	PO Box 2345 Rockville, MD 20847	1-800-729-6686	http://ncadi.samhsa .gov
National Council on Alcoholism and Drug Dependence (NCADD)	22 Cortlandt St. Suite 801 New York, NY 10007	1-212-269-7797 (national office) 1-212-269-75101 (fax) 1-800-NCA-CALL (hope line) (counseling and treatment via phone, 24-7)	www.ncadd.org national@ncadd.org

Organization	Address	Phone	Web Address/E-mail
National Inhalant Prevention Coalition (NIPC)	322-A Thompson St. Chattanooga, TN 37405	1-800-269-4237	www.inhalants.org nipc@io.com
Secular Organizations for Sobriety (SOS)	5521 Grosvenor Blvd. Los Angeles, CA 90066	1-310-821-8430	www.secularsobriety .org SOS@CFIWest.org
Smart Recovery	7537 Mentor Ave. Suite 306 Mentor, OH 44060	1-440-951-5357 (check phone book for local listings)	www.smartrecovery .org
Substance Abuse and Mental Health Services Administration (SAMHSA)	1 Choke Cherry Rd. Rockville, MD 20857	1-866-287-2728	www.buprenorphine .samhsa.gov info@buprenorphine .samhsa.gov
Women For Sobriety	PO Box 618 Quakertown, PA 18951	1-215-536-8026	www.womenfor sobriety.org NewLife@nni.com

Appendix B

Further Reading on Starting Treatment

How-To Books

Brown, Stephanie, Virginia Lewis, and Andrew Liotta. *The Family Recovery Guide: A Map for Healthy Growth*. Oakland, CA: New Harbinger, 2000.

Fearing, James. *Workplace Intervention: The Bottom Line on Helping Addicted Employees Become Productive Again*. Center City, MN: Hazelden Books, 2000.

Fletcher, Anne M. *Sober for Good: New Solutions for Drinking Problems—Advice from Those Who Have Succeeded*. New York: Houghton Mifflin, 2001.

Gold, Mark. *800-Cocaine*. New York: Bantam Books, 1984.

Jay, Jeff, and Debra Jay. *Love First: A New Approach to Intervention for Alcoholism and Drug Addiction*. Center City, MN: Hazelden Books, 2000.

Levin, Jerome D. *Recovery from Alcoholism*. Northvale, NJ: Jason Aronson, 1995.

Nakken, Craig. *The Addictive Personality: Understanding the Addictive Process and Compulsive Behavior*, (2d ed.). Center City, MN: Hazelden Books, 1996.

Olitzky, Kerry M., and Stuart A. Copans. *Twelve Jewish Steps to Recovery: A Personal Guide to Turning from Alcoholism and Other Addictions*. Woodstock, VT: Jewish Lights Publishing, 1991.

O'Neill, John, and Pat O'Neill. *Concerned Intervention: When Your Loved One Won't Quit Alcohol or Drugs*. Oakland, CA: New Harbinger Publications, 1993.

Peele, Stanton. *7 Tools to Beat Addiction*. New York: Three Rivers Press, 2004.

Rogers, Ronald L., and Chandler Scott McMillin. *Freeing Someone You Love from Alcohol and Other Drugs: A Step-by-Step Plan Starting Today!* New York: Body Press/Perigee Books, 1992.

Schaefer, Dick. *Choices and Consequence: What to Do When a Teenager Uses Alcohol/Drugs*. Minneapolis, MN: Johnson Institute Books, 1987.

Memoirs

Burroughs, Augusten. *Dry: A Memoir*. New York: St. Martin's Press, 2004.

Hamill, Pete. *A Drinking Life: A Memoir*. Boston: Little, Brown, 1994.

Knapp, Caroline. *Drinking: A Love Story*. New York: Dell, 1996.

Marlowe, Ann. *How to Stop Time: Heroin from A to Z*. New York: Basic Books, 1999.

McGovern, George. *Terry: My Daughter's Life-and-Death Struggle with Alcoholism*. New York: Villard Books, 1996.

Styron, William. *Darkness Visible: A Memoir of Madness*. New York: Vintage Books, 1990.

Index

abstinence: and AA philosophy, 233, 235, 236, 247; flexible approach toward, 172, 176; as goal, 252; and harm reduction, 106–9, 110, 171–72; long-term, 171–72; and peer-led groups, 246, 247; and selection of treatment, 164, 171–72, 176; and substitutes, 252

acamprosate (Campral), 191

acting out, 40, 47–48

Activan, 181

addiction: controllable part of, 104; cross-, 251, 253; definition of, 4, 15; as disease, 18, 37, 241–42; downside of, 57, 93–94, 98; as hereditary, 69; media promotion of, 104–5; "medical," 3, 277–79, 282; as mental illness, 73; models of, 20–24; as not logical, 86–87; physical/biological aspects of, 24–25, 37, 81, 98, 165, 166–67; reasons for, 20–24; signs of, 4–8; stigma/shame attached to, 24, 71–72, 149, 167, 227, 240, 241; "Three C's" of, 14–15; understanding what is, 25–38, 81, 213; and what people become addicted to, 25–38

addicts: as admitting problems, 59–60, 71, 102, 220, 239, 241, 245; autonomy of, 107; "brick wall" of, 109; and convincing addict to seek treatment, 13, 71, 84, 86–110, 121, 153–55, 258, 266, 267, 271; dually diagnosed, 5–6, 17–19, 270–76; elderly as, 267–70, 282; frustrations of, 206; identification of, 3–19; "labeling" of, 9, 149; minimizing of problems by, 108–9, 189, 212, 268–69,

278, 280; professionals as recovering, 82; "protection" of, 209–12; responsibilities of, 18, 23–24, 246; self-identity/image of, 150–51, 231, 233; self-inventory of, 220; teenagers/minors as, 14, 33, 34, 36, 168–69, 237–39, 257–66, 282; understanding of situation by, 56. *See also specific topic*

aftercare plans. *See* follow-up care

"Aha!" moment, 57–58

Al-Anon, 237–39

Alateen, 237–39

Alcohol Use Disorders Identification Test (AUDIT), 14

alcohol/alcoholism: and defense mechanisms, 42; and definition of addiction, 4; detoxification from, 180–82; and diagnosis, 14, 18; and dually diagnosed addicts, 18, 276; among elderly, 267; and family groups/counseling, 237–39; and identification of addicts, 3, 5, 7, 8; and medical problems, 277, 279; medications for, 191, 192; misconceptions about, 280; and MM, 245–47; and models of addiction, 22–23; and pregnancy, 280–82; and strategies to avoid, 245–47, 251; substitutes for, 26, 251; and teenagers, 257–58, 259, 264–66, 282; "tolerance" of, 30; treatment for, 31, 191, 192; as type of addictive substance, 27, 30, 177–78; withdrawal from, 3, 31, 178, 179, 192, 268, 269, 276. *See also* Alcoholics Anonymous; depressants, CNS

Acknowledgments

I am indebted to my teachers, who have pointed the way toward a fuller understanding of the pain addiction inflicts on addicts as well as on their friends and families. I have been particularly influenced by Dr. Marc Galanter's Network Therapy, a method designed to help professional addiction treaters focus loved ones' attention and efforts toward promoting sobriety. This book represents my efforts to extend and apply Dr. Galanter's ideas directly to the friends and families of the "reluctant patient" who rejects the efforts of those who care about him or her. Many other teachers gave—and continue to give—of their experience in helping me modify my treatment techniques to help addicts in need. Perhaps my most important teachers have been those addicts and their circles of friends and family who have allowed me in, and have told me what does and does not help them.

In addition, I am deeply grateful to Rob Kaplan for his patient and persistent work on this book, and to Nancy Hancock for her incisive editing. The confidence and encouragement of Mel Parker, who has gone above and beyond what can be expected from an agent, continuously goading me into making this the absolute best that it could be. My attorney, Eric Brown, similarly pushed me to "go public" with views I have expressed to him many times. And finally, the patience and support of Lisa, Noah, Tali, and Ari while I was "working at the office" have kept me afloat.

About the Author

LAURENCE M. WESTREICH, M.D., is a board-certified psychiatrist who specializes in the treatment of patients with addictions to alcohol and drugs of abuse, and those dually diagnosed with addiction and mental disorders.

In addition to his private practice, Dr. Westreich has served since 1992 on the faculty of the Division of Alcoholism and Drug Abuse, Department of Psychiatry, New York University School of Medicine. His responsibilities there include teaching psychiatry residents, fellows in addiction psychiatry, and attending psychiatrists on the Bellevue wards.

Dr. Westreich is also the author of numerous articles and book chapters on the treatment of addiction, presents regularly to professional groups, and is board certified by the American Board of Psychiatry and Neurology in general psychiatry, addiction psychiatry, and forensic psychiatry, and as an addiction specialist by the American Society of Addiction Medicine (ASAM).

In addition to his private practice and academic responsibilities, Dr. Westreich is the consultant on drugs of abuse to the commissioner of Major League Baseball and serves on the Therapeutic Use Exemption Committee of the United States Anti-Doping Agency (USADA), the drug-testing agency for American Olympic athletes. Dr. Westreich lives in Upper Montclair, New Jersey, with his wife and three children.